T0372652

*The State of Resistance*

While the Iranian nation-state has long captivated the attention of our media and politics, this book examines a country that is often misunderstood and explores forgotten aspects of the debate. Using innovative multi-disciplinary methods, it investigates the formation of an Iranian national identity over the last century and, significantly, the role of Iranian people in defining the contours of that identity. By employing popular culture as an archive of study, Assal Rad aims to rediscover the ordinary Iranian in studies of contemporary Iran, demonstrating how identity was shaped by music, literature, and film. Both accessible in style and meticulously researched, Rad's work cultivates a more holistic picture of Iranian politics, policy, and society, showing how the Iran of the past is intimately connected to that of the present.

ASSAL RAD received her PhD in Middle Eastern history from the University of California, Irvine, and currently works on US–Iran policy. She has written for *Newsweek*, the *Independent*, *Foreign Policy*, and more, and appeared on *BBC World*, *BBC Persian*, *Al Jazeera*, and *NPR*.

# The State of Resistance

Politics, Culture, and Identity in Modern
Iran

ASSAL RAD

CAMBRIDGE
UNIVERSITY PRESS

# CAMBRIDGE
## UNIVERSITY PRESS

University Printing House, Cambridge CB2 8BS, United Kingdom

One Liberty Plaza, 20th Floor, New York, NY 10006, USA

477 Williamstown Road, Port Melbourne, VIC 3207, Australia

314–321, 3rd Floor, Plot 3, Splendor Forum, Jasola District Centre,
New Delhi – 110025, India

103 Penang Road, #05–06/07, Visioncrest Commercial, Singapore 238467

Cambridge University Press is part of the University of Cambridge.

It furthers the University's mission by disseminating knowledge in the pursuit of
education, learning, and research at the highest international levels of excellence.

www.cambridge.org
Information on this title: www.cambridge.org/9781009193580
DOI: 10.1017/9781009193573

© Assal Rad 2022

This publication is in copyright. Subject to statutory exception
and to the provisions of relevant collective licensing agreements,
no reproduction of any part may take place without the written
permission of Cambridge University Press.

First published 2022

*A catalogue record for this publication is available from the British Library.*

*Library of Congress Cataloging-in-Publication Data*
Names: Rad, Assal, 1982– author.
Title: The state of resistance : politics, culture, and identity in modern Iran / Assal
Rad, National Iranian American Council.
Other titles: Politics, culture, and identity in modern Iran
Description: Cambridge, United Kingdom ; New York, NY : Cambridge University
Press, 2022. | Includes bibliographical references and index.
Identifiers: LCCN 2021059851 (print) | LCCN 2021059852 (ebook) | ISBN
9781009193580 (hardback) | ISBN 9781009193566 (paperback) | ISBN
9781009193573 (ebook)
Subjects: LCSH: National characteristics, Iranian. | Iran – Politics and government –
20th century. | Iran – Politics and government – 21st century. | Popular culture –
Iran. | Nation-state. | BISAC: POLITICAL SCIENCE / World / Middle Eastern
Classification: LCC DS268 .R33 2022 (print) | LCC DS268 (ebook) |
DDC 955–dc23/eng/20220405
LC record available at https://lccn.loc.gov/2021059851
LC ebook record available at https://lccn.loc.gov/2021059852

ISBN 978-1-009-19358-0 Hardback
ISBN 978-1-009-19356-6 Paperback

Cambridge University Press has no responsibility for the persistence or accuracy of
URLs for external or third-party internet websites referred to in this publication
and does not guarantee that any content on such websites is, or will remain,
accurate or appropriate.

For Maman and Baba

# Contents

# Figures

# Acknowledgments

I began traveling to Iran as an adult in 2003 to visit my grandparents and extended family, who could not easily secure visas to travel to the United States. At the time, I was still an undergraduate student with so many ambitions and ideas for my future already carved out. However, upon arriving in Iran, those plans quickly changed. As an Iranian American I always felt very connected to my Iranian heritage and believed I was well versed in Iran's history and culture. It was not until I had the opportunity to visit that I understood the enormous gap between my experience and understanding of Iran and that of my Iranian family, who had been a part of its evolving society. It was in that moment I realized that understanding Iran's history and society went far beyond the basic language skills and traditions we kept alive living abroad, and so I decided I would put in the work and study required to do so.

The relationships I built over the years visiting Iran were crucial to my graduate research years later. My Iranian interlocutors, which included among them some of my family and friends in Iran, were most critical to this project for their assistance, bravery, honesty, and extraordinary generosity. They are among the many amazing and kind people who made this book possible and supported me personally, and this project in particular, along the way.

The staff at the Department of History, School of Humanities, and Samuel Jordan Center for Persian Studies and Culture at the University of California, Irvine (UCI) were integral to the most important stages of this project. To this end, I must thank Yuting Wu, Marc Kanda, Amy Fujitani, Amanda Swain, and Saeid Jalalipour for graciously answering countless questions and providing guidance at every turn with patience. The university's faculty and professors were, of course, fundamental to my broader understanding and education, and to the research process that made this study possible.

My professors provided the intellectual challenges and social principles that made them invaluable teachers inside and outside the university. I met my dissertation cochair Mark LeVine as an undergraduate student, when he taught me my first important lesson, that we do not teach history because it mattered "then," but precisely because it matters now. Professor LeVine shared more than just facts: he imparted lessons in humanity that stayed with me and brought me back to UCI to study history as a graduate student. In a climate of uncertainty and wars, he remained steadfast in his views, teaching about conflicts such as in Palestine and Iraq without the inflection of an agenda. Instead, he taught with the commendable goal of building bridges and understanding. This is the same generosity of character I experienced with my other cochair Touraj Daryaee, whom I met for the first time in Iran before my graduate studies began. From our first meeting and throughout these years, Professor Daryaee has continued to inspire me with his devotion to teaching and providing the Iranian-American community a voice. Even when faced with challenges that go beyond the scope of the academy, he has been a source of optimism and strength. For these reasons and more, I am grateful to them both for teaching me significant lessons with implications far outside the walls of the classroom.

I am also greatly indebted to Roxanne Varzi and Nasrin Rahimieh for their thoughtful contributions to my studies and research. While I can certainly thank them for their scholarly works, which I utilized in my research and gave me new ways to think about my own project, what I owe them is more profound. As a woman of Iranian heritage raised in the United States, role models with whom I could identify were not an everyday occurrence. In our contemporary political climate, calls for representation have become ubiquitous. My experience has shown me why these pleas are so important. For me, Professor Rahimieh and Professor Varzi are more than mentors: they are trailblazers and the impact of their presence in the course of my work cannot be overstated.

A list of professors to thank would not be complete without Joseph McKenna. Though Professor McKenna was not part of the team that directly assisted with this project, I worked with him more than any other professor at UCI as a teaching assistant during my graduate studies. His classes in religious studies provided thought-provoking questions for the students and teaching assistants alike. My classes with Professor McKenna helped me realize the significance of teaching and communication. Moreover, our many talks and long discussions honed my own skills and expanded my thinking on numerous topics. I am confident that the work I have produced has been positively influenced as a consequence of my time with him.

Of course, the path to this moment goes beyond my studies at the university. Though it is quite a satisfying feeling of personal accomplishment to have completed a book, I am wholly cognizant of the privilege that has afforded me this occasion. My only hope is to contribute something of worth to a world that has given me so much. These are the lessons that were taught to me throughout my life by my family and friends here at home in the United States. While such an endeavor is often lonely, it is only because of their unwavering encouragement and support that I was able to realize my goals.

I am grateful to my colleagues who supported this project and allowed me the opportunity to bring it to its completion. That process would not have been possible without Chris Rogers from Dunow, Carlson & Lerner Literary Agency, who believed in my project from day one and guided me with patience through an unfamiliar terrain from writing to publication. I could not think of a better home for this manuscript than Cambridge University Press, whose collection on the Middle East and Iran has been a staple of my education and research, and has included such talented authors and brilliant academics. I am so thankful to Maria Marsh, editor at Cambridge University Press, for her support and kindness, and her resolve to pursue this project in the midst of a pandemic with all its added challenges and obstacles. Thank you to Atifa Jiwa at Cambridge University Press for taking over where Maria left off and stepping in at a critical point in the project.

I am indebted to my friend, Pouya Alimagham, for staying a few steps ahead of me in this process and helping to guide me throughout. Our long conversations over shared interests influenced my ideas and kept me motivated to continue my work. I am also thankful to my older brothers, Behdad and Babak, who I could always count on to protect me while nurturing my independence. To Behdad I am especially grateful for his generosity and for giving me a sense of security. To Sanna, my partner in everything, I owe so much for bearing the brunt of my anxieties and somehow finding a way to put me at ease.

But it is to my parents that I owe the most. They always emphasized the value of an education and made it clear that they would go to any length to ensure that I had every opportunity possible. I admired my father's erudition as a child and will be forever indebted to him for sparking my interest in world affairs and Iran's vast history. It is hard to express my gratitude toward my mother, for without her resolute devotion to her children I am certain I would not be writing these words today. Through all the many upheavals that life produced, my mother's determination never wavered. She was a role model for integrity and perseverance. She is not only the strongest woman I know, but the strongest person. Thank you both for the life you have given me: I will always strive to make you proud.

# Note on Transliteration

For transliteration of Persian, I use the *Iranian Studies* scheme as outlined by the Association of Iranian Studies. Names have been transliterated according to this scheme except for cases in which there are commonly used English forms. In cases of Persian names with Arabic origins, the Persian diction is used.

# 1 | *Introduction*

Perhaps the defining political feature of the twentieth century was the proliferation of nation-states in a world previously dominated by a few, mostly European, empires. With the demise of the imperial system at the end of World War II and the growing recognition of ideas such as sovereignty and self-determination in the face of colonialism, new nation-states emerged across the globe. The formation of international bodies such as the League of Nations and then the United Nations sanctioned the creation of these entities with legal language that bound people together in novel ways. William Blake famously wrote, "What is now proved was once only imagined,"[1] a fitting adage for the case of the nation-state, which, though invented, has proven to be a remarkable force in contemporary society.

This study examines the formation of the Iranian nation-state in the twentieth century and the evolution of its national story since then. National identity in Iran is the result of a process of concession and contestation from above and below. As such, this work investigates the oppositional forces from below that challenged the historical production of their governments. Additionally, the study explores the efforts of both the Pahlavi dynasty and the Islamic Republic (IR) to construct national identities that were suitable to their respective nation-building projects.

In the autumn of 1979, months after a revolution had toppled his monarchical rule, the former shah of Iran, Mohammad Reza Pahlavi, finished writing his final account of Iran's national narrative. In the fatefully named *Answer to History*, the shah reveals one perspective of Iranian history and the momentous days of the 1979 revolution. Much like his previous works and efforts to construct an Iranian nationalism that fit the image of his modernizing nation-state, the shah continued

---

[1] William Blake, *The Marriage of Heaven and Hell* (iBooks version, 2014), 13.

even in his final days to utilize symbols of the past and claim a continuity of Persian monarchy:

Contrary to what can be read in most Western history books, Persia was not influenced by Greek culture, although we still have a charming little Greek statue in a museum ... a phenomenon which recurred with subsequent conquerors: the Persians submitted to them but they preserved their own culture and imposed it on their victors.[2]

The shah dismissed the events of 1979 and its revolutionary discourse in order to maintain his emphasis on Persianness as the cornerstone of Iranian identity:

This obliteration of our national identity and the cultural and spiritual heritage of Iran is abhorrent. Our identity and heritage are our greatest advantages, the essential foundations from which everything else can be recovered and without which all will be lost ... Persian culture will rise to the surface again, nourished by the values, creations, thought, talent, and effort of the people.[3]

Despite such rhetoric, the revolution of 1979 successfully deposed not only the Pahlavi dynasty, but also the institution of monarchy that the shah so confidently championed. These events and the populist movement that accompanied them illustrate the complexity of notions like nationalism and national identity.

Like its predecessor, the reign of the Islamic Republic after 1979 imparted an alternative national narrative. Though based on the ideological discourse of the revolution, which developed over decades of struggle for independence, the Islamic Republic constructed a narrow definition of Iranianness as well. Focused on the role of Islam and especially Shiism in Iranian history and culture, the Islamic Republic turned the Pahlavi narrative on its head by repudiating Iran's pre-Islamic heritage. Khomeini, the leader of the 1979 revolution, argued against the institution of monarchy that had long ruled in Iran by using the example of Imam Hossein, the quintessential martyr in Shiite lore:

The Lord of the Martyrs (upon whom be peace) summoned the people to rise in revolt by means of sermon, preaching, and correspondence and caused them to rebel against a monarch ... This struggle and confrontation has

---

[2] Mohammad Reza Pahlavi, *Answer to History* (New York: Stein and Day, 1980), 37.
[3] Ibid., 190.

continued without respite, and the great scholars of Islam have always fought against the tyrannical bandits who enslaved their peoples for the sake of their passions and squandered their country's wealth on trivial amusements.[4]

Khomeini continued to emphasize the importance of Islam and how its message resonated with the masses of Iranians:

The whole nation was unanimous in its dissatisfaction. Muhammad Reza had done nothing to satisfy any segment of the population ... The people, then, were united in their dissatisfaction, and when the demand for an Islamic republic was raised, no one opposed it. The whole country in unison demanded the foundation of an Islamic republic and the abolition of the monarchy.[5]

Despite the different points each stressed, both states shared the commonality of nation building and the manufacture of a coherent nationalism that coincided with the modern conception of the nation-state.

The failure of the shah to craft a meaningful national identity played a significant role in the 1979 revolution by magnifying the grievances of ordinary people and affording space for the shah's opposition to create a powerful counter narrative. Though the Islamic Republic claimed the revolutionary discourse for its cause, voices from below endured and continued to resist authorities in innovative ways.

## 1.1 Framework

This study examines national and political identity in postrevolutionary Iran, while addressing the historical significance of the emergence of the modern nation-state. However, it is imperative to draw a distinction between official state rhetoric that fits specific agendas and the identity of ordinary citizens.[6] How individuals express their

---

[4] Ruhollah Khomeini and Hamid Algar, *Islam and Revolution: Writings and Declarations of Imam Khomeini* (Berkeley: Mizan Press, 1981), 204–5. Also note, after looking at the original sources, I found Dr. Algar's translations accurate and suitable to use in my project. Where Dr. Algar's translations exist, I will use his original translations; however, the other original sources used throughout this work are my own translations.

[5] Ibid., 336–37.

[6] It is also important to note that the use of "state" does not imply that it is itself a homogenous group. Rather, my use of "state" in this context is to distinguish it from common people who have no ties to official institutions related to the government. It will be made clear that the state itself has many fissures.

national identity, both in opposition and in line with the state's narrative, becomes more apparent through an exploration of popular culture and interviews with Iranians.

Of course, the line between state and subject is often blurred as mass movements and revolutions in the modern era have come to be defined in "national" terms.[7] As Benedict Anderson so aptly puts it, "The reality is quite plain: the 'end of the era of nationalism,' so long prophesied, is not remotely in sight. Indeed, nation-ness is the most universally legitimate value in the political life of our time."[8] While the nation may be "imagined" in the sense that it is based on constructed elements without innate or fixed meanings, it is certainly not *meaningless* in that its manifestation has real implications for the lives of individuals, as Anderson elaborates:

> It is imagined as a *community*, because, regardless of the actual inequality and exploitation that may prevail in each, the nation is always conceived as a deep, horizontal comradeship. Ultimately it is this fraternity that makes it possible, over the past two centuries, for so many millions of people, not so much to kill, as willingly to die for such limited imaginings.[9]

Thus, wars are fought and often changing borders defended in the name of the shared commune of the nation-state.

In addition to Anderson's theories on the nation-state, Eric Hobsbawm's ideas are crucial to this study. As both Anderson and Hobsbawm observe, "nations" are not as old as history; in terms of human history, they are quite new, as the concept developed in Europe in the eighteenth century.[10] To understand how this idea spread in the greater part of the world and in Iran in particular by the twentieth century, it is necessary to recognize its origins. Both authors also note the importance of having a working definition of the term "nation." Although there is much debate, Anderson and Hobsbawm's respective takes can facilitate our understanding of the term. For Anderson the nation is:

> An imagined political community – and imagined as both inherently limited and sovereign ... It is *imagined* because the members of even the smallest

---

[7]  Benedict Anderson, *Imagined Communities: Reflections on the Origin and Spread of Nationalism* (New York: Verso 2006).
[8]  Ibid., 3.        [9]  Ibid., 7.
[10] Eric J. Hobsbawm, *Nations and Nationalism Since 1780: Programme, Myth, Reality* (Cambridge: Cambridge University Press, 1992).

nation will never know most of their fellow-members, meet them, or even hear of them, yet in the minds of each lives the image of their communion.[11]

Hobsbawm adds a practical twist stating that "any sufficiently large body of people whose members regard themselves as members of a 'nation' will be treated as such."[12] Both authors also recognize the dynamic nature of the nation; it is by no means a fixed or static idea. Despite the routinely rigid language of nationalisms, nations are continuously changing and adapting to new circumstances. In fact, the nation, as a political entity, is the result of the confluence of several local and global factors.[13]

In the case of modern Iran, the state and community have been imagined *and* contested, legitimized *and* challenged, through the interaction of the state and the people within the global context of colonialism and modernity. By understanding the complexity of this interaction, we can hope to ascertain a better understanding of national identity in modern Iran, which moves past both the essentializing nature of the often-depicted bipolar identity between Islam and pre-Islamic civilization, and the more recent proclivity in scholarship to reject both identities as inauthentic.[14]

Iran in the early twentieth century had many of the criteria that Hobsbawm posits is needed in the creation of the nation. Iran had a long territorial history and links with empires and monarchies of the past that shared a linguistic heritage and had a long-standing cultural elite. Throughout the territory's history its landmass contracted and expanded. However, of central concern to this study is Hobsbawm's claim that, "*nationalism comes before nations*. Nations do not make states and nationalisms but the other way round."[15] This idea informs one of the central arguments of this study: that while the Pahlavi dynasty is often cited as the architect of the modern Iranian nation, its failure to proffer a nationalism that resonated with the masses of

---

[11] Anderson, *Imagined Communities*, 6.
[12] Hobsbawm, *Nations and Nationalism*, 8.
[13] Ibid. See Hobsbawm's work as he elaborates on criteria for a nation by adding a historic association with a current state or lengthy past, the presence of a cultural elite with literary lingo, and aptitude for conquest.
[14] The work of John L. Jackson Jr. unpacks the notion of authenticity and draws a distinction with sincerity. These ideas will be elaborated within the larger argument.
[15] Ibid., 10 (emphasis added).

Iranians contributed to its overthrow and made the need for a suitable nationalism paramount to the nation-state project.

Moreover, Hobsbawm notes the dual phenomenon of the nation, as it is constructed from above *and* below. Again, the Pahlavi narrative lacked the support from below that is crucial to nationalism and national identity. The shah's image among his subjects as foreign-controlled, and arguably disconnected or alien, can explain the absence of such validation.[16] As Hobsbawm argues in his discussion of nationalism and the creation of nations from the late nineteenth to early twentieth century, "there is no more effective way of bonding together the disparate sections of restless people than to unite them against outsiders."[17] The revolutionary discourse in Iran that developed over several decades leading up to 1979 utilized this sense of foreignness to create a populist movement and advance a new sense of nationalism shaped from below through the collaboration and joint efforts of Iranian men and women.

## 1.2 Background

Many scholars have argued that Iran did not truly take form as a nation-state until the rise of the Pahlavi dynasty in the 1920s.[18] The Qajar dynasty (1796–1925) preceded the Pahlavi era and, though unpopular, they brought a certain sense of stability to the country after decades of power struggles following the collapse of the Safavid dynasty in 1722.[19] The Qajar state was highly decentralized and the geopolitics of the time gave a great deal of power over Iranian affairs to Britain and Russia.[20] The Pahlavi monarchy promulgated these images and highlighted the Qajar reign as a time of concessions and tribal systems of power. Though the Pahlavi narrative emphasized the

[16] Further discussion of the shah's foreignness and foreign control of Iran will continue in subsequent chapters and throughout this study. Also, further discussion will show the shah's cognizance of the significance of Iran's independence from foreigners and the importance of reform and revolution.
[17] Ibid., 91.
[18] Ali M. Ansari, *Modern Iran Since 1921: The Pahlavis and After* (London: Pearson Education, 2003).
[19] Nikki R. Keddie, *Modern Iran: Roots and Results of Revolution* (New Haven, CT: Yale University Press, 2003).
[20] Ibid.

Qajar's inability to modernize Iran, such attempts were actually set into motion under Qajar rule.

However, their situation became worse during World War I as allied powers occupied Iran, making the Qajar state appear powerless. With the end of World War I and the fall of the Ottoman Empire, the region saw many modernizing movements. Reza Khan, an Iranian army commander, made strides in organizing and modernizing the military. Eventually Reza Khan consolidated power to depose the Qajar dynasty and replaced them with a new monarchical house, in which "he took the name of Pahlavi, evoking a heroic ancient dynasty."[21] As historian Nikki Keddie states,

For all its relative backwardness, Iran in 1925 felt a great pressure for change. To exist as an independent nation, Iran needed a civil service, army, and efficient tax system ... modernizing measures were launched by Reza Shah before he became monarch and formed the basis for further modernization.[22]

For Reza Shah it was crucial to implement projects and policies that would quickly bring Iran up to speed with other nation-states such as those in Europe.

The choice of "Iran" for the official name of the state fit very well within Reza Shah's definition of Iranian identity, which focused on the pre-Islamic past, secular ideas, and cultural and political ties to the West.[23] As a cognate of the word "Aryan," the title Iran connected the nation-state to the Aryan race and moved away from the association of Iranians to Muslims and Arabs.[24] This new state discourse was intended to bring the various minorities and ethnic groups together under one unified hallmark for the nation. Under the new state, Persian became the official language in an effort to create a homogenous national population.

While the Pahlavi shahs facilitated the formation of a modern Iranian state structure, both tangibly and rhetorically, the twentieth century tide of anticolonial and prodemocratic movements reached Iran as well. Throughout the century different strands of resistance

---

[21] Ibid., 86.   [22] Ibid., 87.
[23] Firoozeh Kashani-Sabet, "Cultures of Iranianess: The Evolving Polemic of Iranian Nationalism," in Nikki R. Keddie et al., eds., *Iran and the Surrounding World* (Seattle: University of Washington Press, 2002), 162.
[24] Reza Zia-Ebrahimi, "Self-Orientalization and Dislocation: The Uses and Abuses of the 'Aryan' Discourse in Iran," *Iranian Studies* 44, no. 4 (2011), 445–72.

emerged that were against the repressive nature of the monarchy and the lack of openness of the political system. Significant figures of the 1979 revolution, such as Khomeini and Shariati, challenged the national narrative of the Pahlavi dynasty and utilized Shiite and Islamic symbols and language to assert a more "authentic" Iranian identity. After the revolution, under the Islamic Republic, this discourse became official state rhetoric. For instance, during the war with Iraq (1980–88), Shiite symbols of martyrdom and the image of the most revered martyr, Imam Hossein, were used by the government to rally support from the people.[25]

Thus, Iranian identity in the last century vacillated between two opposing camps. On one side were those who emphasized the place of Shiite Islam as the foundation of Iranian identity and the history of Islam within Iran.[26] The contrasting school of thought focused on the linguistic and racial ties to Europe and Aryanism, as well as the 2,500-year monarchy and civilization established by Cyrus the Great in the Persian Empire. These two narratives are often depicted as mutually exclusive; from which the Iranian must choose which identity is truer.

Closely tied into these historical narratives is the role of the state in facilitating and encouraging a certain image and set of values. However, as mentioned before, nationalism cannot be understood by examining only the agenda from above, there is also the need to investigate the current from below within the larger society. These viewpoints can be seen in the ideology and discourse of the 1979 revolution as well as similar political iterations in postrevolutionary Iran. Additionally, the expression of popular culture can serve as another lens to further our understanding of the complexities of Iranian identity. The second central theme of this study then, investigates these various sections of Iranian identity construction, examining it both from above and below in the postrevolutionary era.

## 1.3  What's to Come?

While the rest of the chapters focus on the period following the revolution of 1979, the next chapter is intended to provide a historical

---

[25] Christopher De Bellaigue, *In the Rose Garden of the Martyrs: A Memoir of Iran* (London: HarperCollins, 2004).
[26] Mehrzad Boroujerdi, "Contesting Nationalist Constructions of Iranian Identity," *Critique: Critical Middle Eastern Studies* 7, no. 12 (1998) 43–55.

backdrop leading to that groundbreaking moment. The twentieth century saw the rise of the nation-state model as the preeminent way of organizing human societies. As the world of empires, in their classical sense, broke down, it gave way to a new world order in which the ideas of independence and sovereignty were not just European catchphrases, but believed possibilities for all peoples. Though it was never formally colonized, Iran was part of the global system of colonialism, power, and economics that tied the now "international" community together.

Nation-states were often formed through revolutions that toppled old institutions of monarchy in favor of new concepts such as citizen and republic, or through independence movements to overthrow the dominance of foreigners in the internal affairs of these newly born nation-states. These novel entities were accompanied by, and often preceded by, innovative tales of national histories that helped form new identities. To be a modern nation-state required a cohesive national identity and complimenting narrative. The significance of that account was not lost on the Pahlavi family, whose monarchs tried to formulate a long and uninterrupted history of Iranian grandeur and dominion.

Therefore, Chapter 2 relies heavily on a close reading of the words of Mohammad Reza Pahlavi, to shed light on the shah's rationale for upholding this narrative. The shah understood quite well that Iran could not forge its independence and image as a modern nation-state without freedom from foreign control. In fact, the shah carefully tailored an image of the preceding Qajar dynasty as beholden to outsiders and depicted his father as the savior of Iran from such foreign controlled despots:

A gifted and individualistic people, we had disintegrated into lethargy and political and social anarchy. It required the strength and iron determination of a man of action like Reza Shah to lift us out of the morass into which we had sunk and set us upon the road to national regeneration. Awakening us to the necessities of modern times, he literally created a new Persia with the aspirations and will-power of a modern state and with a recognized position in the community of nations.[27]

According to the shah, it was his father who "created" the modern Iranian state and saved Iran from the ineptness of its previous dynasty.

[27] Mohammad Reza Pahlavi, *Mission for My Country* (London: Hutchinson, 1960), 12.

This chapter also challenges the shah's account and explores how his subjects saw him as foreign and as a symbol of Iran's capitulation to external powers. The shah's failed nationalism left space for his opposition to produce an alternate narrative that captured the imagination of the masses of Iranian people. The chapter examines works by Iranian dissidents and popular literature of the time to show how people were interpreting events. Chapter 2 lays the foundation for the sections that follow by presenting not only the newly constructed image of Iranian nationalism, but also why it was needed in order to advance the cause of independence.

The chapter that follows shifts the focus to the postrevolutionary era and how the revolutionary ideology and the national identity it inspired were used and misused by the new Islamic Republic. Chapter 3 also looks at how the Iranian people continued to appropriate and challenge the state's ideology and representation. The chapter goes on to discuss the significance of the Iran–Iraq War (1980–88) in the early years after the revolution. While the Iranian revolution utilized Shiite discourse to galvanize the Iranian masses against the shah, the war afforded the newly established government an opportunity to solidify its power and further propagate a set of images that they would use to define the Iranian nation-state thereafter. Though the history and state remained the same, the opposing narratives offered by the old and new rulers speak to the nature of constructed national identities. As Gramsci explains, the state and its institutions are critical in creating a specific type of citizen:

If every state tends to create and maintain a certain type of civilization and of citizen (and hence of collective life and of individual relations), and to eliminate certain customs and attitudes and to disseminate others, then the Law will be its instrument for this purpose (together with the school system, and other institutions and activities). It must be developed so that it is suitable for such a purpose – so that it is maximally effective and productive of positive results.[28]

In this view, the state has a stake in the narrative as well as how that account is received by the populace. While the Pahlavi dynasty maintained a discourse of monarchical ancient Iran and Persian supremacy,

---

[28] Antonio Gramsci, Quintin Hoare, and Geoffrey Nowell-Smith, *Selections from the Prison Notebooks of Antonio Gramsci* (New York: International Publishers, 1971), 246–47.

the new Islamic Republic made use of the Karbala paradigm[29] and the martyrdom of Imam Hossein, which played especially well into the context of war and attack from an external force. For the Islamic Republic, it became imperative to forge a novel image that broke away from the shah and re-appropriated portions of Iran's past into a new and meaningful image. By focusing its efforts on some aspects of Iran's past, the new state – like the old – underplayed other parts, recalling Gramsci's discussion on the founding of a new state: "Cultural policy will above all be negative, a critique of the past; it will be aimed at erasing from memory and at destroying."[30]

During the war, the story of Imam Hossein's martyrdom provided the perfect icon for the war effort and connected the people to their new government through a shared past of Shiite culture. The dispute over succession after the death of the prophet Muhammad continued between Ali and Mu'awiya and was eventually fought by their respective sons, Imam Hossein and Yazid, leader of the Umayyad caliphate and Islamic empire in 680 CE. Shiites believe that those who opposed Yazid's corrupt and oppressive rule wished to overthrow his reign, and have Hossein take his rightful place as leader of the faithful. After Imam Hossein agreed to taking up the task, he gathered seventy-two supporters and left for Medina. Once they reached Karbala, a desert in southern Iraq, the rest of his followers did not come to their aid as Yazid surrounded the small band of men. Though greatly outnumbered by Yazid's large army, Imam Hossein refused to submit allegiance to Yazid. Knowing their fate would be death, Imam Hossein and his seventy-two supporters did not relent for the ten days that they were in the desert of Karbala. All were killed in brutal fashion, and on day ten, the tenth day of the month of Muharram, Imam Hossein was killed. Henceforth, Imam Hossein became the martyr of martyrs, the ultimate symbol of sacrifice and piety for Shiite Muslims.

It would be misleading to claim that these images are inauthentic or a simple fabrication of the past. Instead, this study explores how Shiite discourse was appropriated, first by Iranian people in order to resist the shah's authority, and then by the Islamic Republic in order to legitimate its rule and mount a defense in the war. In both cases the context and

---

[29] Kamran Scott Aghaie, *The Martyrs of Karbala: Shi'i Symbols and Rituals in Modern Iran* (Seattle: University of Washington Press, 2004).
[30] Gramsci, Hoare, and Nowell-Smith, *Prison Notebooks*, 263.

interaction of forces played roles in how the national narratives were formulated and how they were understood and received by the masses.

The chapter expands the discussion to the Islamic Republic's penchant to utilize regional geopolitics, as well as other political struggles, to align itself with resistance movements around the world. The Islamic Republic, as its name implies, used identifiers such as Muslim and Shiite to form its national narrative. Moreover, the state tied this national discourse to the larger region that predominantly identify as Muslims. In the case of Lebanon, the Islamic Republic used historical ties and their commonality as Shiites to establish greater relations. It does not appear coincidental that two pillars of the Islamic Republic's political discourse are Palestine and Lebanon. In both cases, nationalism and Islamism have been crucial to their resistance movements. National identity is especially critical for Palestine,[31] as seen in the often-used catchphrase "existence is resistance."[32] The Islamic Republic was brought to power by a revolution, whose opposition to the shah was embedded in anti-imperialist and Islamist rhetoric. Echoing Hamid Dabashi's claim that Shiites must be perpetually engaged in resistance to oppression,[33] the state depicts itself as continuously revolutionary and supports regional movements with analogous rhetoric.

Drawing on the work of Fanon, the chapter looks at how nationalism became a key site of resistance and source of identity throughout the twentieth century in the Middle East. According to Fanon, national solidarity is first expressed by striking blows at the enemy: "When it is achieved during war of liberation the mobilization of the masses introduces the notion of common cause, national destiny, and collective history into every consciousness."[34] While Fanon argues that the future culture of the nation should be based upon the struggle for freedom, he recognizes the tendency to glorify the past:

Perhaps this passion and this rage are nurtured or at least guided by the secret hope of discovering beyond the present wretchedness, beyond this self-hatred,

[31] Rashid Khalidi, *Palestinian Identity: The Construction of Modern National Consciousness* (New York: Columbia University Press, 1997).
[32] See www.existenceisresistance.org and http://electronicintifada.net/content/exi stence-resistance/6825 (last accessed July 5, 2018).
[33] Hamid Dabashi, *Shi'ism: A Religion of Protest* (Cambridge, MA: The Belknap Press of Harvard University Press, 2011).
[34] Frantz Fanon, Richard Philcox, Jean-Paul Sartre, and Homi K. Bhabha, *The Wretched of the Earth* (New York: Grove Press, 2004), 51.

this abdication and denial, some magnificent and shining era that redeems us ... Since perhaps in their unconscious the colonized intellectuals have been unable to come to loving terms with the present history of their oppressed people ... they must have been overjoyed to discover that the past was not branded with shame, but dignity, glory, and sobriety. Reclaiming the past does not only rehabilitate or justify the promise of a national culture. It triggers a change of fundamental importance in the colonized's psycho-affective equilibrium.[35]

In forming its national narrative, the Islamic Republic reclaimed Iran's Shiite past and adopted its images to create a discourse of resistance. It continued to portray itself as a revolutionary spokesperson and champion of such causes within the region.

While the Islamic Republic made its stance on Israel–Palestine public knowledge, that language can also be seen in popular culture, such as the collaborative song "Long Live Palestine,"[36] featuring British-Arab rapper Lowkey and Iranian rapper Hichkas. The content of such a song by a popular Iranian artist raises questions about how Iranians interpret and receive the Islamic Republic's discourse and whether or not they identify with these regional causes. This question becomes more complex when we consider a popular slogan from the protestors of the Green Movement[37] that stated, "Na Ghazeh, na Lobnān, jānam fadā-ye Irān" (Neither Gaza, nor Lebanon, my life I sacrifice for Iran).[38] In this instance it appears that the nationalist discourse of the protestors goes against the rhetoric of the state. The interaction of these forces is investigated further in this chapter.

Since identity is formulated from above and below, the next two chapters shift to an examination of popular culture as a lens to understand ordinary citizens. Chapters 4 and 5 investigate how Iranian identity is manifested within popular culture, examining music and filmed media respectively. By looking at popular culture the concentration moves from the state to the people, while keeping in mind the

---

[35] Ibid., 148.

[36] Lowkey, "Long Live Palestine," YouTube video (January 2, 2010), last accessed July 5, 2018, www.youtube.com/watch?v=4PgxMjmKE0c.

[37] Popular presidential candidate Mir-Hossein Musavi used the color green in 2009 as part of his election campaign in Iran. Protestors used this as a symbol of their continued support for Musavi and the rejection of what they believed to be fraudulent election results.

[38] "Rooze Quds dar Shiraz," YouTube video (September 18, 2009), last accessed July 5, 2018, www.youtube.com/watch?v=QhTbN5cAAX4.

constant interaction of these sides. Questions must be raised about the
realities on the ground, how Iranian national identity is expressed and
the implications of its consequences.

Chapter 4 observes popular culture through music and opens
a discussion on the nature of Iranian identity. A combination of field
research and lyrical analysis of the songs reveal elements of identity felt
and communicated by Iranians. Even when the lyrics and style appear
benign, music can speak volumes about people's hopes and anxieties that
lay below the surface. Not only is music a cultural expression, in Iran it
has also been used as a political tool and as part of resistance movements.

Iranians voiced their allegiance with the revolution and their identity as
Shiite Muslims through song-like protest chants and musical tracks. As
Roland L. Warren points out in his study on the Nazis' use of music, the
protest chant and group singing heighten the meaning of words and help
facilitate a sense of unity.[39] These techniques were employed as an emotive force during the revolution and by later generations to proclaim their
identity and, again, as a form of resistance after the controversial election
of 2009. The Green Movement is a pertinent example of how popular
music is utilized by Iranians as a mode of expression.[40] Consequently,
popular music can be used as another tool for investigation.

Chapter 5 continues the discussion of identity and popular culture
with an exploration of Iranian cinema and television. As Eric Egan states
in his study on the films of Makhmalbaf, "Cinema as made of cultural
expression acts as both a product and document of society."[41]
Accordingly, its relevance comes from the local context of social institutions and events. While cinema and television were important mediums
before the revolution, they became especially significant after the revolution as tools of expression and another means by which the newly
established Islamic Republic attempted to legitimate its rule.[42]

---

[39] Roland L. Warren, "The Nazi Use of Music as an Instrument of Social Control,"
in R. Serge Denisoff et al., eds., *The Sounds of Social Change: Studies in Popular
Culture* (Chicago: Rand McNally, 1972), 72.

[40] One example is the use of the politically motivated song "Yār-e Dabestāni-ye
Man" (My Schoolmate) in protests from 2009 (YouTube video, last accessed
July 5, 2018, www.youtube.com/watch?v=9sRGGXfGUqI). This topic will be
discussed further in the chapter on music.

[41] Eric Egan, *The Films of Makhmalbaf: Cinema, Politics & Culture in Iran*
(Washington, DC: Mage Publishers 2005), 15.

[42] Ibid.

The significance of cinema after the revolution became particularly evident during the Iran–Iraq War, since war is a key location for producing spectacle and emotion, while fomenting perceptions.[43] The war helped consolidate the power of the Islamic Republic and the use of still and moving images were crucial in its development.[44] While media has been used and often tightly controlled by the Islamic Republic for its own ends, artistic expression since the war became gradually more relaxed and Iranian cinema began to flourish in the late 1990s.

In spite of its international acclaim however, cinema in Iran still operates with structured guidelines and artists have come under severe pressure from authorities.[45] Again, we see the interaction of the state and the people in the contest over media and identity formation. Hamid Naficy recognizes the fissures in the hegemony of postrevolutionary cinema stating that it "is not Islamic in the sense that it is not by any means a monolithic, propagandistic cinema in support of a ruling ideology."[46] In fact, Naficy claims, two different kinds of cinema have developed side by side: one populist that upholds the Islamic Republic's values and one art cinema that engages and critiques such values.[47]

The chapter examines popular Iranian cinema and expressions of identity manifested in these films, while incorporating interviews with artists in the Iranian film industry and ordinary citizens. While popular films such as *Āzhāns-e Shishehi* (*The Glass Agency*) and *Ekhrāji-ha* (*The Rejects*) picked out themes from the Iran–Iraq War, both films also challenged stereotypes and depictions of the war, engaging the audience in a dialogue. Films such as *A Separation* and *About Elly* captivated Iranian audiences for their realism in portraying multifaceted characters and stories of everyday life. The characters in these films questioned the simple binary of good and bad often depicted in

---

[43] Paul Virilio, *War and Cinema: The Logistics of Perception* (London: Verso, 1989).

[44] Roxanne Varzi, *Warring Souls: Youth, Media, and Martyrdom in Post-Revolution Iran* (Durham: Duke University Press, 2006).

[45] One example is the arrest of Jafar Panahi in 2009 and his consequent twenty-year ban from making films. This and other related topics are discussed further in the media chapter.

[46] Hamid Naficy, "Islamizing Film Culture in Iran: A Post-Khatami Update," in Richard Tapper, ed., *The New Iranian Cinema: Politics, Representation and Identity* (London: I.B. Tauris Publishers, 2002), 30.

[47] Ibid.

war films. Instead, they added layers and nuance to the nature of Iranian people, the lives they lead, and the complexity of their identities.

Chapter 6 outlines the conclusions of this study, highlights the lasting impacts of modern nationalist discourse on Iran, and examines contemporary examples of resistance through the agency of Iranian citizens. Additionally, it looks at how the Iranian state and its people have come to understand their political landscape and foreign relations through this historical perspective. The intention of these chapters is to further our understanding of national identity formation in Iran over the last century and how that narrative informs the psyche of the Iranian populace today. In doing so I have argued that it is necessary to examine the actions of those in power as well as ordinary people.

Following the conclusion, an epilogue examines the importance of this account in relation to recent events and spotlights female Iranian voices. Though the topic of Iran is a staple of our mainstream media and foreign policy debates in the United States, knowledge of Iran's history, which informs our current state of affairs, is commonly absent from the discussion. The epilogue thus draws on this study to examine the present circumstances of US–Iran relations.

## 1.4 Conclusion

It is evident that Iranian identity has various expressions and is influenced by different forces inside and outside its borders. In both popular iterations and state rhetoric, the symbols used tended to vacillate between the Aryan lore of pre-Islamic Persian civilization and the Islamic account of Shiism. The competing images that were deployed within the last century must be examined and considered within a changing global setting that saw various shifts and opposing views, such as democratic national movements, the emergence of communist parties, and radical shifts in Islamic thought. As various peoples in the Middle East, including Iranians, attempted to gain more control over their fate and develop as modern nation-states, contrasting visions of the future and the past intersected in forming national identities.

The manifestation of national and political identity in Iran was closely tied to resistance movements. In the face of varied histories of illegitimate powers, both internal and external, Iranians stood in defiance and confronted the cultural hegemony of these authorities.

Therefore, these chapters examine the context in which the opposing poles of Iranian identity emerged, how they were accepted and challenged, and how this national identity exhibited itself in postrevolutionary Iran.

This study claims two central arguments: first, the modern nation-state of Iran was established in 1979 with the revolution that instilled an indigenous and independent nationalism, produced by Iranian dissidents, and eradicated the vestiges of foreign power that were linked to the shah; second, the national identity created by Iranian people during the decades preceding the revolution was the most resonant and inclusive because it infused the Shiite symbols ignored by the Pahlavi dynasty, and overused by the Islamic Republic, into populist elements of Iranian society. Despite the political turmoil of the Islamic Republic, that fusion and plurality endure. While the various chapters explore their own specific themes, these ideas run as threads throughout the work to tie the pieces together.

# 2 | The Foreign Shah and the Failure of Pahlavi Nationalism

This chapter focuses on the construction of Iranian national identity under the Pahlavi monarchy. Additionally, it gives attention to the dissident voices that challenged the shah's narrative. Central to the argument is the idea that nationalism was an integral part of building a nation-state, which the Pahlavi shahs were cognizant of and therefore used in their efforts to create the state of modern Iran. However, as the chapter illustrates, the Pahlavi attempt to produce a nationalism that united Iranian masses failed. Opposition movements against the monarchy made use of alternative narratives and depicted the shah as a foreign puppet to help usher in a new nationalism and revolutionary government.

The fact that the shah was viewed as alien, or disconnected from many of his subjects, was a key component of his failure and the rising momentum of the revolution. The twentieth-century anticolonial discourse of resistance and nationalism revolved around the notion of independence and sovereignty. Consequently, exerting control over a nation's resources and extinguishing external powers became a rallying cry for peoples around the world. As Hobsbawm points out, "Those who strove for liberation were 'nationalists' only because they adopted a western ideology excellently suited to the overthrow of foreign governments."[1] The European ideas that were in many cases imposed on Indigenous populations were appropriated and used against those same forces of dominance.

In order to produce an alternate national consciousness and movement, the Iranian opposition to the shah highlighted his detachment from ordinary citizens and his submission to foreign authority. In doing so they succeeded in portraying an overthrow of the monarchy as analogous to defeating foreign powers and establishing their

---

[1] Eric J. Hobsbawm, *Nations and Nationalism since 1780: Programme, Myth, Reality* (Cambridge: Cambridge University Press, 1992), 137.

independence. Ramin Jahanbegloo, reflecting on the shah's shortcomings, argues that, "[c]arried forward on a wave of popular support, the Iranian revolution toppled what was considered by many to be a *pseudo-modernist monarchy* of the Shah."[2] Despite the Pahlavi attempts to propagate their image as saviors of Iran and architects of the modern nation-state, the shah struggled to uphold this persona.

A close reading of the shah's words reveals that he understood the significance of Iran's freedom from foreign powers. This analysis also shows how he tried to depict himself as a revolutionary figure and protector of Iran's sovereignty. An examination of works by the shah's dissidents helps shed light on why, in spite of his efforts and convictions, the monarch fell short. However, before looking at this literature, it is important to provide some perspective into the Iranian consciousness and how fear of external forces, submission, and weakness became prevalent ideas in the public sphere.

## 2.1 Background: Foreign Power and Iranian Decline

The historical land of today's Iran housed several powerful and long-lasting empires. Such bygone preeminence created a high bar to measure Iran's contemporary successes and failures against. While the Safavid Empire (1501–1722) brought a period of prosperity to Iran and helped shape its cultural and religious character with the conversion to Shiism, its fall brought a period of decentralization and tribal rule.

The Safavids succeeded at warding off Ottoman advances and helped maintain a distinct Iranian character by converting the masses to Shiism, distinguishing them from their Sunni Ottoman rivals. The Safavids gained from this competition as contending European powers sometimes formed alliances against the Ottomans to restrict their growing power.[3] In the peak of its success, under Shah Abbas (1587–1629), the Safavids established strong ties within international trade and turned the city of Isfahan into a bustling new capitol. However, economic decline from changing trade routes, wars with the Ottomans,

---

[2] Ramin Jahanbegloo, *Iran: Between Tradition and Modernity* (Lanham, MD: Lexington Books, 2004), ix (emphasis added).
[3] Nikki R. Keddie, *Modern Iran: Roots and Results of Revolution* (New Haven, CT: Yale University Press, 2003).

and tribal conflicts within Iran weakened the Safavids, who were then easily conquered by Sunni tribal Afghans.[4]

The period following the collapse of the Safavid dynasty was one of tribal conflicts. Though the Zand rulers were popular and brought some stability to Iran, they were also tribal and competed with other tribal federations such as the Qajars, who fought for control over Iran. As historian Nikki Keddie argues, though unpopular, the Qajars were able to reunify Iran, "ending the civil and other wars and economic disruptions of the eighteenth century."[5] However, the sense of calm during the Qajar reign was tenuous at best. As Ervand Abrahamian points out, the Qajars had limited power without a structured bureaucracy or organized military.[6] Most of their power was in fact concentrated in the capital, Tehran, while aristocrats and landowners wielded considerable control and proved to be a formidable force. Additionally, without an established state patron, Iran's Shiite clergy adapted to become self-reliant. The insecurity of the eighteenth century provided a new level of autonomy for the clergy, who enjoyed independence from the government.

Despite these difficulties, the Qajars made attempts at modernizing projects and reforms that helped centralize their power and the state. Nevertheless, the late eighteenth and early nineteenth centuries brought new challenges that previous dynasties had not faced. The rising tide of colonialism ushered in a new world order, as European powers grew increasingly stronger and world markets became even more interconnected through capitalist endeavors. Moreover, Enlightenment ideas contributed to waning religious influence and facilitated a gradual shift toward a discourse of sovereignty and citizenry.

Though never formally colonized, Iran was certainly not isolated from these massive global changes. As Keddie states:

A new factor in Qajar times was the growing power of a nonindigenous, untraditional group who profoundly affected society – foreigners, and, at long distance, the government and economic groups they represented ... Iran came to be affected particularly by the policies of Great Britain and Russia. In addition to European interest in Iranian trade, and later in

---

[4]  Ibid.    [5]  Ibid., 37.
[6]  Ervand Abrahamian, *A History of Modern Iran* (Cambridge: Cambridge University Press, 2008).

concessions for European economic activity, Britain and Russia had very strong political and strategic interests in Iran.[7]

Britain and Russia's common desire to prevent total control by either single power helped Iran maintain its "formal" independence. Thus, Qajar Iran kept its quasi-independence because the Iranian monarchs submitted to the authority of these two powers. Such a surrender of control was not lost on Iranian intellectuals, especially those who were sent by the Qajars to become educated in Europe during this same period. The conflicting message of sovereignty and capitulation fostered a growing sense of dissatisfaction with the state of affairs in Iran. The later Pahlavi monarchs understood this paradox well and capitalized on the Qajar inability to maintain Iran's independence. The Pahlavi dynasty was haunted later by the same contradiction of independence and foreign control.

The idea of independence and sovereignty in the case of nineteenth-century Iran was not a simple abstraction. Iranians were not only alarmed at the Qajar's lack of authority, but were also appalled by its failure to conserve Iran's geographic integrity. In an era in which notions such as nation-state and citizen became increasingly important in European discourse, Iran suffered land loss and capitulation at the hands of its advocates. According to Hamid Dabashi, it was this encounter with colonialism and modernity that helped frame the Iranian national consciousness. Since the message of the European Enlightenment was brought to Iran by force, they were denied the very agency it promised.[8]

The Treaty of Golestan in 1813 and the Treaty of Turkmenchai in 1828 demonstrated who held real power over Iran. Both treaties ended in loss of land and capitulations for Iran to the advantage of Britain and Russia. As Dabashi claims, land became a symbol of Iran's identity. In contrast to Jews, who made their holy book the core of their identity, for Iranians, whose books had changed many times and who had a diverse ethnic-linguistic background, the land itself became the only constant that tied the nation and its people together.[9]

It is in this context that we see the roots of the significance of land for Iranian nationalism. The trauma of these losses made the land

---

[7] Keddie, *Modern Iran*, 34.
[8] Hamid Dabashi, *Iran: A People Interrupted* (New York: New Press, 2007).
[9] Ibid., 48.

a centerpiece of Iranian identity and the fear of foreign domination a familiar theme in Iranian society. For instance, Dabashi notes that the shah collected Iranian soil to take with him before departing Iran for the last time in January 1979. The notion of exile and separation from Iran is ubiquitous among the Iranian diaspora, summed up by the word "ghorbat," which means longing for one's homeland. In jewelry shops in Iran the map of the country is a popular item that is sold as an adornment for necklaces. Such examples show the importance of land to the Iranian psyche, but of greater focus here is the issue of perceived foreign invasion.

The angst and suspicion of foreign power, especially that of the British, is well documented in Iraj Pezeshkzad's timeless novel *Dāyi Jun Nāpelon (My Uncle Napoleon)*.[10] Written in the 1970s during the reign of the shah, the book's popularity brought a television adaption that was also a huge success. The novel's characters and catchphrases became iconic and are commonly known today as well. Though written as a satire about childhood love and family relations, the novel is a glimpse into Iranian society. The title is the name of the family's central patriarch, though the uncle is unaware of his family's use of the nickname Napoleon, which is meant to tease him about his obsession with the French leader.

While the novel is often lighthearted and amusing in its ridicule of Iranian culture and family dynamics, its titular character reveals an underlying issue of Iranian society and the mistrust of authority, both foreign and domestic. One of the main plotlines in the book revolves around his son-in-law, whom he is at odds with, spurring Dāyi Jun's paranoia of the British. Dāyi Jun recounts stories of his time in the gendarmerie and believes the British are out to get him, as he states, "Yes, if it wasn't for the power of the English I could have done many things."[11] This statement from Dāyi Jun was analogous to the belief among Iranians that the British, and other foreign agents, were behind Iran's political intrigues and failures. In a later statement Dāyi Jun shows again the significance of soil to the Iranian mentality and the fear of outside encroachment:

That hypocritical wolf called England hates everyone who loves the soil and water of his own country. What sin had Napoleon committed that they

[10]   Iraj Pezeshkzad, *My Uncle Napoleon* (n.p.: Modern Library, 2006).
[11]   Ibid., 68.

harried him like that? That they separated him from his wife and children like that? That they broke his spirit like that so that he died of grief? Just that he loved his country. And this for them is a great sin! ... Their enmity for me started when they saw that I love my country ... I'm a freedom fighter ... a supporter of the Constitution.[12]

In this passage the idea of Hobsbawm's patriotism and love of country are also evident. For Dāyi Jun, as for many Iranians, the love of country and soil drove their idea of nationalism, along with fear and scorn for external dominance.

Thus, a variety of sources that were accepted and resisted by the people, such as historical realities, domestic officials, and outside influences, coalesced into forming Iranian national identity. A sense of invention is also seen in the work of Pezeshkzad. In discussing the ongoing squabble between his father and Dāyi Jun, the narrator declares:

Perhaps everyone there had guessed that my father was lying. All of them knew that Dear Uncle's struggles against the rebels in the south, his struggles against foreigners, and his struggles on behalf of the Constitution were his own invention, and they knew that my father believed these fantasies less than anyone. But these empty words of praise made everyone happy, because they believed that my father was doing all this in order to put an end to their differences and quarrels.[13]

Like the Iranian nation-state, Dāyi Jun invented a reality based on his past, and while many in his family were aware of this concoction, they played along for everyone's benefit. Though invention is part of identity construction, the treaties and foreign encroachment of Iran were real experiences. The trauma they exerted in the Iranian psyche resulted in the development of certain anxieties and defense mechanisms to cope with such losses. The monarchs and revolutionaries that followed did everything in their power to allay those fears because they understood that freedom from foreign control was essential to the nation-state project.

While the Pahlavi dynasty emphasized the incompetence of the Qajar monarchs at modernizing the state and their weakness against foreign agents, they were also victims of similar criticisms from opposition forces in Iran. The fact that a novel such as *Dāyi Jun Nāpelon* was

---

[12] Ibid., 68.    [13] Ibid., 191.

written in the 1970s and so popularly received by Iranians indicates not only the brilliance of the humorous writing, but also the author's ability to touch on social anxieties and critiques. The character of Dāyi Jun exemplified the relentless paranoia of an Iranian populace that saw itself as a long-time victim of incursion and conquest. The shah, like other Iranians, suffered from these same anxieties and often mistrusted his allies. In his last book written after the revolution, the shah sounded much like Dāyi Jun when he recounted:

The British had their fingers in strange pies. They were always interested in forging links with diverse groups in nations they wished to control, and they had long exercised a good deal of control over Iran. There is little doubt that London was involved with the Tudeh[14] in various ways and of course the British had ties to the most reactionary clergy in the country.[15]

Though the shah believed he was a casualty of foreign machinations, he spent much of his tenure portraying himself and his father as liberators of Iran and protectors of its national independence. The rest of the chapter concentrates on the shah's views and the image of his apparent foreignness observed by his detractors.

## 2.2 The Shah's Nationalism: Revolution, Independence, and Persian Dominion

In the context of European dominance and colonialism, the shah of Iran was tasked with the challenge of creating a sense of national pride and independence for the developing Iranian nation-state. Though he imagined a historical continuity between the Iranian nation-state and the empires of the past and took pleasure in boasting of the supremacy of Persian tradition, the shah was clear in his admiration for Europe and believed Iran's place was among the most powerful and advanced nations in the world. In this paradox we see the often-debated dichotomy of tradition versus modernity.

For many observers of the Iranian revolution, it was the loss of identity and tradition, more so seen in religious terms, that brought on rebellion and resistance to the rapid changes under the Pahlavi monarchy. However, as Ramin Jahanbegloo argues, this binary is in

---

[14] Referring to Iran's communist party.
[15] Mohammad Reza Pahlavi, *Answer to History* (New York: Stein and Day, 1980), 59.

fact false and misleading.[16] The so-called "antimodernists" are actually part of modern society and so they take part in current debates; their existence and nature are within a contemporary framework, since no state or individual can really live in the past. At the same time, as Jahanbegloo explains, we cannot deny the significance of the past:

> That we cannot return to the past in no way cancels the fact that we have already been there, and so, as historical beings, are somehow still there. Time does not separate Iranian modernity from Iranian tradition at this level; it binds them together. To reject Iranian traditions entirely would be to reject our modernity as well.[17]

Ultimately, the binary is false because tradition and modernity coexist. They are not independent ideas that can be understood separately, but rather, they must be recognized as synchronous.

While Jahanbegloo maintains that the dichotomy of tradition and modernity is fallacious, he also concedes that intellectual thought in Iran over the last 150 years vacillated between these two extremes and perpetuated this misleading way of thinking. In the case of the Iranian revolution, the shah and his opposition took up these contrasting points of view. As the shah accepted European and American superiority and advocated imitation, thinkers such as Al-e Ahmad and Shariati rejected parroting of the West and called for a supposed return to Iranian roots.

At the heart of this contest was the question of authenticity and a struggle to define Iranian nationalism. Though the shah strove to modernize Iran through a Western lens, he was mindful of the dangers in artificial imitation and a perceived submission to Western powers. As a result, his modernizing project was coupled with a national narrative that looked far into the past and underscored authentic Iranian tradition from the days of the first Persian Empire: "as King I promote Persia's unity and solidarity. It was twenty-five hundred years ago that Cyrus the Great established the first unified Persian nation and empire, and ever since then the monarchy has helped to bind us together."[18] The shah was well aware that constructing a cogent nationalism was essential to the nation-state project and he made every effort to ensure that his narrative capitalized on Iranian history to bring the nation together.

---

[16] Jahanbegloo, *Iran.*   [17] Ibid., xi.
[18] Mohammad Reza Pahlavi, *Mission for My Country* (London: Hutchinson, 1960), 171.

In 1958 the shah began writing his first significant book, *Mission for My Country*, after establishing his autocratic rule following the 1953 coup against Prime Minister Mossadeq, and the ensuing crackdown on oppositional political parties. The book covers many themes such as the shah's daily life, the rise of his father, and his plans for Iran's future. One critical purpose of his writing was to establish Iran's national narrative as he understood it: "Now you will find that this book differs from the usual memoirs or reminiscences, for in a sense *I have tried to write the story of a country* and not only of its head of state. I start with a quick and no doubt inadequate survey of our wonderful historical tradition."[19] Like any writer, the shah took creative liberty in picking and choosing the elements of the story he told. To tell a 2,500-year story in a few pages required great liberty indeed. The task of making that story cohesive and pertinent to the contemporary context was a substantial endeavor.

The relevance, of course, was in establishing a national story that would facilitate a resonant national identity. To navigate Iran's place as a developing nation-state in a world with established super powers, the shah focused on Iran's historical glory and the peak of Persian ascendency. Though the continuity of his story was later questioned, the shah attempted to connect the past to the present directly, in the hope of creating an image of modern Iran that evoked the same powerful empire of the past:

Cyrus the Great, who reigned from about 559–529 B.C., was one of the most dynamic men in history. He captured the Median capital, overthrew their empire and, having united all modern Iran under his own rule established one of the world's first nation-states – some would say the first. He then went on to create the empire which, during his own reign and that of his successor Cambyses (*Cambojieh*), became the greatest the world has ever seen.[20]

Using an anachronistic title, such as "nation-state," to describe the Persian Empire illustrates how the shah was trying to show continuity with present-day Iran. The juxtaposition of past and present was also apparent in the images on bank notes printed during the reign of the shah. The 50 rials bill displayed an image of Cyrus the Great's tomb (Figure 2.1), while the 200 rials bill had a picture of Pol-e Veresk (Figure 2.2), an important feature of a railway construction project

[19] Ibid., 12 (emphasis added).     [20] Ibid., 21.

Figure 2.1 A 50 rials bank note of the Pahlavi monarchy, with an image of Pāsārgād, Cyrus the Great's grave outside the city of Shiraz and close to Persepolis, the capital of the Persian Empire.

Figure 2.2 A 200 rials bank note of the Pahlavi monarchy, with an image of Pol-e Veresk in northern Iran, a bridge that connects a mountain range allowing for the safe passage of trains.

under Reza Shah that became a symbol of Iran's progress toward modernity.

In his attempts to emphasize Persian greatness, the shah also made connections between Iran and contemporary Western powers. As if to place Iran geographically, racially, and, in terms of prowess, on par with the West, the shah wrote, "I sometimes think it curious that we are not better known to the West, for we have from an early date exported our culture, much as Americans today provide technical assistance overseas."[21] Not only did the shah try to establish similarities in global influence, he also made claims that linked Iran racially to the West – and in opposition to Iran's geographic neighbors – and even argued for the superiority of Persians:

Many centuries before the discovery of the New World, Persians were using table utensils and decorated ceramic dishes while most Europeans were still eating with their fingers as they sat on the ground. Ours is the world's oldest *continuous* civilization except that of China, and perhaps I can be forgiven for thinking it superior to theirs in some respects ... Certainly no one can doubt that our culture is more akin to that of the West than is either the Chinese or that of our neighbours the Arabs. Iran was an early home of the Aryans from whom most Americans and Europeans are descended, and we are racially quite separate from the Semitic stock of the Arabs.[22]

Though these passages were written in the late 1950s, the shah maintained this air of Persian supremacy even after 1979 and the decades of opposition that preceded the revolution. In his *Answer to History*, written after the 1979 revolution, the shah recounted, "[I]t can perhaps be claimed that there would have been no European Renaissance – or that it would have been quite different – without the work and much earlier example of the Persians, which the Arabs copied with such brilliance."[23] Like this, the shah built his nationalism on the relics of a long-gone empire.

In the context of anticolonial protest, resistance movements, and the realization of the nation-state as the preeminent model for governance, a national story alone would not suffice in the construction of nationalism. Aware of this fact, the shah went to great lengths to depict himself as a revolutionary and his father as the savior of Iran from foreign control. The Pahlavi monarchy pushed the idea that the previous Qajar dynasty was unfit to rule and had almost entirely squandered away and destroyed Iran: "The Qajars, although they lasted until my father superseded them in 1925, were by far the weakest of the major Persian dynasties. They did little to resist foreign infiltration, and even encouraged outside interference in our internal affairs by their indecisive policies."[24] The picture the shah

---

[21] Ibid., 16.    [22] Ibid., 18 (emphasis added).
[23] Mohammad Reza Pahlavi, *Answer to History* (New York: Stein and Day, 1980), 38.
[24] Pahlavi, *Mission for My Country*, 26.

depicted of Iran before his father's rule was quite bleak: "Really it was not a country, for this once proud land now possessed no central government ... There was no modern army ... there was no law and order."[25] In the midst of such chaos, the shah described his father in heroic terms that border on hyperbole: "[I]t was his piercing eyes that arrested anybody who met him. Those eyes could make a strong man shrivel up inside."[26] In fact, throughout much of his writing, the shah came back to the recurring theme of foreign control.

For the Pahlavis, the strongest point of contention was that the Qajar rulers were beholden to foreign powers. The shah asserted that it was his father's gallant patriotism and astute military thinking that brought Iran out from under the grip of external foes, as he wrote:

Imagine how galling it was to him to realize that he marched under the orders that were often dictated from the Russian rather than the Persian capital. I think he developed his intense feeling of patriotism and nationalism because he knew so well the meaning of foreign domination.[27]

The defiant and defensive nationalism the shah ascribed to his father was akin to that which developed among his oppositional forces, who viewed the shah as a foreign puppet. At the time of his writing, such voices of protest had already begun expressing their critiques in public spaces. The shah was mindful of the fact that these worries needed to be addressed, as evident in his statement:

Some extremists claim that the United States has revived the old imperialist tradition of exploitation ... I must frankly say that this has not been our experience. *We demand and receive complete equality of treatment.* America has never tried to dominate us as the old imperialists did, nor would we tolerate that; and the same applies to our relations with all other countries.[28]

Though the shah showed a keen attentiveness to the notion of independence, his policies were often criticized for enabling quite the opposite.

In an ironic foreshadowing of Ayatollah Khomeini's protest of 1964, the shah condemned the Qajars for corrupting the justice system in his 1958 book:

Under the system of capitulations, as I have said, foreigners (including the Bolsheviks who were now infiltrating the country in great numbers) could not have been tried by us for crimes they committed in Persia ... in the midst

---

[25] Ibid., 37.  [26] Ibid., 36.  [27] Ibid., 37.  [28] Ibid., 130 (emphasis added).

of their desolation the then Shah preoccupied himself with his lavish trips to Europe and his other self-centered luxuries. How could a true patriot have felt otherwise than filled with shame?[29]

Years later when the shah granted immunity to all American military personnel and their dependents living in Iran, Khomeini uttered his famous condemnation:

They have reduced the Iranian people to a level lower than that of an American dog. If someone runs over a dog belonging to an American, he will be prosecuted. Even if the Shah himself were to run over a dog belonging to an American, he would be prosecuted. But if an American cook runs over the Shah, the head of state, no one will have the right to interfere with him.[30]

Despite such protests and his eventual overthrow, the shah upheld the narrative of his father's success in establishing Iran's independence as a modern nation-state. In *Answer to History* he wrote: "Equally important was the re-establishment of domestic unity and the removal of foreign interference in Iran's internal affairs ... The stranglehold of foreign monopolies on the economic and social life of the country was gradually broken."[31] Throughout his rule and after, the shah argued his dynasty – which was part of Iran's unbroken 2,500-hundred-year monarchy – had saved Iran from the clutches of outsiders.

Having formulated a national story, in which his father established Iran's independence, the shah needed to make his own mark and so he thoughtfully imagined his legacy. In his vision of Iranian nationalism, the shah depicted himself as a revolutionary. In fact, the idea of revolution was a critical component of his nationalist plan. In the twentieth century, the creation of many independent nation-states came through revolution and revolutionary language became part of these new national identities. The 1960s were a decade of upheaval and protest throughout the world and in Iran. While many Iranians were swept up by revolutionary fervor and global anticolonial nationalism, the shah attempted to appropriate that innovative discourse with his White Revolution.

In the early 1960s the shah introduced his six-point plan to modernize the Iranian nation-state and to implement reforms in order to help improve the lives of the masses. By addressing issues such as land

---

[29]  Ibid., 38.
[30]  Ruhollah Khomeini and Hamid Algar, *Islam and Revolution: Writings and Declarations of Imam Khomeini* (Berkeley: Mizan Press, 1981), 182.
[31]  Pahlavi, *Answer to History*, 52.

reform, education, public health, and women's rights, the shah hoped to curtail the growing dissent among Iranian people, especially leftists who could look to events in Cuba and China as inspiration for their own revolution. Since communists and peasants led those revolutions, land reform became the cornerstone of the shah's development plans, which was called the White Revolution. The use of the term "revolution" was not simply a pithy catchphrase; in fact the language the shah used was prudently chosen and he wrote in depth about his plans in a book of the same name, *The White Revolution*. That he wrote an entire book dedicated to explaining this new campaign illustrates his careful consideration of language and content.

While *The White Revolution* focused on explaining the proposed reforms and their intended consequences, the shah continued with previous themes as well, such as the significance of independence from foreign control and crediting the Pahlavi dynasty with modernizing Iran. However, it is noteworthy that the central premise of the book was to depict these changes as a revolution, using the very language of his dissidents against them:

This revolution was essentially an Iranian revolution, compatible with the spirit and tradition of the Iranian people. We had not delivered this revolution to the people as an *imported item*. For it would be beneath the dignity of a nation which had for several thousand years been the pioneer of thinking, philosophy and religion, to wear anything borrowed.[32]

The shah made sure to exploit revolutionary discourse and address the concern of imported ideas to mollify the calls for radical change.

Throughout the book it is also clear that the shah marked this revolution as a turning point in Iran's history. In fact, he endorsed the White Revolution as the inauguration of "modern Iran":

This "White Revolution" became a reality by legal and democratic means early in 1963. On the ninth of January at the National Congress of Rural Cooperatives held in Tehran I outlined the principles of this Revolution in a six-point plan. On the 26th of January, 1963, equivalent to the sixth of Bahman, 1341, in the Persian calendar, *which must be considered as the starting point of Iran's modern history*, a general referendum was held.[33]

---

[32] Mohammad Reza Pahlavi, *The White Revolution of Iran* (Tehran: Imperial Pahlavi Library, 1967), 17 (emphasis added).
[33] Ibid., 3–4 (emphasis added).

**Figure 2.3** A 50 rials bank note of the Pahlavi monarchy with an image of the shah handing out land deeds to masses of peasants. Land reform was the centerpiece of the shah's White Revolution.

The idea that Iran's modernity was tied to this revolution was weaved throughout his writing, as he stated, "The revolutionary aim which I have presented to my people, and to which my people have responded with decisiveness and clarity, is that, God willing, I should utilize the present opportunity to construct a modern and progressive Iran."[34] The White Revolution was not only thoroughly written about, but also commemorated by images on Iranian currency (see Figure 2.3), which has long been a site for exhibiting national values.

Additionally, the referendum date for the White Revolution was celebrated as a national holiday, known as *Enqelāb-e Shah va Mardom* (The Revolution of the King and the People). The notion of revolution was so important to the shah that he marked two other national holidays based on the same principle: *14 Mordād* (August 4) in honor of the Constitutional Revolution of 1906 and *28 Mordād* (August 19) to commemorate the coup of Prime Minister Mossadeq in 1953, which the shah described as the people's uprising against Mossadeq.

These efforts indicate that the shah was cognizant of the importance of this discourse in legitimizing not only his own rule, but also his project of nationalism. He went to great lengths to portray himself as a patriot of his nation, and a father to his people. The next section

---

[34] Ibid., 24.

continues to examine the shah's writing closely to show why his message failed by appearing detached and alien to his subjects.

## 2.3 The Shah's Naiveté: Disconnect and Foreignness

Despite the shah's attempts to be seen as a father figure to the Iranian people and his rhetoric of independence, he was often criticized for his extravagance and dependence on foreign powers. By looking at his words, the shah's detachment from common Iranian people and his obliviousness to the concerns of his subjects becomes apparent. While many Iranians were displeased with the undemocratic governing methods of the shah, he maintained a line of reasoning that denied such discontent and described himself as a patriarch. His response in an interview that questioned his ability to restrain the people's demand for democracy is revealing:

But who says that my people are demanding the democracy that you have in Britain? Our tradition, just on the opposite way, the people and their king are so close that they feel as the member of the same family. They have, I think, the respect that these families, or children, used to have for their father.[35]

The shah's impression of himself as a loved father to his children, the Iranian populace, shows just how far removed he was from the reality on the ground. The most direct example of his ignorance was expressed by the shah's interpretation of events leading to the downfall of Prime Minister Mossadeq.

As Ervand Abrahamian argues, 1953 was a watershed moment in modern Iranian history.[36] In his research on this period, Abrahamian posits two main points. First he rejects the narrative iterated by the shah and other scholars that Mossadeq's psychology made an agreement with Britain over oil impossible – in fact the core issue was control of oil. Second, he contends that the coup should be understood in the context of the conflict between imperialism and nationalism rather than the conventional Cold War context. Thus, in his analysis, Mossadeq became a national hero as he worked to break free from British control and struggled for Iran's independence. At the same time,

---

[35] "Shah of Iran Criticizing Britain," YouTube video, last accessed July 23, 2018, www.youtube.com/watch?v=imil1iIpIYA.

[36] Ervand Abrahamian, *The Coup: 1953, The CIA, and the Roots of Modern U.S.-Iranian Relations* (New York: The New Press, 2013).

the shah became associated with British control of Iran's oil and was seen as a pawn to foreign power. Despite the shah's conflicts with Mossadeq, he was compelled to appoint Mossadeq as prime minister because of his overwhelming popularity among Iranian people.

As prime minister, Mossadeq launched a campaign to nationalize Iranian oil that put him in direct confrontation with Britain. This was seen by the Iranian masses as a battle for Iran's independence. It forged a new nationalism based on principles of democracy and freedom from external forces, as Abrahamian explains:

> In a ceremony potent with symbolism and similar to dramatic shifts of power in newly independent countries throughout the world, the national flag was hoisted up as the company insignia was taken down ... For some in Britain, the lowering of the insignia marked another step in the dissolution of the Empire. For many in Iran, the raising of the national flag showed the world that *the country had finally gained true independence*. Oil nationalization was for Iran what national independence was for many former colonies in Africa, Asia, Latin America, and the Caribbean.[37]

This image directly conflicted with the Pahlavi narrative that claimed Reza Shah had broken the curse of the Qajars and freed Iran from all foreign control. Moreover, Mossadeq's growing authority challenged the shah's title as leader of the nation and patriot to his people. Eventually this led to direct confrontation between the shah and Mossadeq over who would lead Iran into the future. With the assistance of US and British intelligence services, the shah succeeded in a coup in 1953 that ousted Mossadeq and reinstated himself as the absolute ruler of Iran.

The consequences of the coup were substantial, the denationalization of Iranian oil following the coup brought with it continued dominance from Britain and increased paranoia among Iranians about their state of politics. The popularity and influence of Mossadeq instilled fear in the young shah, who cracked down on political opposition with full force in Iran after 1953. As speculation over the coup increased it also delegitimized the monarchy and contributed to the impression of the shah as beholden to foreigners.

But what is truly spectacular about the coup is the shah's account of the incident. Throughout his decades of writing the shah maintained

---

[37]  Ibid., 79 (emphasis added).

several consistent themes, which portrayed Mossadeq as an antination-
alist usurper and emphasized the magnitude of support for the monarch among Iranians. In *Mission for My Country*, the shah dedicated an
entire chapter to the character of Mossadeq. Throughout the chapter
the shah tried to depict Mossadeq as an outsider: "I also watched
Mossadegh's progressive surrender to the agents of a foreign
ideology."[38] This image was carefully constructed to tarnish any mus-
ings of Mossadeq as a national hero and to show him as an instrument
of foreign powers. The shah even attempted to dismiss the grounded
accusations of a foreign-led coup: "*Rumours* flow unusually freely in
my country, and one had it that ordinary people who rose against
Mossadegh in some instances received American dollars or (according
to another version) British pounds for their help."[39] In his attempts to
taint the image of Mossadeq, the shah went so far as to compare the
prime minister to Hitler, a parallel he revisited years later in his *Answer
to History*.[40]

As the shah reconstructed the narrative of the coup for his own
benefit, describing Mossadeq as psychologically imbalanced and
foreign-controlled, he also tailored the story to fit his rhetoric of
revolution and nationalism. Writing of the people's loyalty to the
crown, the shah recounted, "In overturning Mossadegh and the
Tudeh, they staged a revolution that was inspired by indigenous
nationalism."[41] Whether willfully ignorant or meticulously decep-
tive, the shah portrayed the 1953 joint CIA-MI6 coup of Prime
Minister Mossadeq as a national uprising. In fact, the day of the
coup was commemorated as a national holiday:

Every country makes mistakes. If the Mossadegh experiment taught us how
not to run a country, perhaps in the long run it will have proved worthwhile.
On 19 August each year, my country celebrates Nation Day, commemorat-
ing the fall of Mossadegh and the *routing of alien forces that came within
a hair's breadth of extinguishing our independence.* I hope we never forget its
significance.[42]

The last words of his statement hang ominously as the significance of
the date was not forgotten, but rather remembered as a blow to Iran's
nationalist movement. The irony of celebrating a foreign-led coup as

[38] Pahlavi, *Mission for My Country*, 97.   [39] Ibid., 106 (emphasis added).
[40] Pahlavi, *Answer to History*, 87.   [41] Pahlavi, *Mission for My Country*, 106.
[42] Ibid., 110 (emphasis added).

a day of national independence should not be lost, as it was certainly not lost on Iranian dissidents who saw the coup for what it was and used it as further evidence of a king mired in his own delusions and out of touch with reality.

Of course, the Mossadeq episode was not the only time the shah was out of touch with his people. In his book on the White Revolution, the shah went to great lengths to outline his reform plans that were meant to be a turning point in Iranian history, or, as the shah claimed, the moment of modern Iran's establishment. It is noteworthy that in this critical work the shah consistently cited European and Western thinkers and writers while explaining his ideas for Iran's national future. Immediately following his declaration that this revolution was not an "imported item," since that would be degrading to the nation, the shah quotes the American essayist Ralph Waldo Emerson. While he quotes more famous figures such as Abraham Lincoln and Shakespeare, many of his references are from lesser-known thinkers such as Leon Walras, a nineteenth-century Swiss economist, or La Bruyère, a seventeenth-century French philosopher. He consistently used sources from the West to give legitimacy to his positions:

It is said that Richelieu called the peasant "the people's mule," and this expression seems to reflect the thinking of many of our land-owners ... I could not tolerate such an idea, since in my opinion the people they called peasants were among the purest and noblest in the land ... I found a great sense of humanity in a letter of Seneca to a large Roman Land-owner.[43]

Throughout the entirety of the book, the shah drew his ideas from foreigners and relied heavily on their philosophies.

If the book was meant for an Iranian audience his sources and prose appear questionable, as the selection was most likely less familiar to the Iranian masses. Looking at his writing however, it is reasonable to argue that the book was actually meant for the very Western spectators his text appealed to and those who were more familiar with such thinkers. It could be that his Swiss education made the shah disconnected from the more traditional learning among Iranians and that this gap was simply evident in his writing. Nonetheless, the shah's foreignness went beyond his erudition.

---

[43] Pahlavi, *White Revolution of Iran*, 34.

It was not just that Westerners influenced his writing, or that, in the case of oil nationalization, his politics were bound to foreign powers. Further reading shows how the shah wanted to be seen as part of the West or resembling foreigners as well. As author Reza Zia-Ebrahimi writes, the shah asserted it was "an accident of geography" that Iran was in the Middle East and not closer to its kin in the West.[44] Such claims are supported by the shah's writing, which indicated a strong desire for affinity with the West:

In our individualism we resemble the French (whose taxi men in their willfulness rate a close second to ours), and it is no wonder that Iran has often been called the France of Asia. As individualists we are also much like the Americans, and I am not surprised that Persians and Americans get on so well together. The hundreds of students we send each year to America almost invariably enjoy their stay there, and Americans working in my country mix freely and naturally in our social life.[45]

The shah continued to boast of Iran's French influence: "Many leaders in Iranian life have their training in France, French is widely spoken among Iran's intelligentsia, a French-language daily newspaper is published here."[46] The shah's Francophilia became a point of contention in 1971 during the infamous monarchical celebrations, a topic that is discussed in more detail in the next section.

For the shah, modernization and progress were directly linked to Westernization. He saw imitation of the West as the best possible strategy to advancing the Iranian cause: "To stimulate our entire educational system, I should like us to establish here a university modeled strictly on American lines and with a primarily American staff."[47] Even after the revolution that ousted him in 1979, the shah persisted in paying homage to his foreign backers. The Author's Note in *Answer to History*, his last book written after the revolution, when he was gravely ill and dying, carries pertinent implications: "It is my intention that the American version of *Answer to History* be the definitive text."[48] Reflecting on the events that had come to pass, the shah proved that he was less concerned with addressing the Iranian people and more interested in an audience with the West.

[44] Reza Zia-Ebrahimi, "Self-Orientalization and Dislocation: The Uses and Abuses of the 'Aryan' Discourse in Iran," *Iranian Studies*. 44, no. 4 (2011), 445–72.
[45] Pahlavi, *Mission for My Country*, 29.    [46] Ibid., 113.    [47] Ibid., 262.
[48] Pahlavi, *Answer to History*.

The shah's reliance on Western thinkers and his aspiration to emulate foreigners became a central critique from his opposition. By the 1970s, rebel forces against the shah took the fight to the streets. The Siahkal incident of February 1971 marked the beginning of armed struggle in Iran, as the Marxist group *Cherik-hā-ye Fadāi-ye Khalq-e Irān* (The Organization of Iranian People's Fedai Guerrillas) attacked a gendarmerie and killed police officers. Following the attacks, the shah cracked down further on political opposition and, tone deaf as ever, continued planning his 2,500-year anniversary party hailing Iran's presumed unbroken monarchy. Thus, 1971 marked another turning point, the climax of the shah's obliviousness and foreignness evident in these audacious celebrations.

## 2.4 1971: The Party of the Century and the Apex of Ignorance

A critical aspect of the shah's nationalism project was the idea of uninterrupted Persian dominion and the crown. The shah marked 1971 as the 2,500-year anniversary of the Persian monarchy. His plan was to have an extravagant party, inviting all the dignitaries of the world, to celebrate this magnificent history. He chose Persepolis as its location to highlight the symbolism of the Pahlavi dynasty, as descendants of Cyrus the Great. This party was the culmination of all the shah's attempts at national cohesion, to affirm his monarchical narrative, to show the glory of Iran's past and present, to demonstrate Iran's progress and rightful place in the international community of nations, and, most importantly, to display all of it for the West to behold.

However, the party also laid bare all of the cracks in the shah's story of nationalism. The party's ostentatious design had egregious costs that oppositional forces quickly noted. In spite of the fact that the party was promoted as a celebration of Iranian history and culture, Iranians were notably absent from the festivities. Instead of bringing the nation together in merriment, the party exposed all that was offensive and out of touch about the shah's nationalism project. The so-called "party of the century" became a symbol for the opposition to demonstrate all that was wrong with the monarchy. The party was of such importance in terms of its impact on the shah's rule and the revolution of 1979, that, as recently as 2016, the BBC produced a documentary[49] that suggested the party was the catalyst for the shah's demise.

In an article discussing the documentary, Robert Hardman writes, "Not since Marie Antoinette's immortal (if invented) remark – 'let them eat cake' – has there been such an ill-advised catering directive."[50] Both the recent article and documentary insinuate that the downfall of the shah was a consequence of the profligate celebrations. While the causes of the revolution are in reality more complex, the concern here is how the party became a symbol of discontent and provided further evidence of the shah's apparent ignorance to the needs and desires of his subjects.

As Sally Quin, a *Washington Post* reporter on site for the celebrations, recalled, the cost of the party in light of the still massive amounts of poverty throughout Iran became a point of contention. The documentary notes several excesses of the party, such as building a tent city for the guests, importing 50,000 birds and thousands of trees to make the hot arid climate feel more like an oasis, importing an abundance of food and drinks, and hiring a film crew to document the party. Beyond such overindulgences, the party's design and the controversy surrounding it were indicative of the shah's foreignness and help to illustrate how he appeared alien to the Iranian masses.

What many observers noted in this celebration of Iranian culture and history was the absence of anything Iranian, including the people. For instance, the narrator hired for the documentary film was Orson Welles,[51] a well-known American actor/director. The tent city that was constructed for the sole purpose of the party was imported entirely from France and even the interior designs reflected French sensibilities.[52] While the menu became quite a sensation as newspapers reported on it, critics emphasized that there was no Persian cuisine offered to the

[49] Hassan Amini, dir., *Decadence and Downfall: The Shah's Ultimate Party* (Amber Entertainment, 2016), last accessed July 23, 2018, www.bbc.co.uk/programmes/b07176xr.
[50] Robert Hardman, "Princess Anne and the £1Billion Party That Lit the Fuse of Islamic Terror 45 Years Ago," *Daily Mail* (February 12, 2016), last accessed July 23, 2018, www.dailymail.co.uk/news/article-3445017/Princess-Anne-1billion-party-lit-fuse-Islamic-terror-45-years-ago.html.
[51] Ibid.
[52] Aline Mosby, "The Party Menu: Baked Peacocks and Quail Eggs," *The Chicago Tribune* (October 10, 1971), 9.

guests in this celebration. Instead, in this festival of Persian monarchy, the shah imported food and drinks from France:

Quail's eggs with caviar, crayfish tail mousse, stuffed roast lamb with truffles, champagne water ice, those 90 peacocks baked and reconstructed, feathers and all, nut and truffle salad, creamed figs and raspberries in port wine, and all washed down with the most famous wines of France, including a pink champagne created for the occasion.[53]

If not for the procession of antique dressed Persian soldiers and the hot weather, one might think they were celebrating French supremacy.

The fact that the celebrations drew criticism from his opposition was not lost on the shah; as one student protestor in *Decadence and Downfall* states, the universities were shut down during the celebrations and student activists were detained to ensure the safety and security of the guests and the party. When asked by a French journalist during the days of the celebration if university protests were forbidden, the shah replied, "Which protests? Against what? Against our country's independence? That's not even a question, nobody talks about it."[54] As before, the shah tied his nationalist celebration to the notion of independence, showing that a national project without independence was hollow. In another interview, when asked what ties Iranians together as a nation, the shah replied, "I'm not making any propaganda, but I think it's the crown, the king."[55] Yet again, he fell victim to his ignorance or hubris, since his perceptions of reality seemed to contrast with that of the Iranian people.

The first president after the revolution, Abolhassan Banisadr, sums up well the sentiment of Iranian people surrounding the celebrations: "When you gather all the countries of the world, you're basing your legitimacy on them. Your celebration is not for your people, but for them. They're the important ones, not your own people."[56] Though he had instilled the same sentiment of detachment on other occasions throughout his reign, the 2,500-year celebrations became the peak of the shah's disconnection with his people and exemplified how far removed he was from the lives of everyday Iranians. Hostility toward the celebrations became a key symbol that brought together various political opponents of the shah. But it was not the celebration alone

---

[53]  Ibid.   [54]  *Decadence and Downfall: The Shah's Ultimate Party* (see n. 49).
[55]  Ibid.   [56]  Ibid.

that was the shah's death knell. His inability to construct a resonant nationalism among the masses, based on the principles of revolution, independence, and indigenous Iranian culture that he espoused, gave his opponents the space and opportunity to formulate an alternative narrative. The next sections investigate sources from the opposition that show how the shah was depicted as foreign and how they were able to create a nationalist force that aided the revolution.

## 2.5 The Opposition: Resisting Imperialism

While the struggles between rebel groups and the shah are at times framed in terms of tradition versus modernity, scholars such as Jahanbegloo and Dabashi reject this misleading binary. Dabashi argues that Iranian national identity was the product of transnational interactions and space. Confrontation and contestation with European imperialism brought together various ideas that influenced Iran and the region as a whole, which included anticolonial nationalism, third-world socialism, and Islamism.[57] In contrast to assertions that give full control to European powers and the impression that they simply imposed their will and ideas on docile Indigenous populations, Dabashi's claim is significant for giving agency to Iranian people. Iranians did not merely import and mimic foreign concepts, instead the diverse rebel forces in Iran studied different political ideologies that were popular at the time and appropriated various components to fit their national cause. Thus, the Iranian nationalism that emerged in the twentieth century leading up to the revolution was a product of interaction with the outside world, a process that was simultaneously imported *and* homegrown.

Central to this nationalism was the perceived struggle for independence, often debated in revolutionary language. Since Iran was never formally colonized by an external power, it was the task of the opposition to portray the shah as foreign. In order to substantiate the claim that the shah was the antithesis of Iranian independence and nationalism, the downfall of the monarchy was envisaged as a blow to world imperialism. This was well understood by many of the shah's dissidents and was epitomized by the work of Ali Shariati.

---

[57] Hamid Dabashi, *Iran Without Borders: Towards a Critique of the Postcolonial Nation* (New York: Verso, 2016).

Influenced by the theories of Frantz Fanon, Shariati saw a need for massive reform and revolution in Iran. Fanon's works inspired many colonized peoples to take up armed struggle against the forces of imperialism and exploitation. His anticolonial manifesto, *Wretched of the Earth*, was popular reading among young rebels fighting for national liberation. In light of Fanon's objection to mimicking Europe, his impact on Shariati was evident in Shariati's rejection of both Eastern and Western models of governance. When Shariati stated, "What all the new appeals have in common is a belief that both the roads onto which Western capitalism and communism have driven humanity culminate in a human disaster, that the way to human liberation therefore consists in turning away from both of them,"[58] he echoed the insights of Fanon:

It was commonly thought that the time had come for the world, and particularly for the Third World, to choose between the capitalist system and the socialist system. The underdeveloped countries, which made use of the savage competition between the two systems in order to win their national liberation, must, however, refuse to get involved in such rivalry. The Third World must not be content to define itself in relation to values which preceded it. On the contrary, the underdeveloped countries must endeavor to focus on their very own values as well as methods and style specific to them. The basic issue with which we are faced is not the unequivocal choice between socialism and capitalism such as they have been defined by men from different continents and different periods of time.[59]

However, while Fanon argued that these new developing nationalisms should not look to the past, Shariati believed it was imperative to take back pride in one's cultural roots in order to come together in the struggle for liberation: "Nationalism rests upon the drive for the political independence and *cultural integrity* of the nation in question."[60] Shariati framed his views in a manner that portrayed the shah as an imperialist force representing foreign interests and looked to Islamic discourse as an alternative to the existing European systems, which he saw as exploitative to the masses.

The notion of cultural integrity was permeating Iranian intellectual thought in the decades leading up to the revolution. For Shariati, and

[58]  Ali Shariati, *Marxism and Other Western Fallacies: An Islamic Critique*, trans. R. Campbell (Berkeley: Mizan Press, 1980), 93.
[59]  Frantz Fanon, Richard Philcox, Jean-Paul Sartre, and Homi K. Bhabha, *The Wretched of the Earth* (New York: Grove Press, 2004), 55.
[60]  Shariati, *Marxism and Other Western Fallacies*, 65 (emphasis added).

others, Shiite Islam was a cornerstone of Iranian culture that was neglected by the shah and could be appreciated for its familiarity as a common denominator among most Iranians. As Shariati recounted:

Our nation prides itself on having followed the Ja'fari school and Ali for centuries. From the very first century of Islam, when Iran entered the Islamic community and swiftly discarded its ancient religion in favor of Islam, it has followed the school of Ali, the companions of Ali and the government of Ali, whether officially as is now the case, or practically, with respect to sentiment and belief.[61]

Consequently, Shariati used Shiism as an ideology to challenge Western dominance and as an emblem for Iran's historically rooted national character.

Along with Shariati, social critics, such as Jalal Al-e Ahmad, gained popularity in Iran for challenging the shah's Westernization policies. Like Shariati, Al-e Ahmad was troubled by the loss of Iranian roots and blind imitation of the West, as evident in his words: "He relegates his religion to oblivion the first time he goes to a movie ... The radio has them under its spell constantly, the cinema brings them visions of more sophisticated lifestyles, while that other reality is still there, unnoticed, a reality of religious faith."[62] In his magnum opus, *Gharbzadegi* (*Weststruckness*), Al-e Ahmad advanced the idea that Iran's leadership had failed the masses and introduced what he described as a disease of "Westoxification," which was destroying Iran and its historical personality. Al-e Ahmad noted the conflict between the Islamic identity of the masses and the shah's nationalist project:

Meanwhile, it is for these people that the government, with its organizations, schools, military installations, administrative offices, prisons, and the trumpets and horns of its radios, promotes nationalism, plays a different tune of its own ... The fanfare and propaganda of its radio stations have deafened the ears of heaven with thousands and thousands of never-ending claims to glory; it continually points its canons and rifles into the people's faces and has its twenty-five-hundred-year exhibition in Shiraz.[63]

---

[61] Ali Shariati and Hamid Algar, *On the Sociology of Islam: Lectures* (Berkeley: Mizan Press, 1979), 40.
[62] Jalal Al-e Ahmad, *Gharbzadegi [Weststruckness]*, trans. John Green and Ahmad Alizadeh (Lexington, KY: Mazda Publishers, 1982), 83.
[63] Ibid., 82.

For Al-e Ahmad and Shariati, the shah's nationalism was a falsehood based on foreign imposition and lacked the religious hallmarks of Iranian society.

These sentiments were also manifest in popular literature of the era, such as Simin Daneshvar's well-known novel *Savushun*. Set in the 1940s in Shiraz, the story centers around a middle-class land-owning family and their life difficulties, which include themes of corruption, foreign power, peasant relations, and traditional values. Against a disheartening backdrop of exploitation and struggle, the reader is drawn to the family patriarch, Yusef, who exemplifies idealism and honesty. During a time of food shortages, as officials and other landlords show more concern for the profits they can reap from feeding the soldiers of occupying forces, Yusef is worried about feeding the peasants on his land.

Written in the late 1960s, Daneshvar's novel reflects the attitudes of the era. Though the shah at the time boasted of the successes of his White Revolution and wrote of Iran's progress and independence, Daneshvar highlighted the mistreatment of Iranians at the hands of foreigners and the complicity of officials in allowing such a state of affairs through her character Yusef: "There is nothing surprising and new about the foreigners coming here uninvited ... What I despise is the feeling of inferiority, which has been instilled in all of you. In the blink of an eye, they make you all their dealers, errand boys."[64] The inferiority that Yusef speaks of is comparable to Fanon's discussion of mental disorders resulting from colonialism.

Yusef embodied the qualities that Al-e Ahmad and Shariati hoped to impart on their fellow Iranians. They wished to break free from Western superiority and reclaim their roots and pride, a charge the shah had failed at in their eyes. That Yusef became a martyr at the end of the novel is not surprising, given the motif of martyrdom that prevails in Shiism. Beyond social critics and writers, the image of the shah as an imperialist was infused into political movements as well. Student activists abroad protested more freely, while fighters within Iran in the 1970s became actual martyrs for the cause against the shah.

Organizing in response to the 2,500-year celebration of Iranian monarchy, Iranian students in the United States wrote and distributed pamphlets on university campuses to bring attention to the shah's

[64] Simin Daneshvar, *Savushun* (Tehran: Kharazmi, 1976), 31.

repression. These students claimed that their efforts were vital because though the propaganda machine of the shah spent a fortune to paint a picture of stability, progress, and prosperity, this image was losing credibility due to their labors. The pamphlets emphasized the shah's dictatorship, but also underscored the divide between the shah and his people:

The regime of the dictator Shah is celebrating 2,500 years of the dictatorship of the kings and shahs of Iran. This regime has attempted to totally undermine the glorious 2,500 years history of the Iranian people – their culture, art, livelihood, struggle, achievements, and hatred for the regime of the kings.[65]

In discussing the shah's reasons for the decadent party, the students stated that it is "to pretend that unity exists among the Iranian nation and the Iranian government."[66] In complete contrast to the shah's account, that the crown was what bound the people together, the students clearly drew a line of separation between the nation and the king. In this regard it seems, the nation was independent from the king and could only be liberated with his defeat.

The memoirs of famed guerrilla fighter Ashraf Dehghani were a more sobering reminder of the extent of the shah's repression, as she detailed her imprisonment and torture under the shah's authoritarian state. In the introduction given by the Iranian People's Fedai Guerrillas, the link between the shah and imperialism was unequivocal. Moreover, it is evident that Iran's movement against the shah was set in a framework of anti-imperial movements around the world:

Our age is the age of liberation of the enslaved masses exploited by imperialism. It is the age of peoples' liberation movements. Every day the masses of the world open up a new front against world imperialism, and everyday a new blow is inflicted on imperialists ... Now when a warrior is slain in the front against imperialism, many fighting hands reach for his weapon to continue the solemn struggle, which leads to the freedom of the masses. This historic development inevitably claims many martyrs, but that does not deter the revolutionaries. Rather, it makes them more determined ... The young generation in Iran has risen to wipe out the degradation of the past

---

[65] Iranian Students' Association in Northern California, *The Regime of the Shah Steps Up Political Repression in Iran as It Prepares for the Celebration of 2500 Year [sic] of Iranian Monarchy* (Berkeley: The Association, 1971), 1.

[66] Ibid., 14.

two decades; to wipe out the gloom and the doubts; to break the silence, the suppression; to end the, impotence; to condemn looking abroad for all inspiration and patterns of action; to eliminate the sewage of opportunism; to destroy the yoke of imperialism and reaction, and to accomplish the rule of the people in their homeland.[67]

In this statement it is clear that the shah was seen as part of the imperialist world order and that these activists were urging Iranians to look inward for answers rather than parroting systems from abroad. It is also noteworthy that, though they were not a religious group, these students appeared undisturbed by the possibility of martyrdom, which is a central feature of Shiism and was often used by religiously minded revolutionary figures. For these fighters, the rule of the people, a significant nationalist sentiment, was only possible through armed struggle that would topple the shah.

In Dehghani's description of her torture, she was also candid with her language about the shah, describing him as a puppet to his masters abroad: "Thinking about the nature of torture infuriated me. I thought about the cause of all this savagery. The traitor, the mercenary, the servant and puppet of U.S. imperialism, does not stop at any crime to buy more time for his tyranny."[68] Dehghani provided reasoning for the shah's actions by observing that his interests, as part of the imperialist machine, were aligned with that of foreign agents: "From the beginning of the armed struggle, the Iranian regime had seen its own interests and that of its imperialist masters seriously threatened. It was petrified in the face of growing struggle."[69] Such references to the shah as a puppet and imperialist underscore the fact that he was portrayed by various factions of his opposition as somehow foreign or separate from Iranian society.

The people who resisted the shah and his nationalism became heroes and patriots for Iran's version of an anticolonial nationalism, which in the twentieth century had facilitated the establishment of many new nation-states. Seen as an imperialist and a foreigner, toppling the shah became equivalent to a Third World revolution against the old-world order. That revolution became realized in 1979 under the leadership of

---

[67] Ashraf Dehghani, *Torture & Resistance in Iran: Memoirs of the Woman Guerrilla Ashraf Dehghani* (1978), last accessed July 24, 2018, www .siahkal.com/english/part1.htm.
[68] Ibid.    [69] Ibid.

the monarch's greatest critic. Ayatollah Khomeini was the most effective example of a detractor who conceived of the shah as a foreigner. Khomeini successfully convinced the masses that Iran could not be free or hope to advance under the shah's misguided nationalism and dictatorship.

## 2.6 Khomeini's Legacy: A Revolution and Modern Iran

Benedict Anderson observes that revolutions, since World War II, have expressed themselves in nationalist terms. The Iranian revolution of 1979 brought together a diverse set of political ideologies, ranging from Marxism to Islamism, but the central connection between all these schools of thought was a populist message with nationalist overtones. The leader who organized these different ideas into a clear message was Ayatollah Khomeini. Though Khomeini used Islam as part of his core message, his speeches and declarations carried overt nationalist implications, as he defined the Iranian nation-state in terms that resonated with the masses. He used Islam and Shiism as the most common foundation in order to link millions of Iranians together.

The connection to these cultural roots is significant, as Anderson suggests, "nationalism has to be understood by aligning it, not with self-consciously held political ideologies, but with the large cultural systems that preceded it, out of which – as well as against which – it came into being."[70] Anderson notes that the two major cultural systems that came before nationalism were the religious community and dynastic realm. Khomeini associated his nationalism with the religious community and against the monarchy to create a new national identity that challenged the Pahlavi narrative. By carefully crafting the shah's persona as foreign, Iranian activists were able to define their revolutionary movement with nationalist language. The shah's naiveté and contrived nationalism aided the efforts of his dissidents.

While Khomeini remained silent in the 1950s during the nationalist uprising of Mossadeq and the ensuing coup that affirmed the shah's authority, he became outspoken in the 1960s as the shah's White Revolution antagonized the position of Iranian clerics. In a speech delivered in Qom in 1963, Khomeini addressed the shah directly:

---

[70] Benedict Anderson, *Imagined Communities: Reflections on the Origin and Spread of Nationalism* (London: Verso, 2006), 12.

"You have carried out your White Revolution in the midst of all this Black Reaction! What do you mean, a White Revolution? Why do you deceive the people so? Why do you threaten the people so?"[71] In his speech Khomeini offered counsel to the shah and urged him to terminate the policies that were beneficial to his "masters." Again, linking the shah and his father to foreign powers and speaking candidly to the Iranian masses, Khomeini stated:

Iranian nation! Those among you who are thirty or forty years of age or more will remember how three foreign countries attacked us during World War II. The Soviet Union, Britain, and America invaded Iran and occupied our country. The property of the people was exposed to danger and their honor was imperiled. But God knows, everyone was happy because the Pahlavi had gone![72]

By using threats of invasion and occupation, that Iranians had long feared, Khomeini embedded that anxiety into the people's minds. Additionally, the notion of honor was key to Khomeini's ability to appeal to the masses, since it stirred their nationalist sentiments and instigated resentment toward the shah who was characterized as bringing shame to the nation.

After being exiled in 1964, for his speech opposing the shah's capitulations to the United States, Khomeini continued his activism from abroad. While his messages were often couched in Islamic terms, the nationalist undertones were quite clear. In a letter addressed to Prime Minister Hoveyda in 1967, Khomeini painfully stated:

Throughout this long period that I have been away from my homeland because of the crime of opposing the legal immunity of the Americans – *a shattering blow to the foundations of our national independence* – and have been compelled to live in exile ... I have been observing the misfortunes that have been descending on our oppressed and defenseless people. I have been kept informed of the oppression inflicted on our noble people by the tyrannical regime, and I have suffered correspondingly.[73]

The image of suffering as a result of being away from one's homeland is immensely nationalist because it brings value to a particular place, with its unique soil and environment. Like the shah, Khomeini used national independence as a rallying cry; only this time the foreign agent was

[71] Ruhollah Khomeini and Hamid Algar, *Islam and Revolution: Writings and Declarations of Imam Khomeini* (Berkeley: Mizan Press, 1981), 179.
[72] Ibid., 178–79.    [73] Ibid., 189 (emphasis added).

Iran's ruling monarch. As before, the nobility of the people was cited to instill indignation against the shah who had failed to protect the integrity of the Iranian nation.

Over his years in exile, Khomeini's message grew more intolerant of the shah. No longer did he offer counsel or advice, nor did he speak straight to him, but rather his declarations were directed at the Iranian people and the world. By the 1970s, for Khomeini, the shah's state had become nothing more than a tool for foreign interests and he framed his arguments in terms of a revolution against imperialism. In a speech delivered while still in exile in 1978, Khomeini argued:

The imperialists proclaim that man is free only in order to deceive the masses. But people can no longer be deceived ... As for America, a signatory to the Declaration of Human Rights, *it imposed this Shah upon us*, a worthy successor to his father. During the period he has ruled, this creature has transformed Iran into an official colony of the U.S. What crimes he has committed in service to his masters! What crimes the father and this son have committed against the Iranian nation since their appointment by the signatories to the Declaration of Human Rights.[74]

By describing Iran as a colony, Khomeini connected Iran's struggle to other anticolonial battles around the world. Khomeini's description of the shah as a "creature" was also meant to degrade and associate him with nonhuman symbols. This dehumanization process was visible on defiled Iranian banknotes that drew over the shah's picture to depict him as a devil or monster (Figure 2.4). Vandalizing the currency carried a potent meaning for its literal imagery and the figurative significance of humiliating the monarchy.

In addition to his compelling speeches, Khomeini appealed to many not for his ideology, but because of his staunch stance against the shah. As Dabashi argues, even secularists and Marxists were attracted to Khomeini for his genuine asceticism, which was antithetical to the shah's image of pomp and flash.[75] Though the revolutionary ideology that facilitated events in the 1970s was influenced by a diverse array of political groups and intellectuals, Khomeini rose[76] to the position of leader by engaging

---

[74] Ibid., 214–15 (emphasis added).
[75] Hamid Dabashi, *Theology of Discontent: The Ideological Foundations of the Islamic Revolution in Iran* (New York: New York University Press, 1993).
[76] As other studies have already argued, other factors contributed to his rise, such as his exile that gave him the ability to speak without fear of retribution from the

**Figure 2.4** A bank note of the Pahlavi monarchy. The text penned in the corner reads "The blood-sucker of history" (Khun āshām-e tārikh).

the masses in a populist message while using their religious proclivities to speak a language they understood. In exile, longing for his homeland, Khomeini became an epic nationalist figure, whose eventual homecoming was likened to the return of the twelfth Imam in Shiite tradition. With this mystical aura, Khomeini became a perceived hero in Iran's national story, while the shah became the antagonist of the plot.

## 2.7 Conclusion

When the image of the shah as a foreign imposition reached its climax, the call for his overthrow became a revolutionary slogan for national independence. Though Iran had experienced periods of political upheaval and economic woes throughout the twentieth century, by the late 1970s, revolutionaries had created an innovative discourse and forged a novel national identity that pushed the country toward revolution. As Mansoor Moaddel argues:

Neither the economic difficulties nor the social discontents explain the emergence of the revolutionary crisis of the late seventies. Revolutionary crisis occurred when the actions of the discontented groups were shaped by Shi'i revolutionary discourse . . . . Nor is it correct to argue that Shi'i ideology and religious institutions constituted *preexisting* organizations that were utilized

state, and the fact that the shah had cracked down on other leftist and nationalist dissident groups.

by the revolutionary actors ... the ideology of Islamic opposition was *pro-duced* by diverse intellectuals.[77]

Therefore, Iranian dissidents designed a discourse and ideology that was not a return to the past, but rather a fresh way of formulating the mechanics of the modern nation-state. In doing so they also managed to construct a national narrative to replace the shah's story of monarchy. In both cases, their actions were not shaped by a traditional model of the past. As Jahanbegloo argues, the dichotomy of modernity versus tradition is futile, since even the position of so-called "anti-modernists" is ultimately modern in its nature.[78] Accordingly, the revolutionary movement used traditional cultural roots to implement a new concept for their modern and independent nation.

As Hobsbawm and Anderson suggest, imagined nationalism is essential to the nation-state endeavor, since the existence of the abstract entity is predicated on the shared vision of a community. In fact, nationalism can exist in the absence of a territorial state, as the Palestinian and Kurdish cases illustrate. However, few nations exist with no form of nationalism. An examination of the shah's words and deeds shows that the shah understood how establishing national independence, a strong national narrative that included Iranian cultural traditions, and revolutionary zeal were vital in the construction of a modern-nation-state. That the shah failed in these attempts in the eyes of his opposition gives credence to the argument that his modern nation-state failed as well.

Popular Iranian musician Mohsen Namjoo, in a song entitled "Reza Khan," captured the shortcomings of the Pahlavi monarchs, as well as their major attempts at modernizing Iran. Much like the scholarly narrative that credits the Pahlavi kings for establishing modern Iran, Namjoo sings, "Oh nation, he brought modernity and the temperament of a dog."[79] Though the Pahlavi dynasty was successful at erecting modern structures, their ideology and nationalism did not succeed in convincing Iranians, who saw them more often as foreign puppets. In the twentieth century atmosphere of anticolonial nationalism and

---

[77] Mansoor Moaddel, *Class, Politics, and Ideology in the Iranian Revolution* (New York: Columbia University Press, 1993), 24.
[78] Jahanbegloo, *Iran*.
[79] "Mohsen Namjoo – Reza Khan," YouTube video, last accessed July 24, 2018, www.youtube.com/watch?v=xOLGTkNGqGE.

revolution, the people's will could not be ignored for long, as the shah presciently concluded years before his downfall:

With the growth of education and of political parties in Iran, a good king will be able to serve his country more effectively than ever before; but a mediocre or bad king would no longer have the means to cause damage, for the enlightened people of this country would not tolerate it. They would oblige him to reform or to relinquish his throne in favor of his constitutional successor. Persian public sentiment, I am convinced, will ever be alert to the country's needs.[80]

Responding to their need for independence and cultural integrity, Iranians protested in mass and led a revolution that shook the world.

While Namjoo ridiculed the Pahlavi king, the song also subtly alluded to the idea that despite changes on the surface, there was a great deal of continuity between the monarchy and the new revolutionary government. Like the Pahlavi monarchs, the newly established Islamic Republic carefully crafted a national narrative to fit their tastes. The next chapter examines the process of the Islamic Republic's historical production.

---

[80] Pahlavi, *Mission for My Country*, 328.

# 3 | The Islamic Republic and Its Culture of Resistance

The greatest success of the Iranian revolution was in extinguishing what many Iranians understood as the influence of foreign powers and becoming an independent state. The national narrative that Iranian dissidents crafted over several decades brought together diverse groups to create a shared imagining of Iran's story. However, once in power the newly formed Islamic Republic government, under the leadership of Khomeini, embarked on a similar endeavor of nationalist construction that the shah had attempted. Like the shah, the new government participated in the production of history. As Michel-Rolph Trouillot asserts, power makes some narratives possible while silencing and trying to erase others.[1] But it is not power alone that is responsible for this production; common people, with their agency and imagination, also contribute to this process by accepting and resisting different facets of these narratives. This is evident in the fact that so many Iranians resisted the account of the shah and continued to challenge the history presented by the authorities of the Islamic Republic.

The fear of erasing the past was exhibited in the works of Shariati and Al-e Ahmad who believed that they were witnessing the disintegration of Iranian, and especially Shiite, culture. As the Islamic Republic rectified that absence, inevitably it worked to erase others. As Trouillot explains, "Silences are inherent in history because any single event enters history with some of its constituting parts missing. Something is always left out while something else is recorded."[2] The fear of such erasure is still seen in creative expressions of Iranian artists (see Figure 3.1).[3] In this image the transition from colorful traditional

---

[1] Michel-Rolph Trouillot, *Silencing the Past: Power and the Production of History* (Boston, MA: Beacon Press, 1995).
[2] Ibid., 49.
[3] Hamideh Razavi, Instagram post (October 31, 2014), last accessed August 6, 2018, www.instagram.com/p/uzuoPtuRjx/?hl=en.

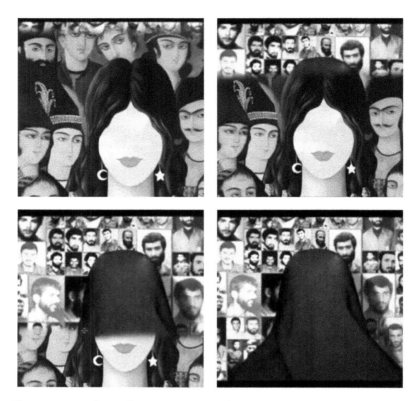

**Figure 3.1** "Veiling of Women." Created using screenshots from the video posted by Ms. Razavi to create an impression of the content.

Iranian art, with an uncovered woman in the foreground, to black-and-white photos of martyrs and the woman concealed in a veil, speaks volumes to the anxieties of Iranians in this new era of historical production.

The task of the historian is not necessarily to uncover the "correct" narrative, but to explore these varying accounts and question the motives behind them. Trouillot outlines this objective:

Between the mechanically "realist" and naively "constructivist" extremes, there is the more serious task of determining not what history is – a hopeless goal if phrased in essentialist terms – but how history works. For what history is changes with time and place or, better said, history reveals itself only through the production of specific narratives. What matters most are the process and conditions of production of such narratives. Only a focus on that process can uncover the ways in which the two sides of historicity intertwine in a particular context. Only through that overlap can we discover the differential exercise of power that makes some narratives possible and silences others.[4]

The changing nature of history and the making of specific narratives are exemplified in the images presented in schoolbooks, which through nationwide education all members of a society are meant to see. As Figures 3.2 and 3.3 show, the messages conveyed by the shah and the Islamic Republic displayed clear similarities as well as stark contrasts.

**Figure 3.2** Pahlavi third-grade schoolbook, 1960: Its message reiterated the idea of the shah as a "father" to the people; in one part it reads, "The shah is like a kind father, and the people are like his children ... We love our king."

---

[4] Trouillot, *Silencing the Past*, 25.

استقلال و آزادی در پیروی از قرآن کریم و رسول اکرم (ص) است.

امام خمینی «قدس سره الشریف»

**Figure 3.3** Islamic Republic seventh-grade schoolbook, 1995: The statement below the image of Khomeini reads, "Independence and freedom comes from following the great Quran and its message."

Both textbooks opened to a picture of the nation's designated leader in order to remind young students of the state's authority, but also subtly implied the people's acceptance of that authority with the accompanying text. Of course, the images diverged in other ways, as one emphasized the supremacy of monarchy and king and the other esteemed independence and Islam. The opposing historical narratives presented by the shah and the Islamic Republic illustrates the significance of context and how Iranian history was produced to support the ideological outlook and agenda of those wielding power.

However, it is important to note that historical *production* is not the same as *fabrication*. As Stuart Hall argues, representation and culture are imperative to how human beings "make sense of things." In other words, cultural meanings are not just "in our heads."[5] Instead, cultural

---

[5]   Stuart Hall, *Representation: Cultural Representations and Signifying Practices* (London: Sage/Open University, 1997).

meanings facilitate how we interpret information and help organize social practices. In terms of national character, relevant ideas and images must be attached in order to represent such identities. As Hall explains: "Members of the same culture must share sets of concepts, images and ideas which enable them to think and feel about the world and thus to interpret the world, in roughly similar ways."[6]

So, while meaning is constructed, symbols and signifiers must be somewhat stable in order to make communication possible. These meanings become fixed through social conventions and bounded within specific cultures. In this sense, representations of national identity and the meanings attached to them, must be conveyed in a way that the masses in a population can "read" and understand. Through this system of mutual understanding, meanings become constructed and set, though they change over time and geographical space. Thus, the national identities constructed by those in power are based within the spectrum of social cues and cultural symbols available to them.

As Trouillot shows, national narratives and histories are always tied to power and while they promote one vision, they silence others. It is crucial to examine the spaces in between in order to understand why some such endeavors succeed and others fail. Where the shah of Iran failed at producing a national identity that the masses of Iranians could "read" and understand, his critics and Iranian revolutionaries thrived. Off of this success the newly formed Islamic Republic government appropriated these symbols and built an innovative foundation for Iran's narrative, rooted in Shiite cultural images and the ideas of independence and revolution that the shah espoused, but could not deliver. In an era of independence movements and mass populist mobilization, the Islamic Republic aligned itself with resistance movements around the world. In fact, the promotion of resistance culture became the bedrock of the Islamic Republic's nationalist narrative, ingrained in the most epic story of resistance and sacrifice that the vast majority of Shiite Iranians were familiar with: the martyrdom of Imam Hossein in Karbala.

In the seventh century CE, when Imam Hossein took up the call from the people of Kufa to challenge the oppressive rule of the Umayyad caliph Yazid, he became a symbol of protest and justice. When faced with certain death at the hands of Yazid's forces in Karbala, his choice

---

[6] Ibid., 4.

not to pledge allegiance to Yazid and instead die for his cause made him the ultimate icon of martyrdom for Shiites. According to Hamid Dabashi, in Islamic history Shiism is the model of revolt, based on the archetype of tragic hero and martyr.[7] Dabashi notes the connection of Imam Hossein's story to the 1979 revolution when he recounts a banner from 1979 welcoming Khomeini's return to Iran that read, "We are not the people of Kufa."[8] The reference carried a clear and potent message: unlike the people of Kufa who failed to come to Imam Hossein's aid, the Iranian revolutionaries were prepared to fight and be martyred.

For Dabashi, the paradox of Hossein's story is that he succeeded by failing. Imam Hossein's sacrifice did not end in a political victory, but a moral triumph that endures in the actions of his proponents centuries later. Consequently, Shiism is honorable and prosperous when it is politically defiant and seeks social justice. According to Dabashi, in Shiism:

We witness a permanent state of deferred defiance – a defiance in the making, a defiance to come. What the Shi'is have deferred in the aftermath of the murder of their primordial son is not obedience – it is defiance. Because the central trauma of Shi'ism is the killing of a primordial son and not a primordial father, Shi'ism has remained a quintessentially youthful religion, the religion of the young revolutionaries defying the patriarchal order of things ... the enduring revolutionary zeal that produced the revered pages of the Shi'i theology with blood and in battlefields of its combative history – Karbala.[9]

Understanding this, Khomeini also expressed the idea of Shiism as a religion of protest, which is persistently confronting injustice and oppression:

The Lord of the Martyrs (upon whom be peace) summoned the people to rise in revolt ... Whenever a vital and alert nation gave them support, they were successful in their struggle. If we too are vital and alert now, we will be successful.[10]

The shah's dissidents tapped into the cultural symbols and meanings that masses of Iranians understood and identified with by using similar rhetoric for the revolution. However, the paradox they created for the

[7]  Hamid Dabashi, *Shi'ism: A Religion of Protest* (Cambridge, MA: The Belknap Press of Harvard University Press, 2011).
[8]  Ibid., 16.    [9] Ibid., 23.
[10] Ruhollah Khomeini and Hamid Algar, *Islam and Revolution: Writings and Declarations of Imam Khomeini* (Berkeley: Mizan Press, 1981), 204–5.

new state was in sustaining an image of political protest while simultaneously silencing all challenges to their own position of power.

The architects of the Islamic Republic constructed an image as the gatekeepers of Imam Hossein's message of integrity and martyrdom by emphasizing incidents and parties outside of its borders and silencing injustices within their own. The Islamic Republic used the United States and Israel as symbols of world power and continued colonialism. The struggles for freedom in Palestine, Lebanon, and South Africa all became symbols of resistance against the world's oppressors. The invasion of Iran by Iraq in 1980 and the ensuing eight-year war became the rallying cry for the fragile new administration to bring the country together and fight back as a united front. All the while, Shiite symbolism and motifs, especially notions of martyrdom, were utilized to give specific meanings to these events. By using Shiism, a religion founded in protest, the Islamic Republic connected its ideology and Iran's national story to the idea of enduring dissent and a continuous fight for justice. Like the revolution, the events that transpired after it were interpreted and explained by the new leaders of the Islamic Republic in ways to fit the image of rising up against oppressors, as they formulated their culture of resistance.

## 3.1  1979: The Islamic Republic's Permanent Revolution and Iranian Independence

Despite the shah's attempts at portraying his dynasty as the pioneers of Iranian independence and himself as revolutionary, oppositional forces in Iran exposed the weakness of his claims. After the revolution, the proponents of the Islamic Republic, under the leadership of Khomeini, moved quickly to construct a new narrative for Iran that addressed the importance of revolution and independence as the foundation of national identity. While the shah celebrated January 26, 1963 (Sixth of Bahman) as the White Revolution, the Islamic Republic celebrated February 11, 1979 (22 Bahman) as a real revolution. For the shah, the 1953 foreign-led coup, which removed Prime Minister Mossadeq and gave the shah full control of the government, marked a national day of independence from external forces. For the Islamic Republic, Iran's Independence Day is April 1, 1979, marking the referendum vote that made Iran an Islamic Republic.[11] On

---

[11] "About Iran: Other Facts," Daftar, last accessed August 6, 2018, www.daftar.org/eng/aboutiran_eng.asp#National%20Anthem.

that day Khomeini made clear that Iran was establishing its independence from foreign powers: "The country has been delivered from the clutches of domestic and foreign enemies, from the thieves and plunderers, and you, courageous people, are now the guardians of the Islamic Republic."[12] The idea of independence and resistance from foreign control became the central theme of the revolutionary narrative.

The significance of such images was evident in revolutionary songs and the discourse of Iranian ideologues. Collections of songs can be found on commemorative CDs sold in Iran that celebrate the revolution. In one such collection,[13] the song "Ey Artesh" (Oh Army) recounted the idea of freedom from dependency:

> *The revolution unified the nation*
> *Ripped apart the curtains of our division . . .*
> *Your day, my day, our day has come . . .*
> *Dependency is over, the homeland is free*

The notion of freedom was a recurring theme in Iran's revolutionary tracks. In the song "Bekhān Hamvatan"[14] (Sing Fellow Countrymen), the blood spilled in the path to freedom invoked the topic of martyrdom as well:

> *Sing my fellow countrymen,*
> *In the name of freedom . . .*
> *The homeland is covered in martyrs and blood*
> *For freedom*

Though imbued with religious motifs, these revolutionary songs had clear appeals to Iranian national identity and the meaning of homeland. This can be seen in the title of the song "Man Irāniam Ārmānam Shahādat,"[15] which means "I am Iranian, my ideal is martyrdom." There is no elusiveness in the link between Iranian identity and Shiite traditions of martyrdom. Freedom, unity, and blood were poetically entwined in the song of Iran's most renowned singer, Mohammad Reza Shajarian. While Shajarian became a critic of the Islamic Republic, his activist song, "Ey Irān Sarā-ye Omid" (Oh Iran, Land of Hope) is still found on CD collections that memorialize the revolution.[16]

---

[12] Khomeini and Algar, *Islam and Revolution*, 266.
[13] Various Artists, *Faryād-e Enqelāb* (Tehran: Arman Cultural Center, 2015), CD.
[14] Ibid.    [15] Various Artists, *Peyk-e Sorush* (Tehran: Sorush-e Iran, n.d.), CD.
[16] Various Artists, *Faryāde Enqelāb* (Tehran,: Arman Cultural Center, 2015), CD.

Its inclusion is fitting given its lyrics, which echo the narrative of the revolution as the moment of Iran's national freedom:

*Unity, Unity is the key to victory ...*
*Peace and freedom live forever in the world*
*In memory of the blood of the martyrs*

After the failures of the shah, it was imperative for the Islamic Republic to tie its revolution to ideas of independence and freedom. The cultural heritage it chose to represent Iranian sensibilities was Shiite Islam, which as Dabashi has argued, requires a perpetual state of political defiance in order to sustain its moral integrity. As such, the themes of independence and an enduring struggle for justice were essential to the discourse of Iranian revolutionaries and the architects of the Islamic Republic. Even before the revolution, Shariati, who is credited as a central figure in Iran's revolutionary ideology, spoke of Islam as the antithesis of global hegemony and of its proclivity toward defending the powerless. For Shariati, Islam and foreign dominance were by nature opposites:

Islam has such a relationship with colonialism and imperialism, meaning neither want the other to exist because in terms of principles, ideals and goals, they are opposites. Islam believes in helping, freedom, human perfection, in peace and justice, while the other believes in colonizing peoples and nations, and in discrimination and the destruction of humans.[17]

In other instances, Shariati illustrated Dabashi's paradox of Shiism and its success in defeat: "Islam ... it has been shown that anytime it has had the support of the powerful it has resulted in its decline and death, and in the case of attack it has come alive and gone on the offensive."[18] In other words, Shariati showed that Shiism is most effective when it is defending something, not when it is in a position of power. This paradox is rooted in the figure of Imam Hossein, who for Shariati "is the greatest failure to have been victorious in human history."[19] Imam Hossein's triumph was not in defeating his opponent, but in his martyrdom and sacrifice for the cause of justice. His victory was secured with his death, a premise that was harnessed by the Islamic Republic for decades to come and continues to this day.

[17] *Goftogu-ye Chahār Jānebe* (Tehran: Enteshārāt-e Sadrā, 2014), 13.
[18] Shabanali Lam'ei, ed., *Eshārāt-e Sokhanān-e Gozide va Payām-ha-ye Kutāh-e Doktor Shariati* (Tehran: Ramand Publication, 2015), 97.
[19] Ibid., 107.

Writing after the revolution, Mostafa Chamran, an iconic revolutionary and war martyr, recounted:

This revolution took shape in order to burn the roots of imperialism, tyranny, and colonialism, to bring social justice, to end poverty, ignorance, oppression and corruption ... We revolted to gain our *true independence* after centuries of abjection and degradation. Our dear country Iran was under the power of foreigners, America and Israel controlled the destiny of our people.[20]

With Chamran, the balance of Islam and nationalism was seen in his approach to the revolution and the continued fight of the oppressed classes. He argued that Iran's revolution was for Muslims around the world: "We have come to unite all the Muslims of the world, to help the deprived and oppressed of the world."[21] However, he also noted the impact of colonialism and the value of homeland: "Most revolutionaries in the world fight against the yoke of colonialism and foreign enemies in order to free their homeland."[22] For Chamran, the Islamic ideology of the revolution was the best suited to defeat colonialism because it focused on spirituality over materialism.

In the case of the Iranian revolution, nationalist sentiments were interwoven with Shiite discourse in order to create a third way to govern and organize society, which rejected both Soviet communism and US capitalism. Shariati was a vocal champion of the phrase "neither East nor West," as he advocated an Iranian identity and ideology deep-rooted in Shiism and free from foreign influence. Though he promoted the benefits of an Islamic ideology, Shariati was cognizant of the importance of infusing it with Iranian national identity: "Our Iranianness has become Islamic Iranianness and our Islam has become Iranian Islam."[23] Iranian revolutionaries and the new state prudently shaped a national identity that blended these elements together. Speaking in front of a large crowd after the revolution, Ayatollah Taleghani, another staunch dissident of the shah, combined national and religious views in his address:

Oh, children who lay at rest, oh young ones whose bodies and hearts were torn apart by the bullets of the enemy, oh honorable women who came to the front lines, with their children in tow, who went into the line of fire. We have come

---

[20] Mostafa Chamran, *Kordestān* (Tehran: Bonyād-e Shahid Chamrān, 2006), 15 (emphasis added).
[21] Ibid., 22.   [22] Ibid., 161.
[23] Mortezā Motahhari, *Nām-e Tārikhi-ye Ostād Motahhari Be Imam Khomeini* (Tehran: Sadrā, 2010), 30.

after one year to renew our vow ... the ideals that you went after, against idolatry and for the freedom of Iranian people, Muslims and all people of the world, we renew that alliance and vow ... we renew our alliance against any form of tyranny and colonialism, and for the freedom of all humans.[24]

Like Chamran, Taleghani connected Iran's revolution with independence movements around the world and portrayed an image of Iran as a defender of injustice for all people.

The hyperbole of such an endeavor is apparent in substantive terms; however, the ambitious aim was conceivable within the confines of rhetoric. In its construction of a new national narrative, the Islamic Republic's goal was less about the actualization of all human freedom, and more about image making. They associated themselves with international causes and against the most powerful nations of the world. As Chamran explained it, "The success or failure of Iran's Islamic revolution is analogous to the success or failure of an ideal humanity, for the realization of a complete social system in which true human freedom and social justice are guaranteed under spirituality."[25] By affiliating itself with social justice, the Islamic Republic could preserve its persona as the hero for the downtrodden.

The supreme leaders of the Islamic Republic were alert to the fact that keeping such an image required constant vigilance. For instance, Ayatollah Khamenei, who succeeded Khomeini as supreme leader in 1989, emphasized the need to continuously discuss Islamic ideology: "There is no doubt that no matter how much we show or discuss Islam or Islamic ideology – by writing or by actions – we have not done enough."[26] The discourse and actions of these leaders were meant to keep the memories of the revolution, and later the war, alive in people's minds. After the assassination of Morteza Motahhari, a favored Khomeini disciple, Khomeini spoke of martyrdom and the revolution: "This movement must stay alive and it will stay alive with these sacrifices. Spill blood, we will survive, kill us, our nation will wake more. We are not afraid of death and you will gain nothing from our death."[27] It seems another paradox in Shiism that one can ascertain is that in martyrdom you are more alive after death. Since the foundation of the Islamic Republic's history of Iran was embedded in Shiism and

---

24  *Imam Abuzaresh Khānd* (Tehran: Rezvān Rasāneh, n.d.), DVD.
25  Mostafa Chamran, *Binesh Va Niyāyesh* (Tehran: Bonyād-e Shahid Chamrān, 2004), 28.
26  *Goftogu-ye Chahār Jānebe* (Tehran: Enteshārāt-e Sadrā, 2014), 29.
27  Motahhari, Nām-e Tārikhi-ye Ostād Motahhari Be Imam Khomeini, 28.

the notion of a permanent revolution, the Islamic Republic needed to maintain an appearance of struggle against oppression or risk becoming seen as the new oppressor. To play the part of the guardians of Imam Hossein's message, they took on a role of protagonist in various freedom and independence movements. But its definitive model of resistance was seen in the Iran–Iraq War.

## 3.2  The Ultimate Resistance Campaign: The Holy Defense

The Islamic revolution in Iran was a significant world event that reverberated throughout the region. The impact of Islamic revivalism, which was a strong oppositional movement in the postcolonial Middle East, was demonstrated in the establishment of an Islamic Republic. More than any other country, Iraq under Saddam Hussein felt threatened by the developments in Iran. This new Shiite revolutionary ideology was especially encouraged in Iraq for two reasons. First, Iraq was a majority Shiite state. Second, Iraq was one of the most powerful states in the Persian Gulf. With power in the hands of the Shiite clerics in Iran, Hussein felt the pressure of dissatisfied Shiites in Iraq, who were repressed politically by the Sunni minority and Saddam Hussein's Baath Party.

Though Iraq initially attempted to be friendly toward its new neighboring government, Hussein eventually began expelling Shiites and supporting separatist movements in Iran. The Algiers Agreement of 1975, which was established during the reign of the shah and quelled the conflicts over the Shatt al-Arab, a strategically significant waterway that divided Iranian and Iraqi control over the Persian Gulf, re-emerged as an issue. The agreement drew final lines of sovereignty over the Shatt al-Arab, however, since the power of the shah was greater in 1975, Hussein felt he had conceded too much of Iraq's fair share. Soon after the Islamic Republic was established in Iran, conflicts arose over the status of the Shatt al-Arab. Such quarrels and border disputes were an untimely challenge for Iran, which was still trying to recover from a revolution and stabilize its new government.

In what was later assumed a great blunder in judgment, Hussein saw Iran's instability as an opportunity to take back control of the waterway, gain some oil rich land in Iran's south, and destroy the Islamic Republic in the process. If successful, Hussein would ensure his power and stability in the region, since Iran was the only real challenge to his authority. Seizing on what seemed a favorable moment, Hussein declared the 1975 Algiers Agreement "null and void." Conflicts continued between the two states until finally on September 22, 1980, Iraq began its invasion of Iran through the southern province of Khuzestan.

Along with Iran's weakened state, Hussein had other advantages, which included superior military numbers, an organized army, and most importantly, the support of the international community. Hussein had the support of the Arab states in the region along with Iraq's most powerful ally during the war, the United States. Additionally, the United Nations was seen as a tool for the US agenda to support Iraq's invasion.[28] Though Iranians were the victims of a foreign attack, the world continued to turn a blind eye to Iraq's violations of sovereign borders and wartime abuses. In Iran the government scrambled to organize its personnel and mount a counterattack.

The goliath task of developing a counteroffensive was not lost on Iranian leaders, as Khamenei recalled: "Every form of support, money, political support, and others were at the discretion of one side of the war, which was the Baath regime, and everything was collected there. On the other side was the Islamic Republic, alone, truly alone; this is one dimension of the war."[29] While resources, soldiers, and weapons were necessities of war, the Islamic Republic tapped into another foundation of support for its war effort through the ideology it espoused during the revolution. The picture of Iran being attacked by the overpowering arsenal of Iraq, with its massive aid from others, was likened to the imbalanced battle in Karbala with ease. The heroic image that soon appeared was none other than that of Imam Hossein, just as he had through centuries of Shiite rituals, the revolution, and now the war. But rather than eradicating the Islamic Republic and its revolutionary fervor, Iraq's attack helped to bolster the Islamic Republic, since times of war call for solidarity and support. Iranians were forced to look to their new leaders for answers, which they received in condemnations of foreign powers and calls to mobilize a *defense*.

The notion of defense suited the Islamic Republic well as it continued to project an image of unending struggle and resistance against oppression. Imam Hossein, as the quintessential martyr and tragic hero, became the key figure in the war effort. As Roxanne Varzi argues, the war defined the

---

[28] Ford Foundation, *The United Nations and the Iran-Iraq War: A Ford Foundation Conference Report* (New York: Ford Foundation, 1987).

[29] Ali Akbari-Mozdabadi, ed. *Hazrat-e Yār* (Tehran: Yā Zahrā, 2015), 155.

Islamic Republic as an image-making machine.[30] From transforming the public space with billboards and portraits, to filmmaking and music, the Islamic Republic used every available medium to control the appearance of the war and the new state, which were both an extension of the revolution and its core message of defiance.

The Islamic Republic's title of "Holy Defense," for the Iran–Iraq War, was indicative of its two central themes: religious dispositions and resistance. It was crucial for the Islamic Republic to maintain its depiction as a protector and never the aggressor. This is evident in the war discourse of its leaders and the modes of image production. In the song "Parcham-e Khunin"[31] (The Bloodied Flag) these concepts were present:

> *We fight to protect religion*
> *We don't desire war*
> *We are the friends and part of the community of Islam*
> *If we attack it is to defend our country and religion ...*
> *We learned about justice from Ali*
> *We learned about martyrdom from Hossein*

Mixed with national sentiments, the song's key message was that Iranians did not wish for war; for them, it was instead a war of defense. The image of Hossein was often woven into these songs, which highlighted the homeland and ideas of liberation. Speaking about the martyrdom of young soldiers, the songs recounted the value of their sacrifice: "Because of your efforts, the homeland has become restored and victorious."[32] Another song, found on a commemorative war DVD, illustrated how the legacy of Hossein lived on in Iran's war effort: "Oh symbols of pride, because you are the followers of Hossein ... We are free and liberated even when captives."[33] Yet another song captured the idea of oppression and stressed the endurance of the martyr's life after death: "You are an everlasting spring, oh martyr, you are forever pride, oh martyr ... because of you the palace of oppression has fallen."[34]

Over and over, we see that the focus of the war was portrayed in defensive terms and as a battle of the martyrs against tyranny in the tradition of Imam Hossein. Khomeini used metaphors such as stars and

---

[30]  Roxanne Varzi, *Warring Souls: Youth, Media, and Martyrdom in Post-Revolution Iran* (Durham: Duke University Press, 2006).
[31]  Various Artists, *Faryād-e Enqelāb* (Tehran: Arman Cultural Center, 2015), CD.
[32]  *Ganjine-ha-ye Khāki* (Tehran: Bonyād-e Hefz-e Āsār Va Nashr-e Arzesh-ha-ye Defā'-e Moqaddas, n.d.), DVD.
[33]  Ibid.    [34]  Ibid.

light to describe the impact of martyrs, who lasted long after their earthly lives and revealed the history of the war. This history was framed not only in religious expressions, but also in national terms and more broadly as a fight against subjugation. Thus, Khomeini described the soldiers as "the oppressed who bravely defended rights and took the power from the oppressors."[35] The soldiers fighting in the war echoed the fusion of religion, nation and defense when discussing their reasons for participating:

Because they assaulted our country and we fight with them with the consent of Islam. One of the important tenants of Islam is jihad, we come for jihad for God, for the Quran, for Islam, and so Islam stays alive; and for this to be a slap in the face of the aggressors and a lesson for the superpowers to not assault our Islamic nations.[36]

In his declarations about the war, Khomeini alluded to the notion of an endless fight, entrenched in the history of Shiism:

We the ever oppressed of history, the disadvantaged and barefooted, we have no one except God, and if we are broken into a thousand pieces, we will not cease in our fight against oppressors ... So, there is no way, except to fight; thus we must break the hold of superpowers, especially America. And it is necessary to choose one of two paths: martyrdom or victory, both of which in our belief are victorious.[37]

The statement also highlights the idea that martyrdom was a triumph, a critical part of the war's rhetoric that is discussed further in the next section.

The influence of the war and the Islamic Republic's production of meaning had contemporary consequences. Iterations of the image of defense and struggle continue to be seen, whether on a pin found in a bookstore in Iran that reads "While there are unbelievers and blasphemy there will be struggle, and while there is struggle, we are here,"[38] or in the dedication of an Iranian artist in his CD jacket:

As an Iranian musician facing the disaster of the war in Khorramshahr and the bombing of Halabcheh, which can be frankly seen as a world disaster,

---

[35] Saeed Golshenas, ed. *Cherāgh-ha-ye Furuzān Dar Tāriki* (Tehran: Nashr-e Sobhān, 2005), 5.
[36] *Ganjine-ha-ye Khāki* (Tehran: Bonyād-e Hefz-e Āsār Va Nashr-e Arzesh-ha-ye Defā'-e Moqaddas, n.d.), DVD.
[37] Ruhollah Khomeini, *Jām-e Zahr* (Tehran: Mo'asese-ye Farhangi-ye Khākriz-e Imān Va Andisheh, 2015), 9.
[38] The pin was on sale in a bookstore in Tehran in September 2015.

I felt responsible to keep alive their memory. Not just for Iranians, but also for the world, through my best musical efforts. The story of Khorramshahr's occupation and the bravery of men in the south in defending their homeland, honor, and ideals are well known. These men sacrificed their lives in this path to free their homeland and secure the peace and lives of the people.[39]

Despite the criticisms against the postrevolutionary government, the invasion of Iran's borders by a foreign foe quickly incited the anxieties of Iranians. They were compelled to support the new state, which vowed to protect the independence of the nation and its people. The war played well into the Islamic Republic's narrative of defense and gave them a fresh adversary in lieu of the shah, who was no longer a factor. With this new challenge, the Islamic Republic continued to paint the image of perpetual battle in pursuit of social justice. National liberation, righteousness, and resistance became a unifying call for the Iranian nation, behind the iconic martyr who embodied the narrative of political defiance. As a result, the war with Iraq became akin to Imam Hossein's battle in Karbala.

## 3.3 Victory in Death and the Campaign of Martyrdom

By all measures, Iraq's invasion of Iran in September 1980 should have ended in a quick victory for Iraq. The initial attack waged by Iraq was successful and after only a month Iraqi forces occupied Khorramshahr. The international community stood still, anticipating a short struggle and hoping for the destruction of the revolutionary Islamic government in Iran. However, in the midst of continuing turmoil from the revolution, the Islamic Republic was able to shift their focus to defending the Iranian border in the south. Young boys who volunteered their services and their bodies for war soon answered their calls and the war's mobilization force, the Basij, was formed.

Though often poorly trained and disorganized as a consequence of the disorder from the revolution, the Basijis made up for their inadequacies through their devotion. As one young soldier put it, "Last night we started our attack with 'Allah O Akbar' and 'Yā Hossein,' 'Yā Mahdi,' 'Yā Zahrā,' that is how we started."[40] The philosophy of

---

[39] *Poem-e Samfoni-ha-ye Khorramshahr Va Halabcheh*, composed by Hooshang Kamkar (Tehran: Noufeh Music, 2011), CD.

[40] *Ganjine-ha-ye Khāki* (Tehran: Bonyād-e Hefz-e Āsār Va Nashr-e Arzesh-ha-ye Defā'-e Moqaddas, n.d.), DVD.

martyrdom (*Shahādat*), which was long a part of Iranian culture because of its Shiite background, found the ultimate setting to flourish. The Islamic Republic did not simply fabricate this history for its own use, but as Hall has argued, it attached meanings based on a "circuit of culture." Even before the establishment of the Islamic Republic, Shariati spoke of the cultural resonance of martyrdom: "In one word, martyrdom, which is against the history of others that see it as an incident, a struggle, an imposed death of a hero and a tragedy, in our culture is an honor."[41] Shariati claimed that Hossein's request for help was not meant for his time, since he knew he would be martyred. Instead, his plea was for the future, for honorable Shiites to take up arms against injustice.

The nation's Supreme Leader, Khomeini, understood the power of this rhetoric, as he stated, "These people are certainly unaware of the unseen world and philosophy of martyrdom and they do not know that someone who has gone for jihad and for only the happiness of God, the immortality, and survival of their higher cause will not be harmed."[42] Emphasizing the belief of victory in death, Khomeini maintained the discourse of martyrdom throughout the war to aid their efforts and bring soldiers to the front:

Many of the soldiers who come to me cry for me to pray for them to become martyrs and I pray that they are *victorious*. When this kind of spirit is found in an individual or individuals, this is victory. And this was the spirit that was found because of the spirit of Islam.[43]

Aware of the importance of his image in the war effort, Khomeini spoke of his leadership in terms of equal sacrifice: "If a bomb hits my house and kills the revolutionary guards around my house while I stay alive in an anti-bomb room, then I will not be a suitable leader. I can be the people's leader when I live like them and we are together."[44] As the leader of the revolution, Khomeini used his position to frame martyrdom as an ultimate goal: "In Islam ... Martyrdom is welcomed,

[41] Shabanali Lam'ei, ed. *Eshārāt-e Sokhanān-e Gozide va Payām-ha-ye Kutāh-e Doktor Shariati* (Tehran: Ramand Publication, 2015), 132.
[42] Khomeini, *Jām-e Zahr*, 19.
[43] *Hekāyat-ha-ye Talkh Va Shirin* (Tehran: Mo'asese-ye Farhangi Honari-ye Qadr-e Velāyat, 2012), 96 (emphasis added).
[44] Ali Ahmadpour-Turkamani, ed. *Simā-ye Āftāb* (Qom: Daftar-e Nashr-e M'āref, 2011), 47.

because they believe after this natural world is a higher and brighter world. Believers are imprisoned in this world and freed after martyrdom."[45] By making death, or martyrdom, analogous to victory, Khomeini and the Islamic Republic employed the greatest weapons in their arsenal: manpower and faith.

Though Iraq's technological strength outweighed Iran's, the morale gained from notions of martyrdom helped Iran get the motivation it needed to engage in battle.[46] The fact that Iran's most useful weapon in the war was faith was not lost on those fighting, as the memoir of Shahid (Martyr) Sayyād Shirāzi revealed: "A secret of our victory in the war of good versus evil was that we fought for God, while the enemy fought for the Devil."[47] While the Islamic Republic facilitated and promoted this narrative for the war, young men saw their stories as a continuation of Imam Hossein's battle in Karbala. One soldier recalled his memory of being in battle with Mostafa Chamran as a parallel to Imam Hossein's experience: "Because it was the night of Ashura, I remembered Imam Hossein and his companions. Doctor [Chamran] in that moment was like Imam Hossein, as the bullets of the enemy came from every direction toward him."[48] It is easy to see how the solider inserted himself in the memory as Chamran's "companion" and by extension the companion of Imam Hossein. The idea that these young men were fighting for God and in the tradition of Imam Hossein was illustrated in edicts and representations concerning the "Holy Defense."

The power of song, hymns, and rhythmic chants that had evoked the emotions of revolutionaries were used in full force to arouse young soldiers and the masses of Iranians to embrace the idea of sacrifice in the face of injustice. Imam Hossein's legacy and influence was captured in a song that stated, "War is war, come until we break the enemy's lines ... Our path is the path of Hossein, with his hatchet we will break the idols."[49] After death, hymns were sung to memorialize the

[45]  Motahhari, *Nām-e Tārikhi-ye Ostād Motahhari Be Imam Khomeini*, 37.
[46]  James A. Bill, "Morale vs. Technology: The Power of Iran in the Persian Gulf War," in Farhang Rajaee, ed., *The Iran-Iraq War: Politics of Aggression* (Gainesville: University Press of Florida, 1993), 198–209.
[47]  Mohsen Kazemi, *Yādāsht-ha-ye Safar-e Shahid Sayyād Shirāzi* (Tehran: Sureh-e Mehr, 2011), 124.
[48]  Davood Bakhtiyari-Daneshvar, *Pāveh-e Sorkh* (Tehran: Sureh-e Mehr, 2007), 80.
[49]  *Ganjine-ha-ye Khāki* (Tehran: Bonyād-e Hefz-e Āsār Va Nashr-e Arzesh-ha-ye Defā'-e Moqaddas, n.d.), DVD.

individual martyr and his triumph: "Your pure heart was fascinated by martyrdom ... God has taken you to his highest places to fulfill his promise to the martyrs."[50] To boost morale and energy, soldiers often used chants on the frontlines. For instance, they chanted, "The advocate of heroes, resistance, resistance. The fight of heroes, resistance, resistance,"[51] or, "Be prepared, be prepared, for endless fight, be prepared, be prepared. Oh, army of Imam Zamān [twelfth imam in occultation], be prepared, be prepared. For meeting with God, be prepared, be prepared."[52] These chants underscore the importance of defiance and perpetual battle, which became the cornerstone of the Islamic Republic's national narrative of resistance culture.

As Roxanne Varzi has shown, the medium of film was one of the most highly valued avenues for disseminating information and images of the war. However, while documentary films such as *Ravāyāt-e Fath* (Narration of Victory), claimed to show the "reality" of war, Varzi argues that all films make choices through editing and framing and in effect help to create a specific reality.[53] The meanings conveyed in these various films echoed the themes of nation, resistance, and especially martyrdom that the Islamic Republic attached to the war, as part of the broader national narrative. It is noteworthy that on the cover of the DVD for "[A]'lamdār," a segment of Āvini's *Narration of Victory*, rather than a picture of the war, there is an image of Āvini behind the camera looking at the audience. The fact that Āvini was killed during filmmaking and considered a martyr, blurs the lines between subject and object. However, the cover photo reminds us of the nature of filmmaking and image production, despite the films attempt at authenticity. These films, along with other modes of communication, were intended to generate unambiguous meanings and facilitate the Islamic Republic's identity construction.

Though martyrdom emphasized Shiite cultural symbols, Shiism was well integrated into Iranian culture. The architects of the Islamic Republic carefully fused these elements together in order to create

[50] Seyyed Mortezā Āvini, dir., *[A]'lamdār* (Tehran, 1987), DVD.
[51] Seyyede Azam Hosseini, *Dā: Khāterāt-e Seyyede Zahra Hosseini* (Tehran: Sureh-e Mehr, 2015), 287.
[52] Hassan Nikbakht, dir., *Ravāyāt Az Khorramshahr* (Tehran: Bonyād-e Hefz-e Āsār Va Nashr-e Arzesh-ha-ye Defā'-e Moqaddas, 2002), DVD.
[53] Varzi, *Warring Souls*.

a national story for Iran. For instance, Khomeini discussed the revolution as a national cause, since it was at the hands of the Iranian people:

When a revolution is done by the people of a nation, this cannot be undone by a group or even an army . . . If America comes and takes Iran, if they can, it will not be able to continue this way. They can send their airplanes and fighters and bomb the cities, but when they are on the ground the people will destroy them with teeth and nails. Those who thought they could return Iran to before, they do not know or understand Islam or the Iranian people.[54]

That Islam and Iran were understood as symbiotic was not odd to the leader of an Islamic revolution. Iran's proclivities toward Shiism gave the Islamic Republic a critical tool in combating the invasion of Iran at a time when it was most vulnerable. However, despite all its appeals to Shiism, the war was still considered in terms of Iran's sovereignty and national borders. After all, the country they were fighting had a majority Shiite population as well.

Such nationalist sentiments are evident in memoirs and films of the war, for instance in *Ravāyāt Az Khorramshahr*, the film ends with footage of people in the streets with Iranian flags and newspapers that read "Khorramshahr Freed." As the celebrations continued, chants of "Allah O Akbar" blended into the nationalist song "Ey Iran." In *Dā*, the best-selling memoir of the war that emphasizes the role of women, Zahra Hosseini described religion *and* nation as causes for fighting, "in the path of God and for this *water and land.*"[55] Zahra captured national feelings about the war when she stated, "Khorramshahr belongs to all of Iran. Saddam has come to take all of Iran. If we do not stand in front of him, today he will take Khorramshahr, tomorrow he will come occupy this. Then we must defend our country with tooth and nails."[56]

With all the odds stacked against it, Iran continued to engage in battle. Armed with the power of Karbala, Iranian forces took back Khorramshahr by May 1982 and soon began to push their campaign into Iraqi territory. As the war went on for many years, both sides saw numerous casualties and estimates point to hundreds of thousands of dead. According to Dilip Hiro, Iranian casualties account for more

---

[54] *Hekāyat-ha-ye Talkh Va Shirin* (Tehran: Mo'asese-ye Farhangi Honari-ye Qadr-e Velāyat, 2012), 311.
[55] Hosseini, *Dā*, 318 (emphasis added).   [56] Ibid., 189.

than twice that of Iraq's.[57] However, while Saddam tried to shield the Iraqi people from the war, the Islamic Republic increasingly publicized the war and the martyrs who fought for the cause of country, justice, and Hossein. Though the many casualties were a difficult weight to bear, the philosophy of martyrdom and the belief that soldiers were in fact victorious in death helped alleviate the burden. The effort to venerate the war continued long after its end and continues through today. In their labors to maintain the image of defense and resistance, the Islamic Republic went to great lengths to keep the martyrs and the war alive through films, tributes, museums, and the transformation of public space. The apex of this memorialization is found in the Holy Defense Museum in the capital Tehran.

## 3.4  The Holy Defense Museum

As Richard Handler and Eric Gable show in their study on museums and history telling, museums are social spaces that produce meanings by displaying what are assumed to be real and authentic objects.[58] The implicit validity of these objects, as part of the past that the museum is trying to represent, provides a sense of authority for the specific narrative being displayed. Handler and Gable challenge the legitimacy of this endeavor and argue, "You cannot point to the past; it is not embodied in objects. 'The past' exists only as we narrate it today. The past is above all the stories we tell, not objects."[59] Like the documentary films of the war that were intended to present the "reality" of events, war museums were meant to give the viewer or participant a taste of actual warfare. However, like those films, which were edited and framed in order to convey a particular story, the war museum was carefully designed to uphold the Islamic Republic's picture of the Holy Defense.

Centrally located in Tehran, the twenty-one-hectare grounds and massive structure are hard to miss. To assure the attention of spectators, the main expressway that leads to the museum has a large sign that engulfs the overpass bridge to advertise. In a densely populated city, the

---

[57]  Dilip Hiro, *The Longest War: The Iran-Iraq Military Conflict* (London: Grafton Books, 1989).
[58]  Richard Handler and Eric Gable, *The New History in an Old Museum: Creating the Past at Colonial Williamsburg* (Durham: Duke University Press, 1997).
[59]  Ibid., 224.

**Figure 3.4** Defense museum: flowers in rifles. The flowers at the end of the rifles support the claim that Iran was not the aggressor. Instead, Iranians are peaceful and their fight was *defensive*.

government spared no space or expense in building this modern structure. The intent of the Islamic Republic is made clear with the words "promotion of resistance culture," which appear on the overpass sign and the pamphlets you can find inside the museum. Built nearly two decades after the war, the aim of the Holy Defense Museum was to keep the essential messages of the Islamic Republic's national narrative – defense and resistance – alive (see Figure 3.4).[60]

Despite its focus on the war, the museum was also a tribute to the revolution, since these events were thought of as interdependent within a broader history of Iranian defiance against injustice. The fusion of these events along with the Islamic Republic's blending of religion and nation are illustrated in the museum's pamphlet, which states, "When we look at the history of the Islamic revolution, it is all bravery. When you look back at the history of the Holy Defense, you

---

[60]  All the photos from the museum are my own and were taken in September 2015.

can see the days of brotherhood, self-sacrifice, and fighting for the homeland." The museum was meant to lay bare that history for all to see and experience.

The significance of participation was unmistakable in the museum's design. Again, the official pamphlet confirmed these intentions, stating, "These halls have a supplementary aspect. Visitors can observe the events of the eight-year Holy Defense in a tangible way. Weapons and war spaces are shown in real size." As you walk through the different halls of the museum, you can observe the history of the revolution and the war unfolding. Additionally, pathways were created to simulate the experience of the war (see Figure 3.5). These reproductions were the tangible elements that the curators of the museum hoped would induce a physical reaction for the spectators, who were meant not just to observe, but also to partake in the experience.

**Figure 3.5** Defense museum: mine field. The glass walkway is meant to simulate the feeling of walking across a minefield.

The idea of keeping the memory of the war alive was literally transformed into a space in which the audience could feel part of the event. Displays showed real-scale replications of bedrooms and classrooms that were destroyed in the war, actual toys of children found in the rubble, as well as uniforms and boots, still dirty and worn from battle. At the core of this memorialization were the martyrs. In fact, one of the key philosophies of martyrdom, as we have seen, was that martyrs lived on after death through their legacy, as was the case with Imam Hossein. The everlasting nature of martyrs was touched on in songs, like "Qebleh-e Shahādat"[61] (The Qibla of Martyrdom):

> *Martyrs, your path is honor*
> *Your name will stay forever*
> *You're respected eternally*
> *Your martyrdom is the roaring of our time*

The soldiers were cognizant of the immortality of their names (see Figure 3.6). Zahra Hosseini's recollections in *Dā* showed her brother's anticipation for martyrdom and his desire to be remembered: "I took this picture for when I am martyred, to put in my memorial so everyone can know the path that I chose was from my heart and soul."[62] Like

**Figure 3.6** Defense museum: street signs. Each sign adorned with the name of a soldier represents an actual street renamed for a martyr.

[61] Various Artists, *Peyk-e Sorush* (Tehran: Sorush-e Iran, n.d.), CD.
[62] Hosseini, *Dā*, 67.

films and music, pictures of martyrs became a prevalent medium for broadcasting the war. Hosseini recalled speaking to a photographer about his photos of the martyrs and the war; for the photographer the photos were important in keeping these stories alive in history.[63]

Nowhere is the war more animated than the Museum of Holy Defense. As you walk through the halls, walls spring to life with projected videos. Other displays incorporate audio tracks to engross the spectator and bring the scene to life. The modern décor at times subtly reminds you of the human losses Iran suffered in the war. One such ceiling display in a corridor is an abstract reminder of the martyrs, whose presence saturates the entire museum (see Figure 3.7). The impact of the war on people's actual lives is dramatized with emotive images of mothers embracing their

**Figure 3.7** Defense museum: dog tags. What looks like a decorative ceiling piece is really a collection of dog tags representing martyrs.

[63] Ibid., 160.

**Figure 3.8** Defense museum: a mother's embrace. A mural in the museum shows a mother's warm embrace.

brave sons, some as they leave on the path of glory and martyrdom and others returning after being held as POWs (see Figure 3.8).

The theme of women, and especially mothers affected by the war, was significant for its emotional potency and capacity to capture people's attention.[64] Hosseini's *Dā*, which means "mother" in Kurdish, highlighted the role of women during the conflict. In one of the many documentaries about the war, an edited video of young soldiers was overlaid with the audio of a song with the lyrics:[65]

---

[64] These themes appear in recent films as well, such as female director Narges Ābyār's 2013 film, *Track 143*, which focuses on the role of women and especially mothers in the war. Such examples echo the work of Yuval-Davis who argued that war, despite its male-centered depiction, was never a strictly male space. Women always play a role, though not the same as their male counterparts.

[65] *Ganjine-ha-ye Khāki* (Tehran: Bonyād-e Hefz-e Āsār Va Nashr-e Arzesh-ha-ye Defā'-e Moqaddas, n.d.), DVD.

*Oh, kind mothers, your children, your children*
*The flowers you gave, the war front you sent them to*
*Now they come back in coffins ...*
*The mothers want to open their coffins*
*And caress their children*

Considering the power of these images then, the museum in Tehran did not just display pictures and objects to tell a dispassionate history of the war. But rather, it imbued these objects with specific meanings and often played on the strong feelings associated with war and loss.

Like the other instruments used to create a history of the war that fit the Islamic Republic's national narrative, the museum emphasizes Iran's Shiite roots while infusing it with nationalist sentiments. The streams of national flags waving around the whole site quickly create an atmosphere of nationalism; an intended effect according to the museum's pamphlet that says the flag tower is "a symbol of Iranian honor." One of the museum's displays pays homage to the religious minorities who were martyred in the war, which underlines the fact that Iran's struggle was national, rather than religious in character (see Figure 3.9). Additionally, the main entrance of the museum exhibits a large archway as a shrine to Unknown Soldiers (*Shahid Gomnām*). As Benedict Anderson argues:

No more arresting emblems of the modern culture of nationalism exist than the cenotaphs and tombs of Unknown Soldiers. The public ceremonial reverence accorded these monuments precisely *because* they are either deliberately empty or no one knows who lies inside them, has no true precedents in earlier times ... Yet void as these tombs are of identifiable mortal remains or immortal souls, they are nonetheless saturated with ghostly *national* imaginings.[66]

The museum's pamphlet also notes that recognizing Unknown Soldiers is a common practice in other countries around the world. Again, we see the point of the tribute was not necessarily religious in nature, but rather nationalist.

The sheer volume of songs, images, and videos taken of the war and the revolution indicates the fervent efforts of the Islamic Republic to capitalize on notions of defense and independence. They depicted the war as a holy and national battle in order to encourage their narrative

---

[66] Benedict Anderson, *Imagined Communities: Reflections on the Origin and Spread of Nationalism* (London: Verso, 2006), 9.

**Figure 3.9** Defense museum: minority martyrs. Screenshots from a video that shows the pictures of martyrs from different religious backgrounds, including Christian, Jewish, and Zoroastrian. In the background of the martyr photos are symbols of their religious identities.

of Iranian national identity, as an identity of resistance established in its history and Shiite culture. The willingness to be martyred for country, God, and honor echoed Shiite sentiments as well as Anderson's idea of a fraternity that is willing to die for its imagined kin. While the Islamic Republic continued to stress the revolution and the war – as can be seen in the call for an architectural competition[67] as recently as 2015 for yet

---

[67] "Open Call: International Architecture Competition of Islamic Revolution and Sacred Defense Museum," *Arch Daily* (October 23, 2015), accessed August 7, 2018, www.archdaily.com/775925/open-call-international-architecture-competition-of-islamic-revolution-and-sacred-defense-museum.

another museum memorializing both events – the passions associated with them ebbed with the passage of time. Consequently, the Islamic Republic looked to other contemporary events outside its borders to promote its resistance culture. In its claim of an eternal pursuit of justice, the Islamic Republic took on the most powerful nations in the world and propagated its image as the guardians of the oppressed.

## 3.5 Challenging Power: The Endless Search for Yazid

One tactic of the revolutionary opposition to the shah was to tie the monarch to foreign powers. By doing so, the opposition argued Iran was a dependent state in need of liberation. After the revolution that toppled the shah and established the Islamic Republic, those in power continued to uphold an image of enmity toward the nations they criticized for supporting the monarchy. Claiming to always be on the side of justice, the Islamic Republic held its position against the most powerful nation in the world, the United States, and its most valued ally in the Middle East, Israel.

As the shah's opposition had done before the revolution, the Islamic Republic maintained the discourse of anticolonialism and continued to designate the United States as the greatest imperial power of the world. Additionally, Israel's legitimacy was called into question because it was recognized as a colonial entity. The Islamic Republic's staunch opposition to both states was a reminder of Imam Hossein's challenge to Yazid's formidable empire and superior armed forces. Much like the epic tale of Hossein's heroism against all odds, the Islamic Republic seemingly resisted the most powerful and corrupt empires of its contemporary era. Thus, the Islamic Republic's quest was not fulfilled with the revolution or the war, but rather, it continues to this day in the endless pursuit of justice and always in search of a new Yazid.

Khomeini's protests against the shah's policies toward the United States were discussed in Chapter 2 and are well known. However, revolutionary figures were also outspoken about the ethics of Israel, and were quickly detained by the shah's forces for it. For instance, Motahhari was arrested in the 1970s for signing a document that aimed to raise money for Palestinians.[68] In another instance, Khamenei recalled being arrested for discussing Quranic passages about Israel:

[68] Motahhari, *Nām-e Tārikhi-ye Ostād Motahhari Be Imam Khomeini.*

When questioned by authorities, they claimed I spoke against Israel and Jews. Are you paying attention? That means if someone discussed a Quranic Surah about Israel and spoke about it, they would have to answer why they presented this information ... Meaning the state of politics was such, it was difficult and politicians were against the people and dependent on their masters.[69]

The internationally recognized struggle of Palestinians against Israeli occupation played well into the Islamic Republic's rhetoric of resistance. As such, the Islamic Republic continued to focus its attention and public discourse on Israel as a symbol of colonialism, and Zionism as a corrupt political ideology.

Mostafa Chamran went to the core of the Islamic Republic's stance by arguing, "The tyrant *Israel came into existence in this region through colonialism* to facilitate the program of colonists and prevent unity and progress of the people in the region."[70] Chamran argued that Iran's revolution was the biggest blow to imperialism and Zionism because it marked a day of victory for the oppressed against the colonizers of the world. As supreme leader of the Islamic Republic, Khomeini capitalized on this discourse and connected Zionism with the immoral political systems of capitalism and communism:

We are seeking to dry the corrupt roots of Zionism, capitalism, and communism. We have decided, with the grace of God, to destroy the forces of these three foundations and to promote the forces of the messenger of Islam – peace be upon him – in this arrogant world. Sooner or later captive nations will witness this.[71]

Khomeini also openly criticized the United Nations for its acquiescence in the face of Israeli violations of international law:

Right now, Israel is standing in front of all Muslim nations and saying "do not step out of line." Is this not wrong? Are they not human, those who Israel stands in front of and says "do not but in"? They came and took Beirut and committed crimes and destroyed the organizations of freedom ... America is the head in all those crimes and the crimes committed in Beirut were at the hidden hands of the U.S. and the appearance of Zionists.[72]

---

[69]  Ali Akbari-Mozdabadi, ed., *Hazrat-e Yār* (Tehran: Yā Zahrā, 2015), 23.
[70]  Chamran, *Binesh Va Niyāyesh*, 30 (emphasis added).
[71]  Khomeini, *Jām-e Zahr*, 7.
[72]  *Hekāyat-ha-ye Talkh Va Shirin* (Tehran: Mo'asese-ye Farhangi Honari-ye Qadr-e Velāyat, 2012), 300.

Khomeini's language was intended to humanize the victims of Israel and to pronounce the role of the United States as the world's superpower.

In its attempts to emulate the legacy of Imam Hossein, the Islamic Republic confronted the established world order. Khomeini, in his role as leader, did not mince words. Like his protests against the shah, he maintained a steadfast attitude toward other centers of power: "These superpowers do not recognize any borders or lines and laws, and they encroach on the interests of others. They justify colonialism and slavery of nations and see them as logical and reasonable principles within the international order of their own creation."[73] While the Islamic Republic emphasized their principles of justice in broad terms, leaders were also careful to articulate this message with nationalist tones. Standing in front of the United Nations in 1987 as Iran's president, Khamenei roused national sentiments with an ode to Iran's ancient civilization:

I am the president of a country that was the cradle of civilization and center of human culture during one of the longest and most significant eras of history, and now it is a system that has been built on that strong foundation ... Our revolution proved that it is possible to stop dominant powers and not pay tribute to them, as long as we rely on something stronger than materialism ... Oh Lord, let experience guide the nations to real independence that is inalienable and, in the end, completes the negation of dominant world powers.[74]

Again, while highlighting the revolutionary zeal of Imam Hossein's Shiism, the Islamic Republic blended nationalist elements to make Shiism the cultural foundation of its national narrative.

As the most powerful country in the world, the United States, and its allies and policies, were often used as a point of contention and as the representation of Imam Hossein's foes. In a political track that lambasted the United States and used the infamous "death to America" (Marg Bar Amrikā)[75] chant as its title, the imagery of Karbala is clear:

*Everywhere has become Karbala*
*Hatred for the killers of children*
*And Harmalas [killer of Imam Hossein's son] of time.*

---

[73] Khomeini, *Jām-e Zahr*, 5.
[74] *Namāhang* (Tehran: Daftar-e Hefz Va Nashr-e Āsār-e Hazrat-e Ayātollah 'zma Khamenei, n.d.), DVD.
[75] Various Artists, *Faryād-e Enqelāb* (Tehran: Arman Cultural Center, 2015), CD.

The Islamic Republic went beyond rhetorical metaphors by weighing in on specific issues within the United States. For instance, Islamic Republic public television and news, Press TV, broadcasted an in-depth segment on the Black Lives Matter movement in the United States, in order to underscore the hypocrisy of the United States as a beacon of freedom and democracy.[76] The Islamic Republic doubled down on their efforts by holding a conference in Tehran in October 2015 discussing police brutality in America.[77] In line with its defense of the oppressed, the Islamic Republic drew attention to the plight of Black Americans.

Purporting to fight against all oppressive world systems, such as Zionism, colonialism, and racism, the Islamic Republic could tap into various geopolitical affairs to portray its image as protector of the downtrodden. For instance, a main boulevard in central Tehran still commonly known in Iran as "Jordan," was renamed Āfriqā (Africa) after the revolution and in more recent years renamed Nelson Mandela Boulevard in honor of South Africa's illustrious leader. Khamenei used Iran's revolution as an example for South Africa to follow in the 1980s: "Our experience is exceptional, and I believe South Africa has no other option than to have the people go to the streets, unafraid, and put pressure on the leaders."[78] Like the Black Lives Matter movement in the United States, the struggle of South Africa's Black majority against its apartheid government suited the Islamic Republic's promotion of resistance culture.

Despite all the Islamic Republic's rhetoric against the United States and Israel, there has been no direct confrontation, or war, with these states. However, in other cases the Islamic Republic went beyond posturing and took express action. Looking to the conflicts of its neighbors, the Islamic Republic claimed to align itself on the side of the oppressed in many of the struggles that plagued the region. Perpetuating its constructed image as guardian, the Islamic Republic continued its quest for social justice outside its borders. By funneling

---

[76]  Seen on Press TV in Iran in September 2015. For more segments from press TV go to www.presstv.ir/Detail/2016/10/01/487148/Black-Lives-Matter-Malcolm -X (last accessed August 9, 2018).

[77]  Yusef Jalali, "Iran's Capitol Hosts Conference on US Police Brutality," *Press TV* (November 2, 2015), last accessed August 9, 2018, http://presstv.com/Detail/2 015/11/02/436049/Iran-conference-US-police-brutality.

[78]  Ali Akbari-Mozdabadi, ed., *Hazrat-e Yār* (Tehran: Yā Zahrā, 2015), 143.

human and material resources into political movements and organizations in Palestine, Lebanon, Syria, and Iraq, the Islamic Republic revealed that they were not just searching for Yazid, but also acting as Hossein.

## 3.6 The Shadow of Hossein: Perpetual Quest for Justice

With the revolution and war behind them, the Islamic Republic used the Shiite idea of endless struggle to divert attention from its own rise to power since, according to Dabashi, anyone in the position of power becomes immediately questionable:

On the primordial model of Yazid, *zulm* [tyranny] is universally rampant and must be resisted by any means necessary. No political power is ever immune from a Shi'i accusation of tyranny – all are constitutionally illegitimate unless proven otherwise. Shi'ism is thus in effect an unending metaphysics of revolt against tyranny, with Imam Hossein and Yazid ibn Mu'awiyah as the archetypal representations of this cosmic battle. It is for that reason that Imam Hossein represents the ideal type: a revolutionary hero who revolts against *zulm*.[79]

In maintaining their image as Imam Hossein's deputies, the Islamic Republic needed to portray itself as the arbiters of virtue in a world of injustice. The architects of the Islamic Republic were cognizant of the expansive reach of such a claim and often spoke in broad terms. The language Khomeini used illustrated this all-encompassing idea, "Today a war of right and wrong, a war of poor and rich, a war of oppression and arrogance, and a war of the barefooted and affluent has begun. I kiss the hands and arms of all the loved ones in the world who have taken on the burden of this fight."[80] This broad rhetoric gave the Islamic Republic countless opportunities to insert itself into global affairs and represent the ceaseless crusade of Imam Hossein against tyranny.

In maintaining the discourse of anticolonialism, the Islamic Republic made the Palestinian struggle against Israel's occupation a keystone of its political ideology. Anticolonial nationalism was a central theme for Iranian revolutionaries such as Ali Shariati, who argued, "No other power in the world has been victimized by colonialism as much as

[79] Dabashi, *Shi'ism*, 83.    [80] Khomeini, *Jām-e Zahr*, 11.

Islam."[81] The combination of anticolonialism and independence from foreign powers, Islamic discourse, and Shiite leitmotifs, brought to fruition the national narrative the Islamic Republic had endeavored to construct. The image of Iran as the custodians of justice played out in the Islamic Republic's unwavering support of Palestine's national resistance movement.

Leaders of the revolution employed the Palestinian cause as a symbol of resistance and simultaneously showed Israel as the emblem of tyranny. Palestine was often invoked in the statements and language of Iranian leaders, such as Mostafa Chamran who recalled, "From Palestine to Vietnam, everywhere we see the pride of those fighting against colonialism."[82] International recognition of Israel's occupation helped bolster the Islamic Republic's position. However, despite the significant secular quality of the Palestinian national movement, Iranian leaders underlined the Islamic elements of the cause, as evidenced in Chamran's assertion that, "Even oppressed Palestinians, in their occupied homeland, utilize Islam in their fight against Israel."[83] By emphasizing the Islamic character of the Palestinian cause, the Islamic Republic attempted to build solidarity and reinforce the strength of its rhetoric, which was embedded in Islam. Khomeini drew direct parallels between Iran's struggle for independence from the shah and Palestine, noting:

The saga of the Palestinian people is not an accidental phenomenon. Who does the world imagine has composed this saga? And now what ideals do the Palestinian people lean on to resist the violent attacks of Zionism without fear and with empty hands? ... There is no doubt that this is the cry of "Allah O Akbar" [God is Great], this is the same cry of our nation that made the shah in Iran and the occupiers of Quds [Jerusalem] hopeless.[84]

The Palestinian struggle became an integral part of the Islamic Republic's image construction, not only because of a perceived Islamic alliance, but also because it fit the archetypical battle of Yazid and Hossein. The portrait of young Palestinians throwing stones at an overpowering and unjust Israeli military force evoked the classic tale of courage in Karbala.

---

[81] Shabanali Lam'ei, ed., *Eshārāt-e Sokhanān-e Gozide va Payām-ha-ye Kutāh-e Doktor Shariati* (Tehran: Ramand Publication, 2015), 116.
[82] Chamran, *Kordestān*, 160.    [83] Chamran, *Binesh Va Niyāyesh*, 30.
[84] Khomeini, *Jām-e Zahr*, 10–11.

The use of such heroic symbolism was prevalent in the Islamic Republic's image production. During the war, missions and operations were often named in honor of Palestine and Jerusalem, such as the operation "Road to Jerusalem."[85] City landscapes in Iran became a canvas for political artwork that put the Palestinian fight on display. The public space in Tehran inundates pedestrians and drivers with constant reminders, such as Palestine Square in central Tehran and its statue of the Palestinian map, a bus station named Quds, or a street named after Rachel Corrie, an American activist killed by Israeli bulldozers in 2003.[86] In addition to political rhetoric and public space, the Islamic Republic designated a national Quds Day, held exhibitions for cartoons on Palestine, and barred travel to "Occupied Palestine," as stated in every Iranian passport.

The use of Palestinian imagery was so extensive that it entered other mediums of Iranian society. In *Dā*, Zahra Hosseini discussed the plight of Palestinians and likened it to Iran's war: "They want to destroy Iran's revolution and steal Iran's oil. They want to make Iran like Palestine."[87] The history and conflict in Palestine are a common theme of documentary films in Iran as well. Figure 3.10 shows an advertisement for a collection of several such films.[88] The film collection uses the term "resistance" as a descriptor, which is fitting for the Islamic Republic's story of defiance.

The manifestation of these themes in less conservative cultural sites is also striking. For instance, popular Iranian rapper Hichkas collaborated with English-Iraqi rapper Lowkey on the song "Long Live Palestine Part 2" in 2009.[89] The song was a powerful protest statement against Israel and highlighted the human loss and oppression of Palestinians, in spite of the world's knowledge of Israel's occupation and terror. Moving between Arabic, English, and Persian, the song was an international cry for recognition of the state of affairs in Palestine. At the time of its release, Hichkas was one of the best-known rappers in

[85] Mohsen Kazemi, *Yādāsht-ha-ye Safar-e Shahid Sayyād Shirāzi* (Tehran: Sureh-e Mehr, 2011).
[86] AP, "Iran Names Street After Rachel Corrie," *The Guardian* (August 11, 2011), last accessed August 9, 2018, www.theguardian.com/world/2011/aug/11/iran-street-rachel-corrie.
[87] Hosseini, *Dā*, 266.
[88] Image was taken from an advertisement in a bookstore in central Tehran.
[89] Lowkey, "Long Live Palestine Part 2," YouTube video, last accessed August 9, 2018, www.youtube.com/watch?v=4PgxMjmKE0c.

**Figure 3.10** Palestine film poster. The title reads, "Documentary Collection of Palestine's Islamic Resistance."

Iran and was also featured in the popular 2009 film *No One Knows About Persian Cats*. The fact that an artist popular among young Iranians drew attention to the Palestinian cause, shows that Palestine is not simply a tool of Islamic Republic rhetoric. Beyond Islamic Republic propaganda, ordinary Iranians evidently grasp and show compassion for the reality of Palestinian subjugation.

To this end, the Islamic Republic was able to use the case of Palestine as a location of continual resistance by aligning itself on the side of the poor and oppressed. Likening itself to Imam Hossein, the Islamic

Republic claimed to take on the rulers of its time in its mission to combat tyranny. Another crucial site of confrontation aimed against big powers was the case of Lebanon. Its mass Shiite population, and conflict with Israel, made Lebanon the perfect target for the Islamic Republic's resistance campaign. Resembling Palestine, the Lebanese struggle against Israeli occupation in the 1980s afforded the Islamic Republic the opportunity to assert its influence in a regional conflict. While the proposed aim of the Islamic Republic was to support Lebanon's efforts to defend the south against Israeli occupation, the predominantly Shiite south of Lebanon presented the Islamic Republic with a chance to form a lasting alliance based on historical roots and shared religious philosophies. By helping to establish Hezbollah in the 1980s, the Islamic Republic cemented its ties to Lebanese Shiites and continued to play a role in Hezbollah's activities.[90]

Even before the revolution, Iranian ties to Shiites in Lebanon were strong, going back to the work of Musa al-Sadr, who moved to Lebanon from Iran in 1959 in order to help the disenfranchised Shiites of Lebanon. As Sadr worked to organize Lebanon's Shiites and build a militia, he maintained his ties to Iranian revolutionaries like Mostafa Chamran. In fact, Chamran spent time in south Lebanon in the 1970s, training and working with Shiites. The notion of martyrdom that became a staple of the Islamic Republic's identity was employed in Lebanon as well, as Chamran recalled in his experience quelling Kurdish rebellions: "The frightening night in Pāveh reminded me of Lebanon and the feeling of excitement for martyrdom."[91] Shared rituals and practices gave Iranian and Lebanese Shiites a sense of camaraderie, while the marginalized status of Lebanese Shiites gave the Islamic Republic another opportunity to take up the role of protector.

Like Palestine, Lebanon was a site of injustice that the Islamic Republic utilized in its rhetoric of political opposition. Khomeini made use of the Lebanese case whenever the occasion presented itself, for instance after the death of Chamran he declared, "I give my condolences for this tragedy to the noble nations of Iran and Lebanon, and also to Islamic nations and armed forces and those fighting in the path

[90] Augustus R. Norton, *Hezbollah: A Short History* (Princeton: Princeton University Press, 2007).
[91] Chamran, *Kordestān*, 77.

of God."[92] The communal connection of Lebanese and Iranian Shiites is apparent in such a statement. Lebanon's confrontation with Israel in the 1980s gave the Islamic Republic an additional opening to confirm Israel's brutality and reinforce its mutual interests with Lebanon. The fact that Israel's occupation was in the predominantly Shiite southern region of Lebanon was favorable to the Islamic Republic's strategy to take a lead in the conflict. However, in its effort to maintain its influence and an outpost for its resistance culture, the Islamic Republic's position in Lebanon went beyond the conflict with Israel. In later statements about Lebanon, Khomeini took aim at Lebanese officials as well: "Today you can recognize that Lebanon has many problems, there are now real crimes being committed, before directly at the hands of Zionists, and now by Amine Gemayel."[93] Khomeini shrewdly framed issues by using absolute terms like "crimes" in order to justify the Islamic Republic's actions as fair retribution.

The Islamic Republic continued to influence Lebanon in its alliance with Hezbollah, which is evident in the discourse of Hezbollah's leader, Hassan Nasrallah. The rhetoric Nasrallah employed was often identical to the language used by the Islamic Republic, similarly infused with ideas of martyrdom and political defiance indicative of Shiism. During Hezbollah's thirty-three-day war with Israel in 2006, Nasrallah repeatedly suggested that Hezbollah's strength was its Shiite faith, stating:

At this moment I am telling the Zionists, it will quickly become clear to you how ignorant your new government and leadership is; they do not know the end of this affair and they have no experience in this area. You do not know whom you are fighting today. You are fighting with the children of Mohammad, Ali, Hassan, Hossein and the household and companions of the messenger. You are fighting with people with the strongest faith than anyone in this world.[94]

Akin to the case of Iran in its war with Iraq, devotion was Hezbollah's key weapon in fighting Israel. As Nasrallah's statement a year after the war indicated, the idea of martyrdom was an asset for Lebanese Shiites: "From twenty-five years ago and until now, we have been attached to

---

[92]  Ibid., 4.
[93]  *Hekāyat-ha-ye Talkh Va Shirin* (Tehran: Mo'asese-ye Farhangi Honari-ye Qadr-e Velāyat, 2012), 288.
[94]  Siavash Sarmadi, dir., *Jang-e Shishom: Jang-e 33 Ruz-e* (Tehran: Arman Cultural Center, n.d.), DVD.

a school of thought in which its messengers are martyrs, its Imams are martyrs, and its leaders are martyrs."[95] Echoing the songs of war and revolution from Iran, Nasrallah highlighted the everlasting nature of martyrs, arguing:

You are the pride of Ummah [Muslim community]. You are the men of God and with you we will be victorious. I say to Bush and Olmert and all the oppressors of the world, try your best and use all your power, but I swear you cannot erase our memories or names, or destroy us.[96]

Doubling down on the Islamic Republic's rhetoric, Nasrallah painted the picture of heroic martyrs battling against the tyrants of the day.

Behind the extravagant language and ideology, Nasrallah went to the heart of the matter. In his frank discussion of the geopolitical situation facing the region, he stated:

The new Middle East is a place in which America dominates and interferes in its affairs and its most important ally is Israel. In the new Middle East, the issue of Palestine must be resolved and Palestinians must accept whatever Sharon and Olmert say. In the new Middle East there is no place for resistance movements. *The main obstacles against this new Middle East are the resistance movements of Palestine and Lebanon and the governments of Syria and Iran.*[97]

Nasrallah's nod to Iran confirmed that the Islamic Republic's support was tangible and, more than just words, action was taken. The Islamic Republic's persona of political defiance comes full circle with Nasrallah's assertion by demonstrating Iran's real assistance in political movements against oppressors in the region, from Palestine to Lebanon. Nasrallah's language was no coincidence; it was the result of the Islamic Republic's construction of its national narrative and its promotion of resistance culture. The success of promulgating this idea appears in statements by ordinary people as well, as one Lebanese woman declared after the Thirty-Three-Day War, "We gave twelve martyrs, amongst them were children, a young groom, and Alhamdulillah [Praise to God], we are still standing with all of our might. And if the whole world is destroyed on our heads, we will sacrifice ourselves for resistance."[98] The themes of sacrifice and resistance stress the lessons of Imam Hossein and intimate Iran's discourse.

---

[95] *Namāhang* (Tehran: Daftar-e Hefz Va Nashr-e Āsār-e Hazrat-e Ayātollah 'zma Khamenei, n.d.), DVD.
[96] Sarmadi, *Jang-e Shishom.*    [97] Ibid. (emphasis added).    [98] Ibid.

While Palestine and Lebanon were integral parts of the Islamic Republic's political outlook from the beginning of its reign, it continued to find new opportunities to assert its views and uphold the image of revolutionary, embodied by Imam Hossein. The speeches of the Islamic Republic's Supreme Leader, Ayatollah Khamenei, during the tumultuous years of the Arab Spring, beginning in 2010, illustrated the Islamic Republic's continuous search to align itself with resistance movements. Khamenei advanced the idea that these movements were, in reality, against the corrupt powers of the world, stating:

They were surprised, America was surprised by these events, it was a sudden blow for them, for the Zionists as well, and for the pretentious colonial governments of Europe. They were all surprised, but they want to maintain their dominance on the scene in any way necessary.[99]

Moreover, Khamenei was careful to discuss the rebellions in defensive terms and in one address given in Arabic he claimed, "Anyone who understands Egypt, will clearly know that Egypt is now defending its dignity and honor."[100] Throughout the revolutionary wave of protests and demonstrations that spread across the Middle East, Khamenei was an outspoken supporter of the rebels he deemed suitable, who challenged the corruption and despotism of their leaders. In accordance with the Islamic Republic's rhetoric, Khamenei argued, "And because this Islamism is characterized by anti-Zionism, anti-dictatorship, pro-independence, for freedom and pro-progress in light of the Quran, it will be the inevitable path and decisive choice of all Muslim nations."[101] Despite the secular undertones of the Arab Spring, like the case of Palestine, the Islamic Republic tried to stress and infuse an Islamic discourse into these uprisings.

In yet another recent regional conflict that afflicted Syria, the Islamic Republic moved beyond a rhetorical stance. By sending Iranian troops into Syria, it sought to play a more decisive role in the ongoing civil war. Unlike the cases where the government appeared to take the side of the resistance, in the case of Syria the Islamic Republic supported the dictatorship of Bashar al-Assad. Despite this important distinction, the rhetoric it employed remained the same. The Iranian government presented its military undertakings in Syria as part of its wider struggle

[99] *Namāhang* (Tehran: Daftar-e Hefz Va Nashr-e Āsār-e Hazrat-e Ayātollah 'zma Khamenei, n.d.), DVD.
[100] Ibid.    [101] Ibid.

against the United States and its local "allies" against the Iranian-led axis of resistance.[102]

The language used by Qasem Soleimani, who at the time was the commander of Iran's Islamic Revolutionary Guard Corps (IRGC), was reminiscent of Khomeini's words during Iran's Holy Defense. Addressing a small crowd of soldiers in Syria to chants of "we are prepared, prepared ... Mashallah, Hezbollah," Soleimani thanked them for their service and said, "I kiss your hands, I kiss your feet ... you are a source of pride ... your efforts have filled the hearts of the oppressed and the believers with happiness."[103] The fusion of religious tones with the fight against oppression was a hallmark of Iran's revolutionary ideologues, such as Ayatollah Motahhari who argued, "Islam, in being a religion – in being, of all the revealed religions, the seal of religions – exists to institute social justice. It follows that its goal is to liberate the deprived and oppressed and to struggle against the oppressors."[104]

When Iranian soldiers in Syria chanted, "It is a point of pride to die in your path ... soldiers of Ali, in the name of God, in the command of Abolfazl, we are all ready,"[105] they conjured the beliefs of Shiism and the honor of martyrdom familiar from the days of the Iran–Iraq War. Thus, decades after the revolution and war, Iranian authorities continued to advocate the ideology of political defiance that is essential to Shiism. Contending that they were following in the footsteps of Hossein, the Islamic Republic imagined itself in a ceaseless quest for justice.

## 3.7 Conclusion

History, as it is commonly understood in descriptive terms, is an essential part of national identity construction. While an entirely

[102] "Iran: 'We're in Axis of Resistance with Syria,'" *CBS News* (August 7, 2012), www.cbsnews.com/news/iran-were-in-axis-of-resistance-with-syria. Also see: https://farsi.khamenei.ir/news-content?id=41796.

[103] "Iran Qods Force Commander Qasem Soleimani in Aleppo Syria," YouTube video, last accessed August 9, 2018, www.youtube.com/watch?v=QIITSz720mY.

[104] Murtaẓá Muṭahharī and Hamid Algar, *Fundamentals of Islamic Thought: God, Man, and the Universe* (Berkeley: Mizan Press, 1985), 53.

[105] "Iranians of IRGC Chanting in North Aleppo, Syria," YouTube video, last accessed August 9, 2018, www.youtube.com/watch?v=j45XpylCvIA.

fictional and unrelated account would be difficult to accept, subjects of the nation-state certainly imagine and assume some truths about their identities based on the notion of a shared experience. Therefore, while some narratives fail, others may succeed in capturing a meaningful image for that society. In his attempts to foster support for his throne, the shah of Iran often utilized history for legitimacy. In fact, after the revolution of 1979, the shah wrote his *Answer to History* in which he claimed, "My own answer to history, therefore, must begin with the history of my country, the 3,000 years of Persian civilization that, misunderstood, has led to the defeat of Iran's attempt to enter the twentieth century."[106] Despite his overthrow in a massive people's revolution, the shah ignored his critics and argued that the history and civilization of Iran was "misunderstood." While the shah was aware of the importance of historical story-telling in the creation of Iran as a modern state, he failed at creating a national story that met the needs of many Iranians.

After the revolution, the Islamic Republic took up the task of creating its own narrative based on the success of the revolutionaries, who produced a message that resonated with Iranian masses. In contrast to the shah, who seemed enamored by European models, the Islamic Republic emphasized Iran's Islamic and Shiite heritage. The Islamic Republic picked up on the discourse of popular opponents of the shah, like Shariati, who claimed, "If we remove God from nature, Ali from history, and the temple from the earth, nature would be an abandoned graveyard, history a dark corridor, and the earth a cold and ugly landfill."[107] Shariati's statement highlighted the significance of religious character and the fear of removing Iran's Shiite history.

As the Islamic Republic focused on allaying these fears, its eager leaders imposed a national narrative based on Shiite cultural roots and Iran's independence in the revolution. Emphasizing political defiance and the pursuit of social justice, the Islamic Republic endorsed Imam Hossein's martyrdom as the defining moment for Shiism, and in turn, the Iranian nation-state. Moreover, in the image of Hossein, the Islamic Republic stressed Iran's moral responsibility to protect and defend the poor and oppressed of the world. Khomeini repeatedly

---

[106] Mohammad Reza Pahlavi, *Answer to History* (New York: Stein and Day, 1980), 34.

[107] Shabanali Lam'ei, ed. *Eshārāt-e Sokhanān-e Gozide va Payām-ha-ye Kutāh-e Doktor Shariati* (Tehran: Ramand Publication, 2015), 74.

conveyed these sentiments, as one revolutionary guard recalled him saying:

Listen to the words and grievances of the downtrodden and know now that our country, by the want of God, is Islamic. The armed forces must help the underprivileged, they must give 100% of their effort for them and interact with the deprived with Islamic morality.[108]

Consequently, Islam and the nation became intertwined by the shared values of the Iranian people, who represented both.

Though Islamic Republic policies and rhetoric maintained the narrative of resistance culture, these ideas did not go unchallenged. Like the shah, the Islamic Republic was condemned for its policies and Iranians pushed back on the exclusivity of Shiite identity. Recognizing a new set of silences, Iranians opted for plurality and a more complex understanding of national identity. However, it is noteworthy that the style of their dissent was distinct from the opposition of the shah. While there were certainly Iranian political groups who wished for the overthrow of the Islamic Republic, political events in Iran since the revolution paint a different picture. Having lived through one revolution, rather than calling for another, many Iranians participated in the political system and focused their efforts on reform.

The most poignant example of this struggle for change within the system was the 2009 election and ensuing Green Movement that contested its results. The stories and images of people waiting for hours in long lines to vote illustrated the participatory nature of Iranian politics. When Iranians first took to the streets to protest the announcement of Ahmadinejad's victory, "Where is my vote?"[109] was their rallying cry, showing the desire for the system to work properly. As tensions escalated, Iranians began shifting their message using slogans and tactics from the 1979 revolution, for instance, chanting "Allah O Akbar" from their rooftops.[110] By inverting revolutionary slogans, protestors signified that they were holding the Islamic Republic accountable for

---

[108] Ali Ahmadpour-Turkamani, ed., *Simā-ye Āftāb* (Qom: Daftar-e Nashr-e M'āref, 2011), 136–37.
[109] "Where Is My Vote?," YouTube video, last accessed August 9, 2018, www .youtube.com/watch?v=MmZlnzvLbNM.
[110] Olivia Cornes, "How Iran's Opposition Inverts Old Slogans," BBC News (December 7, 2009), accessed August 9, 2018, http://news.bbc.co.uk/2/hi/mid dle_east/8386335.stm.

the aim and discourse of the revolution. One particular slogan that
captured national sentiment and criticized the Islamic Republic's policies was "Na Ghazeh, na Lobnān, jānam fadā-ye Irān" (Not Gaza, nor
Lebanon, I sacrifice my life for Iran).[111] While this chant seemingly
rejected the Islamic Republic's rhetoric on Palestine and Lebanon, the
idea of sacrificing one's life for the nation affirmed the notion of
martyrdom ingrained in Shiism and Iranian culture.

Iranians not only challenged the political system, but also the Islamic
Republic's narrow view of Iranian identity. However, in the decades
since the revolution the Islamic Republic exhibited its ability to evolve
and navigate these situations, but also showed that the state would
resort to violent repression in order to retain its power.

While the Islamic Republic still appears to promote the narrative of
resistance culture and revolution embedded in Shiism, there are some
signs of adaptability, as ordinary Iranians continue to push back. Long-
avoided symbols of Iran's pre-Islamic past made their way back into
officially sanctioned items. In the 2016 Olympics, Iranian wrestlers
donned outfits with a picture of the mythical Iranian bird, Homā, and
the phrase "Yā Ali."[112] The juxtaposition of Islamic Iran and ancient
Iran is apparent on newer currency (see Figure 3.11) and passports as

Figure 3.11 Islamic Republic 1,000,000 rials bank note, which uses an image
of Persepolis, the Achaemenid capital.

[111]  "2009 Iranian Revolution – 'No to Gaza, No to Lebanon, I Only Sacrifice My
       Life for Iran,'" YouTube video, last accessed August 9, 2018, www
       .youtube.com/watch?v=eD7Gca4gHYA.
[112]  "Hassan Yazdani – Highlights," YouTube video, last accessed August 9, 2018,
       www.youtube.com/watch?v=2KDyjve9xcY.

well. Passports and currency are objects often used by states to convey specific meanings in defining the nation. The use of images such as the tombs of Iranian poets and Persepolis indicate the Islamic Republic's expanding attitude toward Iranian identity and the impact of Iranian people in resisting the limited narratives of those in power.

As recent developments and the ongoing efforts of different governments over the last century show, the nature of national identity is malleable. Rather than use fabrications, Iranian leaders used various cultural symbols from the array that was available to them to construct Iran's historical narrative and national identity in the modern era of nation-states. The successes or failures of this enterprise had significant impacts on the Iranian state and people. While state actors had a vested interest in maintaining a particular image, ordinary people also used national identity and nationalist rhetoric to advance social and political causes. Furthermore, for many Iranians, their identity has profound emotional ramifications. Tied deeply to their "imagined community," Iranians often associate struggle with their identity. This attitude of Iranians is best summed up by Shariati: "The nation is the sum of a people who feel the same pain."[113] The next two chapters consider Iranian agency and how they express their identities in popular mediums, such as music and cinema.

---

[113] Shabanali Lam'ei, ed., *Eshārāt-e Sokhanān-e Gozide va Payām-ha-ye Kutāh-e Doktor Shariati* (Tehran: Ramand Publication, 2015), 187.

# 4 | Iranian Identity and Popular Music

Though there is great speculation about a future without nations and a world that transcends borders, the nation-state is still the central organizer of human societies. As Benedict Anderson has suggested, the motivation to sacrifice one's life for the nation is especially remarkable, given that their imagined connection to the homeland and its millions of inhabitants is so limited in scope. The willingness to die, which has become an integral part of nationalism, resonates in contemporary Iran as can be seen with estimates of hundreds of thousands of casualties in the Iran–Iraq War (1980–88).[1] In the age of nation-states and international conflict, nationalist rhetoric requires further inquiry and understanding.

While the previous chapters emphasized the state's role in constructing national narratives, they also highlighted the limits of their imagination. Though all nation-states can be understood as Anderson's "imagined communities," how these communities are conceived is based on the historical and cultural resources at their disposal. In this sense, state authorities cannot simply invent a national identity from fabrications and falsehoods. Instead, the Pahlavi monarchs and its revolutionary successors in the Islamic Republic utilized the local histories and affinities of their people – their language, culture, history, and religiosity – to fashion an Iranian identity befitting a modern nation-state. It could only be through the interaction of these forces that a meaningful Iranian identity developed.

As Hamid Dabashi stresses, identity formation in Iran was a transnational process that emerged out of Iran's public spaces.[2] The swift decline of the Qajar dynasty and the rise of Iranian intellectuals and artists, many influenced and educated outside of Iran, facilitated

---

[1] Anthony H. Cordesman and Abraham R. Wagner, *The Lessons of Modern War, vol. II: The Iran-Iraq War* (Boulder, CO: Westview Press, 1990).

[2] Hamid Dabashi, *Iran without Borders: Towards a Critique of the Postcolonial Nation* (London: Verso, 2016).

a burgeoning public space. These cosmopolitan forces challenged the shah's legitimacy and the Islamic Republic's efforts to define Iranian popular culture with an Islamic character.[3] While both the Pahlavi monarchy and Islamic Republic created histories and narratives for their own purposes and systematically ignored Iran's rich diversity, the Iranian populace resisted their accounts of Iranian identity. It is imperative to examine the agency of these actors and their influence in the construction of national identity.

The contestation of Iranian identity took many forms and manifested in various spaces, however, it is important to understand that the very act of challenging national narratives presented by state authorities is political in nature. Though the Islamic Republic tried to appropriate social movements and political resistance culture for its own use, people continued to defy the image of a homogenous Iranian identity in strictly Islamic terms. Such attempts by the Islamic Republic mirror the shah's efforts to appear revolutionary in the face of a radical movement. Where the shah failed to create a suitable modern nationalism, the Islamic Republic seized on the counternarrative of Iranian revolutionaries. Still, the Islamic Republic's determination to Islamize the Iranian populace after the revolution faced many obstacles.

In the decades after the revolution, many Iranians professed a strong desire for reform and embraced democratic principles in governing. The fact that Iran is under an Islamic system does not prevent it from being democratic, insofar as elected representatives are given the ability to govern based on the will of the people. As Asef Bayat aptly argues, no religion is inherently democratic or undemocratic; instead it is social agents that determine its nature through interpretation.[4] For Bayat, after the death of Khomeini, Iran entered an era of post-Islamism in which people advocated change within the system. According to Bayat, "Post-Islamism is neither anti-Islamic nor un-Islamic nor secular. Rather it represents an endeavor to fuse religiosity and rights, faith and freedom, Islam and liberty."[5] Accordingly, while social agents in Iran resisted opposing national narratives and adopted a more complex and plural view of identity, they did not entirely reject the influence and significance of Islam as part of Iran's cultural fabric.

---

[3] Ibid.
[4] Asef Bayat, *Making Islam Democratic: Social Movements and the Post-Islamist Turn* (Stanford, CA: Stanford University Press, 2007).
[5] Ibid., p. 11.

Bayat emphasizes the critical role of urban youth in Iran's post-Islamic movement and the importance of using social spaces to produce alternative ideas and customs. Therefore, we must explore the social spaces of Iran's urban youth to better understand how they challenged authorities and articulated their Iranian identity. Popular culture is a crucial area that is heavily influenced by urban youth and acts as a vehicle for social change. One sector of popular culture that is examined here is music.

Music is an essential aspect of any culture, since it has the capacity to convey meanings and evoke strong emotions. As Stuart Hall has noted, "Music is 'like a language' in so far as it uses musical notes to communicate feelings and ideas."[6] In the case of Iran, music was used in politics, revolution, and war to create specific images and challenge the powers that be. Under the Islamic Republic, music took on an especially important role in contesting power because of the limited freedoms of artists and the regulations of state authorities. As a result, music itself is a point of civil contention, even when the content appears benign and apolitical. The case of the official selection for Iran's 2006 World Cup song illustrates this conflict.

In 2006 the Iranian national soccer team was among the thirty-two countries participating in the World Cup. For Iranians, as with citizens from all the competing nations, qualifying for the World Cup was a notable event that brought about celebrations throughout the country. One manifestation of their joy was through music. A handful of authorized artists within Iran submitted tracks to be selected as the official team song by the Iranian Federation of Soccer. The government then approved these songs and one entitled "Persian Stars," sung by three soccer players, became the official selection.[7] The song was highly nationalistic, making references to the flag and brave heroes of the country. Not surprisingly, the lyrics played on themes that fit the image of Iran espoused by the Islamic Republic:

*The people's good prayers*
*For their hard work*
*Revive them again*

---

[6]  Stuart Hall, *Representation: Cultural Representations and Signifying Practices* (London: Sage/Open University, 1997), p. 5.
[7]  Sanam Zahir, "The Music of the Children of the Revolution: The State of Music and Emergence of the Underground Music in the Islamic Republic of Iran with Analysis of Its Lyrical Content" (MA thesis, University of Arizona, 2008).

*Love and Battle and Scream*
*Plant another goal*
*In the competitor's end*
*So, the world will tremble*
*With the name of Iran*[8]

In addition to the lyrics, the video also showed images that directly supported the Islamic Republic's vision, including images of the Iranian flag with "Allah" pictured, a pious woman in full cover praying, and pictures of revolutionary leader Ayatollah Khomeini and Supreme Leader Ayatollah Khamenei. Yet, while "Persian Stars" was the official state selection for the World Cup song, YouTube numbers show that the video has only 44,000 views.

This number is in stark contrast to another song by a Swedish-Iranian artist, Arash, also performed for the World Cup of 2006. His song, "Iran, Iran," was not allowed to be officially distributed in Iran, and the song was not played on state television or radio. Nevertheless, Arash's song has well over three million views on YouTube.[9] The popularity of the song was not its only distinction; the lyrical content and video were also markedly different. In Arash's video the Iranian flag simply has the name "Iran" in the middle. This move carries great meaning, given that the center of the flag changed from "the lion and the sun" to "Allah" after the revolution in 1979.[10] Since then, the Iranian flag has been a heated issue for opposing political factions in the diaspora. Arash's choice to use neither the old nor new flag represented a deliberate effort not to align himself with any political doctrine. Like "Persian Stars," "Iran, Iran" invoked nationalist sentiments, yet the themes exhibited were noticeably different. Arash's song made references to pre-Islamic Iran, the land of an ancient civilization, and of Aryans:

*Generation after generation Aryan*
*Warm and down to earth, without malice*
*Anywhere I am, anywhere in the world*
*My life I would sacrifice for the grains of Iran's soil*

[8] "Persian Stars," YouTube video, last accessed March 23, 2020, www.youtube.com/watch?v=gAjapbkrRdk.

[9] Arash, "Iran, Iran," YouTube video, last accessed July 23, 2018, www.youtube.com/watch?v=L_1maePHaZk.

[10] Nikki R. Keddie, *Modern Iran: Roots and Results of Revolution* (New Haven, CT: Yale University Press 2003).

*Cyrus the Great is a Sultan*
*Arash the Archer is from Iran*
*My life I would sacrifice for the culture*
*And 2,500-year civilization of Iran*

The music video for "Iran, Iran" pictures a group of young people watching a soccer game on the beach where there are men and uncovered women in the audience intermixed. These images would not be allowed to air on Islamic Republic state television, since Iranian women must be covered in appropriate Islamic headdress in all public spaces. It is evident that Arash's song and video did not comply with the strict rules that govern authorized music in Iran. Though the song was significantly more popular[11] and the content was appropriate for a national sports team, it had no place in the Islamic Republic's public discourse.

While the use of music as a medium of expression is not unique to Iranians, the Islamic Republic's control over music distribution distinguishes it from many other nation-states. Under the guidelines of the Islamic Republic, not all music is approved for distribution. The Ministry of Culture and Islamic Guidance, also known as Ershād, must accept the musical content and lyrics before artists are allowed to officially distribute their CDs to the public. Approval is granted if the ministry deems the music is within the parameters of Islamic morality and law.[12] As a government entity, Ershād has the authority and motive to block approval for content that it views as being outside the image of Iranian nationalism that the Islamic Republic champions. Despite these limitations, the overwhelming national pride evoked by the World Cup resulted in several songs by various artists that captured the passion of the moment.

What are the implications in this case? And why is it important to consider the gap between the state's official selection for a World Cup song and the popularity of an *unauthorized* World Cup song? In the United States it is difficult to imagine that someone would have to

[11] Though the song is from the 2006 World Cup, it continues to be the unofficial anthem for the Iranian national team. This was evident in the team's celebrations after their victory against Morocco in the 2018 World Cup. As the clip shows, the players expressed their euphoria and sang Arash's "Iran, Iran." https://instagram.com/p/BkDdB9hnzQP/ (Last accessed August 25, 2018).
[12] Ministry of Culture and Islamic Guidance, last accessed March 23, 2018, www.Ershad.gov.ir.

illegally purchase a national song created for an international soccer tournament. Artists in the United States are free to express their feelings and political views, even those that go directly against the government, as a right protected by the first amendment of the constitution. Musicians in Iran do not have the same luxury. Instead, their work is impeded by what authorities allow and authorize to be distributed in accordance with their interpretation of Islamic morality. It is precisely because of the Islamic Republic's attempts to control such artistic outlets that music is a site of contestation. As Nahid Siamdoust insightfully argues, in postrevolutionary Iran:

Music has served as an important alternative political, societal, and ideational space, and Iranians, music producers and consumers alike, have imbued it with great significance. The soundtrack of revolutionary Iran tells the story not just of matters that have lain at the center of the people's and policy makers' negotiations about politics, religion, and national identity, but also the story of the evolution of the Islamic Republic itself.[13]

Thus, music is a critical instrument in identity construction, both from the top down and from the bottom up. In the Islamic Republic's efforts to facilitate a particular notion of Iranianness, conflicting identities were silenced and censored. To understand the nature of Iranian identity under the Islamic Republic, it is necessary to analyze these discrepancies where they exist.

In my examination of Iranian identity, I look at the lyrical content of popular music, focusing on how the notion of Iranianness is discussed and represented in the music that urban youth enjoy. The music's popularity is determined based on the number of views and downloads on websites such as YouTube, and Radio Javan, a website for Iranian music and artists. Additionally, my findings are supported by field research conducted over many months and spanning more than four years from 2011 to 2015.[14] This fieldwork includes interviews with urban youth living in Tehran, which helped provide more information on how Iranians regard their national identity. The bulk of my investigation focuses on a selection of songs taken from a large archive acquired in Iran and collected from various sources inside Iran.

---

[13] Nahid Siamdoust, *Soundtrack of the Revolution: The Politics of Music in Iran* (Stanford, CA: Stanford University Press, 2017), 2.
[14] Fieldwork in Iran was also conducted in the mid-2000s and contributed to this research.

As a mode of communication that reflects the shared experiences of members in a society, music is a fitting source when studying national identity. The following analysis looks at lyrics of popular Iranian music and presents several themes regarding Iranian identity, such as the need to assert national identity and identity as a form of political resistance. Music offers an excellent medium for interpreting culture because it is an expression of both our individual self and our collective existence.[15] An exploration into popular music reveals a world that goes beyond official rhetoric and emphasizes the role of ordinary people as agents of their identity construction.

## 4.1 Need for Identity

The need for identity has a psychological factor. For Erik Erikson, identity is a process both on the individual and collective level, and a sense of identity is a crucial part of human existence, "For man's *need for a psychosocial identity* is anchored in nothing less than his socio-genetic evolution."[16] One manifestation of this necessity is reflected in modern-day society as a need for national identity, since the nation-state is a fundamental part of the contemporary world. The need for such an identity is a product of a global community, membership of which requires a national identity. Hence, identifying as "Iranian" reveals a necessity to assert a national consciousness. This was a process that occurred on an individual level among ordinary citizens and was simultaneously constructed through the modernizing project of the Iranian nation-state, an undertaking that the Pahlavi monarchs vigorously attempted.

However, because simply creating the label of Iranian was not sufficient for producing an identity, Reza Shah worked to implement policies and laws that would give substance and meaning to the word. For example, he implemented cultural changes as part of his modernizing campaign to bring Iran closer to Western and European society. The secular ideology implemented by Reza Shah undercut the cultural influences of Islam by imposing invasive laws, such as banning certain types of Islamic dress, like the chador, a traditional sheet-like garb that

---

[15] Observed in Simon Frith, "Music and Identity," in Stuart Hall et al., ed., *Questions of Cultural Identity* (London: Sage Publications Ltd., 1996), 108.

[16] Erik H. Erikson, *Identity: Youth and Crisis* (New York: W. W. Norton, 1968), 41 (emphasis added).

covers the entire body and form of the female, and enforcing a Western dress code.[17] Indoctrination of the body was also a part of the shah's cultural mission, by creating organizations dedicated to athletics and physical fitness and supporting national sports.[18] In the musical arena, Reza Shah, not surprisingly, promoted Western models and even brought European musical teachers so that Iranians could learn their superior technique.[19]

However, no program was more essential to this cultural production than the area of education and language. As a key component to culture and a modern state, having a unified language was crucial to Reza Shah's crusade. He emphasized the superiority of Persian and established language institutes and a public national education campaign to solidify national identity based on shared language, culture, and history. In 1932 the shah organized a group to create new scientific words and terms in Persian. Reza Shah also established a Language Academy that focused on replacing non-Persian words from use.[20] During this process he ignored the ethnic and linguistic diversity of Iran in pursuit of creating a nation united under one identity with one common language. The primacy of Persian related directly to the creation of a national education program that ensured uniformity, in which children learned the official language in a formal setting.

The teaching of Iranian history was also vital to cultural indoctrination, as Afshin Marashi points out: "Education, like the national project itself, looked to an idealized ancient past in charting a course for Iran's future."[21] Pedagogy is a key area in which identity is formed, and central to teaching is the textbook. A study conducted in the mid-1990s explored textbooks from the last decade of the Pahlavi era and the first decade of the Islamic Republic.[22] The authors of the study

---

[17] Firoozeh Kashani-Sabet, "Cultures of Iranianess: The Evolving Polemic of Iranian Nationalism," in Nikki R. Keddie et al., ed., *Iran and the Surrounding World* (Seattle: University of Washington Press, 2002), 162.

[18] Ibid.

[19] Nahid Siamdoust, *Soundtrack of the Revolution: The Politics of Music in Iran* (Stanford, CA: Stanford University Press, 2017).

[20] Mehrdad Kia, "Persian Nationalism and the Campaign for Language Purification," *Middle Eastern Studies* 34, no. 2 (1998), 9.

[21] Afshin Marashi, *Nationalizing Iran: Culture, Power, and the State, 1870–1940* (Seattle: University of Washington Press, 2008), 90.

[22] Patricia J. Higgins and Pirouz Shoar-Ghaffari, "Changing Perceptions of Iranian Identity in Elementary Textbooks," in Elizabeth Warnock Fernea, ed., *Children in the Muslim Middle East* (Austin: University of Texas Press, 1996), 337.

argued that textbooks were significant as a tactical part of education that was controlled by the government. Not surprisingly, the study showed distinctions between the monarchy and the Islamic Republic, especially in the social sciences and humanities. The Pahlavi era textbooks focused on Persian, pre-Islamic history, and had little religious teachings, while the texts from the Islamic Republic focused much more heavily on religion, the history of the revolution, and deemphasized lessons focused on Persian.

Those in positions of power, vis-à-vis the state, had enormous sway in setting Iran's national boundaries, both physical and symbolic. However, the larger populace negotiated and interpreted the actions of officials in order to influence the characteristics ascribed in this process of national identity formation. As one middle-class Tehran youth pointed out, "Reza Shah officially made the country's name 'Iran' to establish it as a nation, like England and France. The Persian Empire is important to our cultural roots, but to be modern is to be a state, not an empire."[23] The young woman's explanation of Reza Shah's actions illustrates the capacity of common citizens to construct meaning. For this Iranian youth, being modern was linked to being a nation-state.

Displays of nationalism are pervasive in Iranian society and exemplify their aspiration to advance and be accepted among the community of nations as a modern state. The prideful need to proclaim their national identity is illustrated through popular music. What is important to note is that these themes are evident in pop songs that are lyrically simple, and meant for dancing and light listening. Even in such neutral musical styles we come across identity features associated with the nation and national identity. For instance, the song, "Dokhtar-e Iruni" (Iranian Girl), from the early 1990s by popular Iranian artist Andy[24] has the lyrics:

[23] Interview conducted in Tehran, December 2012. Subject was female and early twenties.
[24] Andy is part of the US diaspora Iranian music scene that was popular in Iran in the absence of domestic pop music production. By the late 1990s as the Islamic Republic eased restrictions, the domestic pop music scene in Iran was favored over the expatriate artists abroad. However, the expatriate artists continued to be listened to, especially the older songs that have remained staples of party music and evoke nostalgia. Andy has 240 million plays on Radio Javan.
"Andy," Radio Javan, last accessed March 23, 2020, www.radiojavan.com/artist/Andy.

*An Iranian girl is like a flower, oh what colors she has*
*Don't say who is better, every flower has a fragrance*

The song was popular at the time of its release and continued to be played at dance parties and gatherings in Iran with young people feverishly dancing and singing along to the lyrics. The video for the song has over 10.7 million views on YouTube[25] and while the song is light and fun, the lyrical content is all about Iranian girls. The song also mentions many different areas in Iran, but brings them all together under a larger national banner of being "Iruni" (Iranian):

*She is breathtaking and witty, she must be from Shiraz*
*She is a beauty from Khuzestan, she is born from Abadan*
*Oh, how eloquent she is, she is from Isfahan*
*She is abundantly loyal, she is a Tabriz girl*
*Ask her where she is from, from what region*
*Within all the beauties she stands alone, there is no question*
*An Iranian girl is like a flower, oh what colors she has*

In the middle of the song a female voice joins to sing in tandem with the male voice that is, in a sense, courting the woman. She replies in kind, also referring to his identity as "pesar-e Iruni" (Iranian boy):

*The Prince of my fairytales, oh Iranian boy*
*You guard my heart you know my value*
*You, you are my favorite, your love has trapped me*
*You my Iranian companion, born of my country*

The last line is telling for not naming an individual love interest: this ballad was meant for all Iranian women because of their national origin.

This theme was not unique to Andy in Iranian pop; other artists and songs also invoked Iranian identity and exceptionalism in their music. The popular expatriate boy band Black Cats[26] used similar language on more than one occasion. In 2002 the band had a party favorite called, "Āhang-e Man" (My Song), for which the video on YouTube has over

---

[25] Andy, "Dokhtare Irooni," last accessed March 23, 2020, www.youtube.com/watch?v=-05qe1MF5Pg.

[26] Like with Andy, popular songs by Black Cats were often listened to and played at parties inside Iran. Black Cats has 130 million plays on Radio Javan. "Black Cats," Radio Javan, last accessed March 23, 2020, www.radiojavan.com/artist/Black+Cats.

1.5 million views.[27] The male singer makes a reference to the object of his affection by naming her nationality:

*Everybody knows you as beautiful and kind*
*With cuteness and gestures your walk sets fires*
*Everyone loves you and adores you, Iranian girl*
*Oh oh, Iranian girl*

In the mid-2000s Black Cats had another popular song that young Iranians listened to, especially at dance parties, named "Jun-e Khodet" (Your Own Life). The video has over 1.5 million views on YouTube.[28] The lyrics were meant as a love ballad to a girl, but again we see that the girl is specified as a "dokhtar-e Iruni" (Iranian girl). The male suitor is also referred to as "pesar-e Iruni" (Iranian boy):

*Iranian girl who is sweet and breathtaking*
*Listen! To this message from Black Cats*
*You break the hearts of Iranian boys*
*Listen! To the words of his heart*

In both situations the indication is broad; there are no names mentioned or pronouns that would indicate a particular individual. Instead, the songs are dedicated to Iranian girls and boys in general, and allude to their unique and exceptional qualities.

These songs help illustrate the prevalent nature of national identity in Iran. If being modern is equated with being a nation, then the Iranian state over the last century did all it could to construct a crystallized idea of Iranianness. As Theodor Adorno argues in his 1941 piece, "On Popular Music,"[29] this "standardization" of the individual is closely tied to media and the mass appeal of popular music. Adorno is concerned with mass psychology and the systematization of individuals that comes along with the uniformity indicative of popular music. In the case of Iran, standardization of the individual as "Iranian" was a project of the state before 1979. The

27  Black Cats, "My Song," YouTube video, last accessed March 23, 2020, www .youtube.com/watch?v=4E9x2ve1qx4.
28  Black Cats, "Joone Khodet (Ey khanoom koja)," YouTube video, last accessed March 23, 2020, www.youtube.com/watch?v=9xqlLCTWdrI.
29  Theodor Adorno, "On Popular Music," Soundscapes, last accessed August 23, 2018, www.icce.rug.nl/~soundscapes/DATABASES/SWA/On_popular_musi c_1.shtml. Originally published in: *Studies in Philosophy and Social Science*, IX (1941), 17–48.

lyrics we see in popular music today are simply an expression of that normalization.

While these songs are all from after the 1979 revolution, the notion of identity assertion and the nation-state also existed during the Pahlavi era. A look at a couple songs by popular Iranian musician Vigen illustrates this point. Vigen was one of the first Iranian pop singers to become popular in the 1950s and 1960s in Iran, and continued to have a following among young and old Iranians until his death in 2003. His music is still enjoyed by Iranians and covered by younger Iranian artists. His 1975 song, "Ākh Jun"[30] (Oh Life), is a jazzy pop song that talks about the uniqueness of Iran:

> *Only in Iran, Only in Iran*
> *Oh oh how hot it is, the sun of the summer*
> *Only in Iran, Only in Iran*
> *Oh yes, and how nice is the sun of the winter*

Vigen's descriptions all focus on nature, but then go back to the idea that the beauty and nature of the seasons in Iran are somehow exceptional:

> *Its autumn is so beautiful, its trees colorful, anywhere you go is a place*
>   *to behold*
> *Its spring is refreshing, with green and bloom, you want to be with*
>   *your partner*
> *My beautiful spring, my autumn rain, you have overwhelming*
>   *affection*
> *Now the charcoal of my winter, the ice water of my summer, you are*
>   *only in Iran*

This song was remixed into a more contemporary dance song in the mid 2000s by a young Iranian musician and was again well received and played in parties in Iran.

Another popular Vigen song, "Zan-e Iruni"[31] (Iranian Woman), is still a staple at Iranian weddings and, similar to previous tracks, it amplifies the incomparable character of Iranian women. Vigen's use of the word "*hamzabun*" is interesting to note here. Literally translated

---

[30]  Vigen, "Ākh Jun," YouTube video, last accessed August 23, 2018, www .youtube.com/watch?v=cW9B2YX7hp0

[31]  The song has over 6.6 million plays. "Viguen – Zane Irooni," Radio Javan, last accessed March 23, 2020, www.radiojavan.com/mp3s/album/Viguen-Zane-Irooni.

the word means "fellow language," but the connotation takes on a deeper meaning. It can be used to refer to someone who understands you and is therefore of the same tongue, so to speak. Central to its meaning is the emotional weight of someone who appreciates you and speaks the same cultural language. Lyrics from the song are as follows:

> For a *"hamzabun,"* a good and sweet companion
> I searched the world with my heart and soul, every day and every
>     night
> I saw the whole world until I got here
> That I say, nowhere have I seen something like an Iranian woman
> An Iranian woman is exceptional, beautiful, and charming

In light of the Pahlavi nationalizing campaign and the significance given to Persian as a cornerstone of national identity, Vigen's use of the word "hamzabun" in a pop song has greater implications. The efforts of the Pahlavi dynasty to create a specific image of Iranian identity that privileged Persian were evident in several institutions and the effects of those efforts permeated Iranian culture.

As Raymond Williams explains, "culture" is one of the most complicated and contested words in the English language; here I am referring to Williams' third category of usage, in which culture describes the works and practices of intellectual and artistic activity,[32] in this case, music. The cultural and institutional changes executed by successive Iranian governments were part of a project of modernity; a quote from Antonio Gramsci's *Prison Notebooks* speaks to this idea:

If every State tends to create and maintain a certain type of civilization and of citizen (and hence of collective life and of individual relations), and to eliminate certain customs and attitudes and to disseminate others, then the Law will be its instrument for this purpose (together with the school system, and other institutions and activities). It must be developed so that it is suitable for such a purpose – so that it is maximally effective and productive of positive results.[33]

In this sense, we see that the ruling class, who deploys the traditions of a society for specific ends, contributes to the social construction of culture. This continued to be true under the Islamic Republic's reign.

---

[32] Raymond Williams, *Keywords: A Vocabulary of Culture and Society* (New York: Oxford University Press, 1985).

[33] Antonio Gramsci, Quintin Hoare, and Geoffrey Nowell-Smith, *Selections from the Prison Notebooks of Antonio Gramsci* (New York: International Publishers, 1971), 246.

While the state is not secular, it created the façade of democracy. There is an elected legislative body, an elected president, and a constitution. The government continued other modernizing projects, such as advances in science and technology; their contested civilian nuclear program is a relevant example.

Unlike the Pahlavi dynasty, the Islamic Republic's central focus and marker of identity was Islam. While Islam is an identity that transcends borders, even the current Islamic government did not deny the importance of the nation. For instance, during his tenure, president Khatami (1997–2005) tried to create a notion of Iranian identity that fused together both Islam and Iranianness.[34] For Khatami, both pre-Islamic and Islamic identities were important. However, as Shabnam Holliday argues, "Iraniyat" was the prime identity he emphasized: "Thus, it is being Iranian that is ultimately important. In other words, Islam is Iranianised and furthermore the framework for the political apparatus is not simply politicized Islam, but rather *Iranian* political Islam."[35] As a result, Islamic discourse became uniquely Iranian: Islamist-Iranian discourse. Though the features that define Iranian identity were different between the Pahlavi monarchs and the Islamic Republic, the notion of the Iranian nation as a state within the world of nations remained the same.

Nationhood emerged out of the modernizing campaign and made the idea of national identity a requisite for the Iranian citizen. This phenomenon was not unique to Iran. In the period following World War I, the whole region was affected by the war and the dissolution of the Ottoman Empire. The significance of oil reserves in the region made it important geopolitically, while subsequent occupations and colonial projects laid the foundation for nationalist and social movements among various young nations determined to decide their future. As discussed previously, the failure of the Pahlavi monarchs to construct a meaningful national narrative, and their image as pawns of foreign agents, sowed the seeds of dissent that helped to usher in a revolution with an alternative national vision. Regardless of the details of these competing accounts, the individual Iranian showed a necessity for national identity. The psychological need to have an identity and have a place in collective society, along with the project of modernization, made nationality an understandable form of

---

[34] Shabnam, Holliday, "Khatami's Islamist-Iranian Discourse of National Identity: A Discourse of Resistance," *British Journal of Middle Eastern Studies* 37, no. 1 (2010).

[35] Ibid., 4.

identity to desire. The repetitive need to assert one's identity as "Iranian," even in mundane pop music, reflects these deep-seated needs.

## 4.2  Identity as Resistance: Dual Narratives and Glorification of the Past

The political context of turmoil in twentieth-century Iran and changing state narratives made national identity an identity of resistance for many Iranian citizens. Two conflicting notions of national identity existed in Iran, one that emphasized the pre-Islamic and "Aryan" roots, while the other was centered on Islam, especially Shiism. The contrast between these identities must be understood within the historical setting of the Iranian state and politics. The repressive nature and tactics of both the Pahlavi dynasty and the Islamic Republic made identity in Iran a political issue that goes beyond the simple sense of identity that is centered on psychological need. In the tumultuous history of the last century in Iran, identity emerged as a point of opposition to the government. Again, music was used as an outlet for the expression of these conflicts and an avenue for both exploring the nature of identity, and asserting that identity as a point of resistance to the respective state authorities.

While Reza Shah was executing his cultural renewal plans and projects to advance Iran, he did not allow for political openness. Reza Shah used repressive strategies and laws to control the state, his corruption made his family the largest landowner in the country, and made the parliament useless in influencing decisions.[36] Reza Shah's inclination toward Aryan national identity and economic ties made him sympathetic to Germany during World War II. Though Iran did not take sides in the conflict, the allied powers still occupied Iran during the war, forcing the shah to abdicate his throne to his young son and leave the country.[37] The new shah, Mohammad Reza Pahlavi, continued most of his father's policies, especially his cultural projects and the lack of political freedom. Though Prime Minister Mossadeq challenged the young monarch in the early 1950s, the Mossadeq government was overthrown by a CIA-led coup in 1953 that re-established the shah as the head of state.[38] Following the anti-Mossadeq coup, the shah solidified his position as a dictator. With

[36] Keddie, *Modern Iran.*    [37] Ibid.
[38] Stephen Kinzer, *All the Shah's Men: An American Coup and the Roots of Middle East Terror* (Hoboken, NJ: J. Wiley & Sons, 2003).

the help of his secret police, SAVAK, he quelled political dissidence and continued Iran on the path of modernization he saw fit.

With oil revenues the shah attempted to modernize Iranian industry, infrastructure, and society. However, being heavily dependent upon foreign – especially Western – powers, his cultural outlook was also greatly influenced by the West.[39] As discussed in Chapter 2, the shah's concessions to foreign dominance, along with his dictatorial stance and attention to the wealthy classes, led to rebellions throughout the country. While there were several factions involved in the revolution, they shared one commonality, their desire to overthrow the shah. As Nikki Keddie has suggested, once the shah and his dependence on foreign powers became associated with Western culture, it made sense to use themes such as indigenous Islam as a counter narrative.[40] Thinkers such as Al-e Ahmad and Shariati, who attacked Western hegemony and made attempts to combine ideas of freedom and independence with recognizable cultural roots, such as Shiite Islam, also influenced revolutionary thought.[41]

Iranians expressed their allegiance to the revolution and their identity as Shiite Muslims through song-like protest chants and musical tracks that became widely known. As Roland L. Warren points out in his study on the Nazi's use of music, protest chants and group singing heighten the meaning of words and help facilitate a sense of unity.[42] These chants are meant to arouse emotions and have a lasting effect on the participants. This phenomenon was displayed in the protest chants of Iranians, as they marched through the streets during the revolution, shouting rhythmically in mass unison[43]:

> *You traitor Shah, homeless as you are*
> *You ruined our homeland*
> *And killed the offspring of this nation, alas, alas*
> *And you filled the coffins with thousands of youths, alas, alas*
> *Death to the Shah, death to the Shah, death to the Shah, death to the*
> *Shah*

---

[39] Keddie, *Modern Iran.*     [40] Ibid.

[41] For further study see, Brad Hanson, "The 'Westoxication' of Iran: Depictions and Reactions of Behrangi, & Al-e Ahmad, and Shariati," *International Journal of Middle East Studies* 15, no. 1 (1983), 1–23.

[42] Roland L. Warren, "The Nazi Use of Music as an Instrument of Social Control," in R. Serge Denisoff et al., eds., *The Sounds of Social Change: Studies in Popular Culture* (Chicago: Rand McNally, 1972), 72.

[43] See Hossein Torabi's 1979 film, *For Freedom*, which documented the revolution through film: http://simafekr.tv/video/24857 (last accessed August 23, 2018).

In other chants the call to Islam was also evident:

*It's our day of victory today*
*Though our martyrs are no longer with us*

Or:

*Islamic Republic would be our final victory*

In some cases, the sentiments of the revolution took the form of songs that were produced with music and used during and after the revolution. One of the more well-known songs from the revolutionary period, "Iran, Iran," goes as follows[44]:

*Look how everyone is shouting, look how everyone is rebelling*
*Iran, Iran, Iran, Iran, Iran, Iran ...*
*Allah Allah Allah, Allah O Akbar (God is great), Allah O Akbar*
*There is no God, but only one God*
*Tomorrow when spring comes, we will be free and liberated*
*No injustice, no chains, we are high above with God*

Another important song from the period, "Khomeini Ey Imam"[45] (Khomeini O Imam), was dedicated to the leader of the revolution, Ayatollah Khomeini:

*Khomeini O Imam, Khomeini O Imam*
*Khomeini O Imam, Khomeini O Imam*
*O Warrior, O symbol of honor*
*O He who sacrifices his life in the path of purpose*
*For saving humankind is your call*
*Death in the path of justice is your pride ...*
*We are all your companions and allies*

The religious and Islamic overtones in these examples are self-evident. In the face of a dictator who was seen as a puppet of the West, many Iranians sought to re-establish their Islamic identity in spite of efforts by the shah to replace it with a pre-Islamic identity of Persian civilization. For all of his attempts to stay in power, the shah failed to keep his throne. On January 16, 1979 the shah left Iran, opening the door to Khomeini's return on February 1, 1979.

---

[44] "Iran Iran," YouTube video, last accessed August 23, 2019, www.youtube.com /watch?v=HAJF66elXg4.
[45] Sorodhaye Enghelabi, "Khomeini Ey Emam," YouTube video, last accessed August 23, 2018, www.youtube.com/watch?v=MzFnJ3mytRg.

Ten days later the last of the military loyalists relinquished the royal government.[46]

However, the glory of the revolution was short-lived, as the unity of the diverse factions did not last long. The days following the revolution saw instability before Khomeini and his Islamic Republic Party (IRP) were slowly able to consolidate power.[47] While Khomeini initially appointed non-clerics and liberals to important government posts, the drafting of the constitution changed the nature of the revolution that had sought to overthrow the repressive kind of government imposed by the shah. The constitution, which was eventually adopted in December of 1979, made Khomeini *Vali-e Faqih* (Supreme Leader), essentially giving him the same dictatorial authority as the shah. With ultimate power, Khomeini purged the government of any opposition and implemented institutional changes that emphasized Islamic culture and traditions. In many ways, these changes mirrored that of Reza Shah's, in style though not in substance. For instance, the Islamic Republic also enforced a dress code, which became Islamic rather than Western.

Like the cultural renewal of Reza Shah, the Islamic Republic carried out transformations in the landscape, the laws, and education system. Moreover, the new government made these changes based on claims of a true Iranian past and identity, this time concentrated on Islam and Shiism. Both the shah's government and the Islamic Republic made attempts at rewriting Iran's history, while in the process, both also tried to undermine the relevance of its opposing narrative.

As Dick Hebdige argues, while culture is always in a process of dispute, it is important to recognize the role of institutions in constructing meaning and the groups and classes that are behind those institutions.[48] We can examine these cultures through the way they consume culture and construct meaning in objects and styles. Drawing on these insights, a look at Iranian musical tastes after the 1979 revolution furthers our understanding of the dynamic nature of Iranian identity in its historical context.

The use of Islamic themes had clear political implications during the revolution. Many Iranians identified as Muslim not just for religious purposes, but also as an identity of resistance, in other words, in

---

[46] Charles Kurzman, *The Unthinkable Revolution in Iran* (Cambridge, MA: Harvard University Press, 2004).

[47] Keddie, *Modern Iran.*

[48] Dick Hebdige, *Subculture: The Meaning of Style* (London: Methuen, 1979).

opposition to the despotism of the shah, who they saw as foreign. Similarly, in postrevolutionary Iran, popular music uses themes of a pre-Islamic past and Western cultural overtones as a form of resistance to the Islamic Republic's core narrative. As one middle-class youth in Tehran revealed:

The government makes the mistake of purposely de-emphasizing our past civilization, before Islam. If anything, this makes people more disaffected with the religion, rather than encouraging faith. Islam becomes tainted, because it is misused. Cyrus and Darius and Persepolis are part of our culture as well, and should be honored.[49]

As noted earlier, the popular World Cup song by Arash engaged these themes with references to being Aryan, Cyrus the Great, and a 2,500-year civilization. The song associated these attributes directly with belonging to the nation-state of Iran:

*We are children of Iran*
*We will always remain Iranian*
*Together with one voice we will sing*
*With one voice will sing, Iran, Iran, Iran*
*Its flag is in our hands*
*The scream of "Iran" is on our lips*

Referencing ancient Iranian civilization, one that predates Islam, was a part of the Pahlavi state-building project. For Iranians living under the current government, these allusions to the past are a way of opposing the Islamic Republic and its new brand of ideology. The more the Islamic Republic put strict restrictions on musicians and artists, the more young Iranians challenged the state and pushed at the limits of those boundaries. After the election of president Khatami in 1997, some restrictions were eased and Iranians quickly took advantage of their newfound freedom, however limited it was in reality.[50]

In 1998 the mixed gender pop group, Arian Band, was formed as an authorized musical group. Their music reflected quintessential pop, with quick tempos, upbeat styles, ballads, and simple lyrics. It was not the content of their music that made Arian a groundbreaking band,

[49]   Interview conducted in Tehran in December of 2012. The subject was male and in his mid-twenties.
[50]   Laudan Nooshin, "Underground, Overground: Rock Music and Youth Discourses in Iran," *Iranian Studies: Journal of the International Society for Iranian Studies* 38, no. 3 (2005), 463–94.

but the composition of its members. As the first pop band with male and female singers, Arian broke through barriers that were in place since the revolution. According to the law in the Islamic Republic, women are not allowed to sing solo in public or for a mixed audience.[51] In the case of Arian Band, the female vocalists never sang lead vocals, but rather they sang in unison with the male vocalists. Though this may seem like a small victory, the band was immensely popular among Iranians[52] and allowed women into a public space that had been dominated exclusively by men in Iran since the revolution. The band took another successful risk in 2008 by collaborating with British musician Chris De Burgh for the song "Dustet Dāram" (The Words "I Love You").[53] In the video, the female band members, wearing their headscarves, sang in English along with De Burgh. Not only did the band use Western musical styles, but they also used English lyrics and Western artists in their work. Playing by the rules of the game, the band continued to have a successful career in Iran as an authorized group and held concerts around the world.

The name of the group should not escape our attention: "Arian," is simply a cognate of Aryan. Not only did the group challenge the state by having female members and collaborating with English artists, their name also confronted the Islamic Republic's Islamist rhetoric. By calling themselves "Arian," they associated themselves with the monarchic discourse of Iran's Aryan roots and pre-Islamic past, yet their music was for the most part neutral in style and content. In this sense, Arian Band was particularly adept at subtly defying the state, while staying within the confines of the law. A closer look at two songs from Arian helps illustrate their acumen at navigating the musical terrain of post-revolutionary Iran. Their first album released in Iran included a song titled, "Molā Ali Jān" (Master Ali Dear), which was a song dedicated to Imam Ali, a significant personage for Muslims, and a founding figure

---

[51] Wendy S. DeBano, "Enveloping Music in Gender, Nation, and Islam: Women's Music Festivals in Post-Revolutionary Iran," *Iranian Studies* 38, no. 3 (2005) 441–62.

[52] A search on YouTube turns up several videos with hundreds of thousands of views. The band also sang a song with Chris de Burgh; the video has over 800,000 views. On Radio Javan the band's many songs have millions of plays.

[53] Arian Band ft. Chris de Burgh, "Nori Ta Abadiat (Dostet Daram)," YouTube video, last accessed August 23, 2018, www.youtube.com/watch?v=TGGvLsUYhJ4.

for Shiites. The song plainly reflected Islamic themes and was in line
with the Islamic Republic's discourse:

> *You are the light in every darkness*
> *Light up my heart with a look*
> *You are the guide of those who have gone astray*
> *You are the light of the sun that shines up the world*
> *The best man of the mosque and battlefield*
> *O king of men, Ali the God knower*
> *Our beloved master, Ali*[54]

The juxtaposition of these lyrics with a group named Arian is
noteworthy, as it encapsulates the conflicted nature of Iranian identity. In another song by Arian, titled "Iran," we see a different
depiction:

> *Your flag is a pride*
> *Up there in the clouds*
> *Those three pure and beautiful colors*
> *Will always stay with me …*
> *Story of Farhad and Shirin*
> *Story of Siavash's Love*
> *Those heroes in love*
> *Rostam and Kaveh and Arash*
> *Memory of jungle, memory of mountains*
> *Chehel Sotoun and Persepolis*
> *The sea shore and the redness of the sunset*
> *Iran*[55]

Here there are no religious implications and Iran is connected to its past
through Persepolis and stories and tales from classical Persian poetry.
Arian Band walked a fine line between conforming to the rules and
challenging the Islamic Republic's narrative. In doing so it also echoed
the opposing poles that have chronicled Iran's history. An urban youth
I interviewed in Tehran articulated the oppositional quality of Iranian
identity well:

I'm Muslim. I'm Muslim first and then Iranian. But not the state's version of
Islam. Yes, the state wants to embed Islam as our sole identity, and I *am*
Muslim, but not because the state forces me to be. I choose it, and that's the
bottom line; we should have the choice. When you take the choice away you

---

[54]  Zahir, "Music of the Children of the Revolution," 116.    [55]  Ibid., 123.

create resentment, and unfortunately in our country, they have created antipathy toward the religion itself.[56]

Though this young man still identified as being Muslim, he recognized the negative role of the state in trying to enforce that identity, a point that is not lost on other Iranian youth.

The song "Hoviat-e Man" (My Identity),[57] by popular underground rap artist Yas, exemplified the assertion of an Iranian identity that defied the Islamic Republic's vision. Over the last two decades rap music gained a popular following among Iranian youth. Like its Western counter part, a segment of rap music in Iran advocates social justice, with lyrics that reflect the political and social issues of the day. Rappers such as Yas and Hichkas, and rap groups such as Zedbazi and TM Bax, enjoyed popularity, especially among young men. For the rapper Yas, "Hoviat-e Man" was a reaction to the 2006 US film *300*, which depicted Persians fighting Greeks in the battle of Thermopylae. Many Iranians were offended by the image of Persians shown in the film. The song Yas produced in response had marked nationalist motifs and he associated his Iranian identity with the glory of the ancient past:

> *Listen, I want to tell you my intent*
> *They want to erase my identity*
> *The history of the land of the Aryans*
> *Is screaming until we come to it*
> *So now is the time for you to hear*
> *Iran is my land*
> *The country which after 7,000 years*
> *Is still standing*[58]

Later in the song Yas returned to the themes of the past:

> *It was Cyrus the Great that started the peace*
> *Freeing the Jewish from the grip of Babylon*
> *Cyrus the Great wrote the first bill of human rights*
> *That is why I carry my esteem and great pride*
> *For my Iran, the history of my land*

[56] Interview conducted in Tehran in December 2012. The subject was male, middle class and in his early twenties.

[57] Yas feat. Amin, "Hoviate Man," YouTube video, last accessed August 23, 2018, www.youtube.com/watch?v=i6G9-bx7Kbc.

[58] Zahir, "The Music of the Children of the Revolution," 138.

For Yas, the image of Iran was linked to his own image and identity. At the end of the song he stated, "The history of Iran is my identity, Iran, protecting your name is my good intent." Not only was Yas resisting the Islamic Republic's version of Iranian identity, he was also confronting a Western world flooded with inaccurate and negative images of Iran.

Glorification of the past, whether an idealized vision of Islamic virtue or a romanticized dream of an ancient civilization, is evident within the Iranian populace. Inside the changing political climate of the nation-state, various interpretations of Iranianness are visible. The case of Iran therefore illustrates the dynamic process that is identity. As Stuart Hall explicates, "identities are never unified and, in late modern times, increasingly fragmented and fractured; never singular but multiply constructed across different, often intersecting and antagonistic, discourses, practices and positions."[59] As Iranian authorities tried to produce a national identity suitable to their tastes, they silenced others, both figuratively and literally. However, just as the Iranian populace contested the shah's narrative, they continued to challenge and negotiate the boundaries of their identity under the Islamic Republic. Modernity created the need for a national identity, while the political situation defined the terms of that identity, as Iranians formed counternarratives in opposition to the powers that be. The fruition of their efforts can be seen in their cultural fusion and the embrace of pluralism that forced the Islamic Republic to acknowledge a more complex notion of Iranian identity. Forming an identity of resistance, Iranians clung to the most tangible aspect of the nation-state, land.

## 4.3 Vatan: Land as a Fixed Object of Adoration

Throughout several visits to Iran from 2011 to 2015, I conducted numerous interviews in order to investigate how Iranians describe their identity. Using the snowball technique to gather participants, interviews began with a few young urban Iranians in Tehran and expanded to their networks. In some cases, the interviewees were aware of what I was working on and why I was interested in speaking with them. However, I made efforts to conceal the reasons in many

---

[59] Stuart Hall and Paul Du Gay, *Questions of Cultural Identity* (London: Sage, 1996), 4.

cases in order to hear people's answers without engaging them in any political conversation. As an identity of resistance, Iranian national identity is closely connected to the political climate of the country; therefore, I hoped to get answers that were removed from that predisposition. Of course, identity does not exist in a vacuum, nor can it be easily compartmentalized. Nonetheless, by avoiding a formal setting and keeping the interview casual, it was possible to obtain material that sheds more light on the subject of Iranian identity.

The outward displays of Iranianness tended to favor the two conflicting identities that we are already familiar with: Islamic and Persian. Physical presentations of identity include such things as attire and décor. For instance, the Farvahar, an iconic symbol of Zoroastrianism that is carved into the stone ruins of Persepolis, is a popular emblem that Iranians incorporate into their style, used in jewelry, clothing, and even tattoos. Similarly, Islamic representations are used in accessories as well, with jewelry containing stylish calligraphy saying "Allah," "Ali," or "Hossein." In fact, it is common to see both Islamic and pre-Islamic symbols on display in jewelry stores throughout Iran.

Yet, the commentary of ordinary people when discussing what it meant to be Iranian revealed the complexity of identity that went beyond this simple binary. In almost every case of both young and old, people responded that their identity was Iranian because they were born there, when probed further they would elaborate by adding that it is the land of their mother and father. Typically references to being Muslim or Aryan would arise when subjects were asked about it directly, and more often than not that would change the course of the conversation. In one case when I asked a young woman, from an upper middle-class family in Tehran, if she identified as being Aryan, she scoffed and said:

No, I don't believe in any of that, that is the ancient past and it has nothing to do with me. It's not from lack of pride, I love this country and would defend it, it is after all the land of my father and mother and all of my family. I understand why people use those symbols though; we look at our current situation and we're unhappy. Iran has the potential for greatness, but nothing to show for it. So, to make ourselves feel better we focus on something we can have pride in, and that is the past. This way we can say, "look, this is who we truly are," and distance ourselves from the reality of our lives.[60]

---

[60] Interview conducted in January 2013. The subject was in her early twenties.

Others, who saw the veneration of Aryanism as a reaction to the Islamic Republic's historical production, reiterated the sentiment of this young woman. As one man born and raised in Tehran noted:

I don't think of myself as "Aryan," but I do see that age of empire and ancient civilization as a part of Iranian culture. I also think Iranians in the US and Europe cling to the past more to separate them from this government. Looking to the past is a way to resist the current state. That's why I think it is a mistake for this government to underrepresent Iran's ancient history; Islam becomes tainted this way.[61]

Even those who asserted their Aryan or Muslim identity without further questioning, initially answered that being Iranian meant being born in that land, the soil of their lineage.

In many cases, they described their affection for the land and their willingness, and sometimes need, to defend it. Given these responses then, it is not surprising to find so many songs that speak to these ideas. One song that dedicates its entire subject to adoration of Iran's land and love of nation is another example of a light pop song intended for dancing.[62] The song's lyrics do not refer to any ideological or historical characteristics of Iran, but rather focus on concrete aspects of Iran's landscape, such as its forests, birds, the smell of the sea, and the taste of the water. The song's chorus leaves out subtleties, affirming the devotion of Iranians to their country:

> *I die for the smell of your soil*
> *I die for your soil that is pure*
> *I die for the smell of your soil*
> *I die for your soil that is pure*

At the song's climax, the object of its affection is made clear:

> *I am a child of Iran*
> *I adore Iran*
> *I am a child of Iran*
> *I adore Iran*

---

[61] Interview conducted in September 2015. The subject was in his early thirties. Though from a working-class family, he had attained middle-class status through education and work.
[62] The song was found on an unauthorized CD compilation purchased in Iran in 2011.

Throughout the track the lyrics position Iran as the subject of love; however, they do so by referencing its soil or "khāket." It is the land and soil of Iran that is at the center of the pop ballad.

The word "vatan" in Persian can be translated as fatherland or homeland in English, and as many interviewees showed, fatherland and motherland carry an enormous meaning for Iranians and their sense of identity. One historical root for this affinity with land can be seen in the Russo-Persian Wars of the nineteenth century.[63] The Qajar's limited administration caused Iran to lose land in these conflicts and according to Kashani-Sabet:

History writing, in particular, defined as Iranian an expansive territory that had once belonged to the ancient Persian monarchs. Increasingly, intellectuals voiced their attachment to the Iranian homeland (*vatan*) . . . The Iranian *vatan* was thus deified to inspire individual fealty to the homeland.[64]

This love for the homeland was evident among interview respondents who associated their Iranian identity with their place of birth and kinship roots.

Though it is not the official national anthem, the song "Vatanam" (My Homeland) is quite popular among Iranians and is considered an unofficial national anthem. The video for Salar Aghili's "Vatanam" has over 215,000 views on YouTube,[65] but this figure is misleading. While Salar Aghili's version is the most recognized, this song has been sung by different artists and there are many videos on YouTube that reflect a much higher number of views.[66] The song's lyrics are centered on the idea of *vatan*:

*Oh, homeland my world*
*My passion and ecstasy*
*Show yourself in the sky*

[63] Firoozeh Kashani-Sabet, "Cultures of Iranianness: The Evolving Polemic of Iranian Nationalism," in Nikki R. Keddie et al., eds., *Iran and the Surrounding World* (Seattle: University of Washington Press, 2002), 162.
[64] Ibid., 166–67.
[65] Salar Aghili, "Vatanam," YouTube video, last accessed April 13, 2018, www.youtube.com/watch?v=fvZ1P7v6X0s. Aghili has other songs about "vatan" with millions of views. "Salar Aghili – Vatanam," Radio Javan, last accessed March 23, 2020, www.radiojavan.com/mp3s/mp3/Salar-Aghili-Vatanam.
[66] For instance, another video has over 714,000 but the singer is Darya Dadvar. Darya Dadvar, "Vatanam," YouTube video, last accessed March 23, 2020, www.youtube.com/watch?v=hDlMictEQsI.

*Like the everlasting sun*
*Hear the burning of my words*
*I am your companion singer*
*All of my soul and body*
*My homeland, my homeland*
*My homeland, my homeland*
*Listen to the pain of my words*
*For I am the nightingale of this garden*
*All of my soul and body*
*My homeland, my homeland*
*My homeland, my homeland*

As a national anthem the song ends by noting the link to the nation-state:

*All with one name and sign*
*With all different colors and languages*
*All happy and well and singing*
*Because of the strength of young Iran*

The lyrics recognize the diversity of people within Iran, but also note that they all fall under the larger banner of the nation-state, or in this case of the homeland. In other words, what connects Iranians to each other is not their language or appearance, it is lineage and the sharing of a common piece of land.

The lyrical content and themes of "Vatanam" are in stark contrast to the Islamic Republic's official national anthem, which is sung at all state events. Known as the "National Anthem of the Islamic Republic of Iran,"[67] the lyrics focus on the core elements of the Islamic Republic's national narrative, such as revolution, independence, and martyrdom:

*Oh Imam, your message*
*Of independence and freedom*
*Is engraved in our souls*
*Martyrs, your cries echo in the ears of time*
*Islamic Republic of Iran, stand everlasting*

---

[67] This is the national anthem provided in the "Interests Section of the Islamic Republic of Iran" on the Embassy of Pakistan's website for the United States. "About Iran – National Anthem," Embassy of Pakistan, last accessed August 23, 2018. www.daftar.org/Eng/aboutiran_eng.asp?lang=eng#National%20Anthem.

While the Islamic Republic anthem highlights state motifs, the more popular unofficial anthem emphasizes ties to the land and acknowledges Iran's diversity. Though "Vatanam" is not Iran's official anthem, it is often used on state radio and television because its broad national appeal does not necessarily threaten the Islamic Republic's image. However, its popularity also made it attractive to Islamic Republic critics and its lyrics were used in more politically driven tracks, such as an underground rap song, "Moj-e Mosbat" (Positive Wave),[68] which was released before the 2009 election in Iran. The rap lyrics examined Iran's state of affairs, boasted about its potential, and affirmed a willingness to sacrifice one's life for the homeland. The invocation of such nationalist sentiments made the lyrics for "Vatanam" a fitting chorus for the rap song.

As this example illustrates, the notion of *vatan* is seen in more commercial music and in diverse genres such as traditional folk music and underground rap. The 2008 song, "Vatan" (Homeland),[69] by the artist Homayoun Shajarian, son of internationally-acclaimed Iranian traditional vocalist[70] Mohammad Reza Shajarian, is another case. The popularity of both father and son transcends generations and stylistic differences. Their concerts in Iran are quickly sold out and their songs are well known by Iranians of all stripes. In "Vatan," the young Shajarian speaks to the pain of being far from one's homeland:

*Homeland, homeland, look upon me for I*
*Am a stranger sleeping under another sky*
*I have always been with you, I have always been with you*

Later in the song he goes on to say:

*Homeland, homeland, stay forever flourishing for I*
*Am a migratory bird that has flown above your picturesque garden*
*To a hazy distant land*

The lyrics and tenor evoke heightened emotions and portray a special relationship to the land, one that is almost romantic in its tones of

---

[68] Mohammad Bibak and Ehsan Gheibi, "Moje Mosbat," YouTube video, last accessed August 23, 2018, www.youtube.com/watch?v=_uEnF3dSRgo.

[69] Homayoun Shajarian and Dastan Ensemble, "Vatan," YouTube video, last accessed August 23, 2018, www.youtube.com/watch?v=T5fR7ug_sV4.

[70] Shajarian was named one the "50 Great Voices" in 2010. Steve Inskeep, "Mohammad Reza Shajarian: Protest Through Poetry," NPR, 50 Great Voices series, last accessed August 23, 2018, www.npr.org/templates/story/story.php?storyId=130047062.

yearning. Such nostalgic qualities are found in music by other popular folk singers as well, such as Shahram Nazeri's "Bāz Havā-ye Vatanam" (Again the Sky of My Homeland)[71]:

> *Oh, eastern wind, how can I bear being distant form this flower?*
> *I yearn for a petal of a flower from that garden*
> *Again, the sky of my homeland, homeland, homeland, is my yearning*

While the poetic nature of these songs might make it seem as though the subject is unique to the genre, it is also evident in popular rap music. The distinction in songs that rap about "vatan" is in their tone. Rather than arousing nostalgia, their lyrics tend to be more assertive. While there is still the sentimental air induced by "vatan," there is also a note of defense. In fact, in many cases the artist makes direct references to being a soldier or Iranians as soldiers defending their land. Popular Iranian rapper Hichkas had a song entitled "Ye Mosht Sarbāz" (A Bunch of Soldiers),[72] in which he rapped about young Iranian men as soldiers ready to sacrifice their lives:

> *We are prepared to give our lives for four precious things*
> *God, Homeland, Family, and Friends*

Later in the song, Hichkas also rapped about the martyrs who had already gone:

> *I want the martyrs to know that if we are keeping it real*
> *It is due to their blood that was spilled on the ground for us*
> *All the people keeping it real*
> *Know that the flag is flying high*
> *If you are a real man then we are with you*

In some cases, the rapper takes a direct approach in discussing the political issues of the day. Another song by Hichkas, "Vatan Parast" (Patriot),[73] reveals that Iranians are mindful of current events and willing to die for their "khāk" (soil):

> *Swear, swear on the pure blood of Siavash*
> *On the name of Iran and its soil*

---

[71] The video for this song has over 500,000 views on YouTube. "Baz Havaye Vatanam Arezoost," YouTube video, last accessed August 23, 2018. www .youtube.com/watch?v=Kazk8SnlCjs.

[72] HichKas, "Ye MOsht SarBaz 'Bunch of Soldiers,'" YouTube video, last accessed August 23, 2018, www.youtube.com/watch?v=xebK0CrtyuM.

[73] HichKas, "Vatan Parast," YouTube video, last accessed August 23, 2018. www .youtube.com/watch?v=QRnbQ65Aqx0.

*That for this soil, I will give my life . . .*
*Their excuse now is nuclear energy*
*Say why you have nuclear weapons yourself*
*Occupying Iran is not easy*
*There's no doubt in your fear*

Another example of this theme comes from Zedbazi, a well-known rap group in Iran. In their song "Āmādeh Bāsh" (Be Ready),[74] subjects like war, patriotism, and soldiers are evident:

*We Iranians are warriors*
*We don't let the enemy enter our borders*
*Warriors of mountain and desert*
*Are unbeatable in heat and in cold*
*There are a lot of soldiers*
*The country won't be destroyed by strangers*
*If the enemy comes they will destroy him*
*Don't think wrong of my words*
*We Iranians are all patriots*
*We saw eight years of "holy war"*
*If you come now there are still loaders and rifles*[75]

Such a collection of songs illustrates the Iranian propensity for defiance and defense. The enemy they guard against is not always the same. At times their adversary is external and related to foreign conflicts, while in other instances the confrontation is with the state of domestic affairs. Even the idea of being distant or exiled from the nation can pose a challenge for many Iranians. However, in all these cases, the idea of homeland is one element that remains constant. The importance of land and the soil of the nation are imbued in Iranian culture and society, embodied by the ballads for *vatan*.

## 4.4  Fusion: Rejecting Bipolar Narratives

More recent developments in popular Iranian music moved beyond the appropriation of Western musical styles and toward a mixture of indigenous and foreign sounds to create a modern and uniquely Iranian composition. This progress in music is evident in works by

---

[74] Zedbazi, "Āmādeh Bāsh," YouTube video, last accessed August 23, 2018, www .youtube.com/watch?v=AIMAlkjE__4.
[75] Zahir, "Music of the Children of the Revolution," 145.

new artists, people's listening habits, and some easing of restrictions by the state. While music was often used as a defensive tool for political and identity resistance, this new trend of Iranian musical artistry shows a more positive approach to cultural expression. Rather than using subjects and genres that are antithetical to the political landscape, popular music in Iran shifted to a focus on more commonplace topics and original styles.

The popularity of Homayoun Shajarian[76] speaks to this trend. Though he came on to the Iranian musical scene with his father's famous name and hauntingly similar voice, the young Shajarian made a name for himself by evolving his father's genre. Both father and son use traditional Iranian instruments and poetic lyrics, however, Homayoun created tracks that mix Western and Iranian sounds and use more familiar ballad-like structures. While the younger Shajarian sings nationalist songs, his most popular tracks discuss topics such as love and loss in poetic lyrical prose.

Shajarian's video for his song, "Cherā Rafti" (Why Did You Leave),[77] has over 3.3 million views on Radio Javan and features Iranian artists listening to his song for the first time. The video is shot in black and white with familiar Iranian performers sitting against a blank backdrop and listening attentively with headphones. The emotional expressions of these artists affect the viewer along with the lyrics:

> *Why did you leave? Why am I restless?*
> *I dream of your embrace*
> *You did not say how beautiful the moonlight is tonight*
> *You did not see how my soul is intolerant from sorrow*
> *Why did you leave? Why am I restless?*

The simplicity of the video draws the viewer's attention to the music, while the image of the listeners moved to tears creates a shared powerful experience. There is also a parallel American version[78] of the video, where non-Persian speakers are listening with headphones in the same

---

[76] "Homayoun Shajarian," Radio Javan, last accessed March 23, 2020, www .radiojavan.com/artist/Homayoun+Shajarian. Homayoun Shajarian's body of work has over 200 million views on Radio Javan.

[77] "Homayoun Shajarian and Tahmoures Pournazeri – Chera Rafti," Radio Javan, last accessed March 23, 2020, www.radiojavan.com/videos/video/homayoun-shajarian-tahmoures-pournazeri-chera-rafti. The video also has several versions on YouTube with many views.

[78] "Chera Rafti (American Version)," YouTube video, last accessed August 25, 2018, www.youtube.com/watch?v=i2rE9VntuvI.

style as the original video. Despite not understanding the lyrics, the listeners are clearly moved by the passionate melody and Homayoun's entrancing voice. The fact that there is an American version of the video illustrates the universal nature of music and a transformation in Iranian musical identity that is not bound within the borders of the nation-state.

The young Shajarian's concerts are sold out events in Iran, with mixed crowds of young and old, male and female gathering together to enjoy a night of musical entertainment. He used his name and talents to forge a fresh sound in Iran's growing musical industry and helped pave the way for new young artists to play with traditional musical styles. A more open public space for music allowed a burgeoning group of young Iranian musicians from a variety of genres to emerge. One group in particular, Chaartaar, gained a mass following and exemplified the synthesis of Iranian and international musical styles. Their first album, *You Are the Rain*, was produced and distributed in Iran and catapulted the band in 2014 to immediate prominence.[79] The release of their 2015 album, *The Road's Dancing*, was advertised all over Tehran, as Figure 4.1 shows.

Like Homayoun Shajarian, the band Chaartaar is a popular authorized group and sells out large concerts in Iran as well as abroad. Chaartaar is most popular among postrevolutionary Iranian generations with hybrid musical tastes. Even their performances utilize Western influences, as seen in a concert in Tehran where the band sings, "Leylācheh" (The Little Leyla),[80] with a large screen on stage displaying an older foreign film. As the audience watches the unfolding infatuation of a young man for a woman, the singer serenades:

*With you, I plead, do stay*
*Thus, my flight might be kept away*
*From being caged, as it may*
*Your breath gives the moment*
*A taste of melody, nay*
*It haunts the moment*
*By a sweet melody*[81]

---

[79] "Chaartaar," Radio Javan, last accessed March 23, 2020, www.radiojavan.com /artist/Chaartaar. The band's body of work on Radio Javan has 200 million views.

[80] Chaartaar, "Leylācheh (Live in Concert, September 2015, Tehran)," YouTube video, last accessed March 21, 2021, www.youtube.com/watch? v=HSxI3auYOMU.

[81] Chaartaar, *Jādeh Miraqsad* (Tehran: Javān Records, 2015), CD.

**Figure 4.1** Chaartaar posters. One poster pictures the new album cover, while the other pictures the band members. Photo taken in September 2015; these posters were seen across public street walls in Tehran.

The production of the concert, images displayed, palpable enthusiasm of the mixed audience, and the evolving musical trends demonstrates the power of Iranians to shape their public space and discourse.

A discussion of musical hybridity in contemporary Iran would be incomplete without Mohsen Chavoshi. The immensely popular artist[82] made his mark in 2007 with the soundtrack for the film *Santuri*. Though the film was not allowed to be screened in Iran, bootleg copies circulated throughout the country. The soundtrack, and the artist behind it, became more popular than the film itself. Chavoshi's career was launched soon after the *Santuri* soundtrack, as he was finally given

[82] "Mohsen Chavoshi," Radio Javan, last accessed March 23, 2020, www
    .radiojavan.com/artist/Mohsen+Chavoshi. Chavoshi's body of work has
    710 million views on Radio Javan.

permission by Ershād to release an authorized album in 2008. Since then, Chavoshi sold millions of albums in Iran and became one of Iran's preeminent postrevolutionary musicians.

Chavoshi's style is the culmination of Iran's musical evolution. It combines some traditional Iranian sounds with electric sounds and Western instruments. Also noteworthy is that many of Chavoshi's most popular songs use lyrics from Persian poets such as Rumi and Hafez. The lyrics associated with Rumi are highly spiritual, often with mystical and otherworldly themes. Again, this reveals religiosity as an essential quality of Iranian culture, though the nature of that religiosity may contrast with the narrative of the Islamic Republic. Using a mix of electronic sounds and some Iranian folk instruments to create modern ballads with traditional Persian prose, Chavoshi epitomizes the progress toward fusion in Iranian cultural expression.

While the use of poetic Persian prose mixed with foreign musical influences highlight one aspect of this fusion within the domain of popular music, similar instances of such unions are found in less likely places. Another recent trend in the area of Madāhi, which are melodic eulogistic recitations that pay tribute to Imam Hossein, is to perform panegyrics to Imam Hossein using tempos from pop music and rap tunes.[83] Since actual music cannot be used for these recitations, the performers tempo and delivery mimics that of the pop songs. The sounds of the crowd of men thumping their chests or wailing provide a certain harmony. In some cases, the eulogist incorporates similar lyrics that express adoration for Imam Hossein in place of the original song's object of affection.[84] These trends demonstrate how the impact of social fusion pervades other facets of mass culture.

As such examples suggest, bounding Iranian society in any one-dimensional way is misleading. Instead, synthesis is apparent in Iranian culture and in how Iranians define their national identity. In opposition to the classical binary approach of the state, which emphasizes Islamic versus Persian supremacy, and the inclination to vacillate between these two spheres as a form of political resistance, cultural expressions in Iran integrate these narratives. Songs with nationalist

[83] "مداحیه سبک رپ از امیر رضا اسیفی," YouTube video, last accessed August 25, 2018, www.youtube.com/watch?v=Cm-Gn8rPP7o. A search on YouTube gives many similar examples of Madāhi performances with pop beats.

[84] "جدیدترین نوحه مداحی 94," YouTube video, last accessed August 25, 2018, www .youtube.com/watch?v=Hj7oQrHwCNY.

sentiments and political themes continue to be popular among
Iranians, while artists working in Iran stress both their secular nationalist pride and their Shiite heritage.

Two songs by authorized Iranian singer, Farzad Farzin, elucidate this
point. The first song, "Khalij Tā Abad Fārs" (Persian Gulf Forever),[85]
was released in 2012 and had 4.2 million plays on the Persian music site
Bia2. The song was a nationalist response to the political climate in
which references were made to the Persian Gulf as the "Arabian" Gulf.
Farzin's lyrics fit the typical nationalist themes of adoration for land
and soil:

> *My world is Iran*
> *From the roots it is my soil*
> *My tomorrow is Iran*
> *Forever my land*

The song also makes references to the mythical Iranian archer, Arash,
who is often used as a symbol of Iranian national pride that predates
Islam. Such pre-Islamic iconography is not as predominantly found in
authorized Iranian music.

While Farzin's nationalist pop song ignored Iran's Islamic identity, in
a song released in 2017 entitled "Marz" (Border),[86] the artist's video
highlighted Shiite elements of Iranian nationalism. Starting with a scene
of Iranian soldiers fighting, the video shifts swiftly to the theme of
sacrifice ubiquitous in Shiism and Iranian war culture. One soldier
stays behind to fight the enemy in order to help the others escape.
Viewers can quickly observe the parallel to Imam Hossein's knowing
martyrdom and sacrifice. The lyrics for the song match the images:

> *This sacrifice has intimidated the world*
> *If not for these men our borders would be lost*
> *Full of love they gave their hearts to the sea*
> *Their presence on this soil was the pride of the nation*

In the end of the video when the body of the martyred solider is
returned in a flag worn casket and walked through the streets, ordinary
Iranians gather to follow the procession and honor their fallen

[85] Farzad Farzin, "Khalij Tā Abad Fārs," Bia2, last accessed March 23, 2020,
www.bia2.com/music/1797.
[86] Farzad Farzin, "Marz," Bia2, last accessed August 25, 2018, www.bia2.com/v
ideo/Farzad-Farzin/Marz/. At the time it was accessed the song had 3 million
plays.

countrymen. Despite the fact that Iran's war with Iraq ended decades ago, representations of resistance culture remain part of the Iranian social fabric.

In the case of Farzin's songs, competing national sentiments are seen in one artist. However, the 2017 song, "Ey Pahlevān" (Oh Gladiators),[87] by authorized artist Reza Sadeghi,[88] embodied the complexity of Iranian characteristics in one song. In the tradition of tracks for the Iranian national soccer team, Sadeghi's song paid tribute to the players and the homeland with verses that reflected an array of nationalist symbols. Full of the clichéd references one would expect for such a song, including love of the homeland, an undefeatable team, and adoring fans, the lyrics also selected specific features of Iranian culture to encourage the players and characterize the nation:

> *In a battle in which Arash is the Archer*
> *Bullets and shrapnel have no power*
> *Your strength bends the back of your opponents*
> *Like the bow in the hands of the Arashs*
> *You passed under the Quran with love*
> *With the prayers of mothers beside you*
> *Your veins fill with pride*
> *When you utter the name Abolfazl*
> *The love of your flag's colors gives you honor*
> *Your pure heart is filled with faith*
> *We also shout beside you*
> *Keep alive forever Iran*

Sadeghi sang about the epic national hero, Arash the archer, and in the same breath evoked the image of the players walking under the Quran. Looking back at the official song selection for the 2006 World Cup, instead of the more popular song by Arash, it is evident that sanctioned lyrical content has evolved. In Sadeghi's song, he was able to use themes in both songs from 2006 and his music was authorized by the state. Rather than selecting one pole of representation, Sadeghi's nationalist song spoke to both pre-Islamic Iranian mythology and the pious inclinations of Iranian people.

---

[87] Reza Sadeghi, "Ey Pahlevān," Bia2, last accessed August 25, 2018, www.bia2.com/music/55311.
[88] Reza Sadeghi is also a popular artist in Iran, his music has 460 million plays on Radio Javan. "Reza Sadeghi," Radio Javan, last accessed March 23, 2020, www.radiojavan.com/artist/Reza+Sadeghi.

The fact that these subjects are being blended together illustrates the Islamic Republic's capacity to modify its approach, though still with clear limitations, as a result of the attitudes and actions of Iranian people. In its attempts to garner support from younger, reform-minded citizens, Islamic Republic authorities changed their position on the work of one recognized underground rapper/musician, Amir Tatalu. As Iran's nuclear agreement was being finalized in July 2015, Tatalu released a video for his song, "Enerzhi-e Hastehi" (Nuclear Energy).[89] Though Tatalu spent most of his young career making music underground because his rap styles and outer appearance were considered illicit by the Islamic Republic's moral guidance standards, officials eventually allowed him to produce music in Iran. In fact, the video for "Enerzhi-e Hastehi" was produced with the support of the Iranian navy, which gave him permission to film on a naval ship and features Iranian officers chanting, "This is our absolute right, to have an armed Persian Gulf." The song advocated Iran's peaceful nuclear program and featured nationalist sentiments of defense and sovereignty without any indication of Islamic imagery. This shift in policy suggests that the actions of Iranians are not without consequence. As agents of social change, Iranian citizens continue to challenge the narrow visions of bipolar identity, and embrace fusion and plurality.

## 4.5 Conclusion

Simon Frith astutely observed that the significance of popular music is not just in revealing how we express our identities, but also in facilitating the construction of those identities.[90] As the given examples have shown, national identity is no exception. In fact, Frith further posited that one of the social functions of popular music is "its use in answering questions of identity: we use pop songs to create for ourselves a particular sort of self-definition, a particular place in society ... It is not surprising, then, that popular music has always had important

---

[89] "Amir Tataloo – Energy Hasteei," Radio Javan, last accessed August 25, 2018, www.radiojavan.com/videos/video/amir-tataloo-energy-hasteei.

[90] Simon Frith, "Towards an Aesthetic of Popular Music," in Simon Frith, ed., *Popular Music: Critical Concepts in Media and Cultural Studies*, vol. 4 (London: Routledge, 1987), 32–47. Originally published in Richard Leppert and Susan McClary, *Music and Society* (Cambridge: Cambridge University Press, 1987).

nationalist functions."[91] Thus, music has the power to elicit passionate feelings of collective identity unlike any other medium.

The popularity of one song in Iran that has spanned decades illustrates this point. The song, "Yār-e Dabestāni-e Man" (My Classmate), by Fereydun Fo.rughi, was popular in the political context of the revolution because of its nationalist overtones and push for unity against tyranny. Re-recorded after the revolution by a new singer, the track remained an archetypal call for resistance among activists in Iran. It was used as a song of solidarity among Khatami supporters and reform-minded Iranians in the late 1990s and as a song of protest during the contested 2009 elections. Videos created for social media in 2009, in support of Iranian protestors, often used the song as a soundtrack to accompany the images of the demonstrations. Other videos showed university students chanting the lyrics in unison, literally hand in hand with fists raised up, singing,[92] "My hands and your hands must tear down this curtain, who, other than you and I, can cure these ills." In Iran's presidential election of 2017, voters standing in line to cast their ballots spontaneously broke into chants of this all-familiar tune.[93] In all of these cases, it is reasonable to argue that the song was linked to Iranian resistance movements. The use of "Yār-e Dabestāni-e Man" in these various instances substantiates the claim that music is a powerful force of national expression and opposition.

Music in Iran has evolved since 1979, as a gradually opening public space allowed for more artistic expression and varying subject matters. After the Islamic Republic banned pop music following the revolution, music produced outside of Iran by exiled pop artists became especially trendy. Laudan Nooshin highlights the subversive nature of this music, arguing that pop itself, and not necessarily its lyrical content, became a symbol of resistance, challenging the Islamic Republic's control.[94] However, after the election of Khatami, the Islamic Republic reversed

---

[91] Ibid., 38–39.
[92] "Kashan Iran University Yare Dabestani," YouTube video, last accessed August 25, 2018, www.youtube.com/watch?v=9sRGGXfGUqI.
[93] "Voting Day 1396," Facebook video, last accessed August 25, 2018, https://m.facebook.com/story.php?story_fbid=10158879713910195&id=551915194. Another video shows people celebrating with the song after Rouhani's victory. Facebook video, last accessed August 25, 2018, https://m.facebook.com/story.php?story_fbid=10158795841405201&id=642630200.
[94] Laudan Nooshin, "Subversion and Countersubversion: Power, Control, and Meaning in the New Iranian Pop Music," in Annie J. Randall, ed., *Music, Power, and Politics* (New York: Routledge, 2005), 231–72.

its position and allowed for state-authorized pop music. As the reform movement grew along with a generation of new young artists, musicians inside Iran became more popular, especially underground (unauthorized) musicians who explored diverse musical genres, such as rock and rap. These underground artists gained followers because their lyrics were more pertinent to everyday life in Iran than the diaspora musicians.[95] As we have seen, recent forms of popular music in Iran embraced a fusion of traditional Iranian musical styles and poetic lyrics with Western influences. Diaspora music lost its luster, while local musicians, including many authorized artists, had high-selling albums and sold-out concerts, such as Homayoun Shajarian, Chaartaar, and Mohsen Chavoshi.

What we can observe is a fascinating trajectory in which music was utilized as a source of political and national expression. The revolution acted as a vehicle of identity formation that rejected the shah's idea of Iranianness, but after the revolution, as the Islamic Republic fashioned another narrow definition of Iranian national identity, people employed music again as a form of resistance. As Iranians attempted reforms within the political structure of the Islamic Republic, it also forced the state to acknowledge the limits of its narrative. While musical tastes and genres became more diverse and Iranians embraced a pluralistic image of themselves, the state demonstrated its ability to adapt in a changing environment. Like the election of Khatami and subsequent easing of musical restrictions that allowed the emergence of domestic pop music to be produced, Iranians continued to push the boundaries of the state and continued to gain ground. This can be seen in the growth of musical diversity and popularity among more authorized Iranian musicians. To this end, the Islamic Republic is not monolithic or static; instead, it demonstrates some fluidity and at times appropriates tools of resistance for its own purposes.

The elections of Rouhani in 2013 and 2017 illuminate this transformation. Following Rouhani's 2013 victory, Iranian artists produced a song from Rouhani's first speech as president with an accompanying video. As the authors of the post share, the song was inspired by President Obama's "Yes We Can" video dedication and included women uttering the speech in song-like fashion and playing instruments.[96] Rather than promoting

---

[95] Ibid.
[96] "New Voyager President Rouhani," YouTube video, last accessed August 25, 2018, www.youtube.com/watch?v=TYytErqGdC4.

Persian hegemony, the video featured men and women voicing parts of the speech in different dialects and languages spoken in Iran in order to represent the diversity of the populace. Making a direct connection between Rouhani's election and nationalist and revolutionary movements of the past, the video was also interlaced with speeches from Mossadeq and Ayatollah Taleghani. Despite these provocative images, President Rouhani featured the video on his website.

In the 2017 election, Rouhani used Hojat Ashrafzādeh's song "Dobāreh Iran" (Iran Again) as his official campaign song along with the slogan "Iran again, Rouhani again."[97] The song was used at Rouhani's rallies and aroused strong reactions from the thousands of spectators who uproariously sang together[98]:

> *Become the morning light*
> *Leave the darkness of night*
> *Shine and turn the darkness*
> *Smile again, unite again, commit again*
> *Iran again, Iran again, Iran again …*
> *Give your life for the dearest*
> *You and I become "we" again*
> *Again, me and you, again they*
> *Again, the smiles of hope*

Despite its subtle nod to Shiite ideas of sacrifice, the song emphasized a call for national unity in Iranian terms. However, this fact does not diminish the influence of faith in Iranian culture. In another song that was widely popular and used during celebrations after the 2017 election, "Mardom-e Shahr" (People of the City),[99] belief in God was the key to people's euphoria:

> *Whatever you have or don't have*
> *Wear it, dance, and laugh*
> *That tonight at every street there is God*

[97] http://rouhani96.ir/ (last accessed August 25, 2018).

[98] "دوباره ایران," YouTube video, last accessed August 25, 2018, www.youtube.com /watch?v=8CuBl2PFDcU. The song was used during street celebrations after Rouhani's victory as well. Instagram post, last accessed April 15, 2018, https:// instagram.com/p/BUXHZV0hrb2/.

[99] Facebook video, last accessed August 25, 2018, www.facebook.com/Ebrahim .Nabavi.Page/videos/1702898006388743/. The song has over 24.7 million plays on Radio Javan. "Hamed Homayoun – Mardome Shahr," Radio Javan, last accessed March 23, 2020, www.radiojavan.com/mp3s/mp3/Hamed-Homayoun-Mardome-Shahr.

*Write on the wall of your heart, there is God*
*Not once, not ten times, but a hundred times*
*With faith and humility write, there is God*
*There is God, there is God, there is God*

In spite of efforts by opponents of the Islamic Republic in the Iranian diaspora, who called for boycotting the election to undermine the legitimacy of the government, the participation of over 70% of the voting population affirmed the hopes of millions of Iranians in reform, the Iranian nation-state, and the conviction that they are agents of change.

From strict bans, to allowing selected pop music, to using popular music of various genres as part of the official political system, the Islamic Republic's transformation is telling. The evolution of the state cannot be separated from the agency of ordinary Iranians, who continued to push and struggle against the restrictions placed on them and the identities assigned to them by those in power. The next chapter, on popular media, indicates a similar trajectory following the revolution in which cinema and television have evolved. As with the case of music, other mediums of popular culture are both revealing and constructive. Contemporary Iranians actively confirm the multidimensional nature of their national identity by negotiating the boundaries of authoritative narratives and simultaneously accepting and rejecting aspects of both.

# 5 | Media and the Struggle over Representation

As the preceding chapters illustrate, the formation of national identity is a complex process with multiple sites of contestation. For more than a century, Iranians grappled with authorities over the nature of modernity, their political system, and the portrait of their nation. Both the Pahlavi dynasty and the Islamic Republic utilized mediums, such as film and television, to portray a particular image of Iranianness and regulated the media for public consumption. In addition to domestic image production, Iranians in the twentieth century saw themselves through the gaze of Western powers.[1]

Since the notions of nation-state and national identity were foreign imports, the process of national consciousness was heavily influenced by the dominant position of European powers vis-à-vis the Middle East. Thus, Iranians fought on two fronts in forging their collective identity: first against the inferior depiction of Orientalism and second against the narrow view of the Iranian authorities. As they faced external forces vying for control over resources and political influence, Iranians challenged representations imposed by foreign powers. Additionally, despite the efforts of the Pahlavi monarchs and the Islamic Republic to inculcate their respective narratives, ordinary Iranians continued to resist one-dimensional renditions of their culture and identity. As a result, media representations of all varieties were significant sites of struggle in the battle to construct Iranian national identity.

The link between popular culture and politics is evident in the state's role in the production and consumption of this culture, as well as the influence of pop culture on individual behavior and collective identities.[2]

---

[1] Edward Said's work on Orientalism critically explored the impact of Orientalist and Western scholars during European colonialism in shaping the images of the Middle East. The denigrating narrative of the subordinate East adversely affected how the peoples of the Middle East imagined themselves as well.

[2] Tim Nieguth, *The Politics of Popular Culture: Negotiating Power, Identity, and Place* (Montreal: McGill-Queen's University Press, 2015).

Popular culture is not simply for entertainment, but rather, it is crucial in sustaining and opposing prevailing attitudes and ideologies. While there is a wealth of previous scholarship on Iranian films, especially as it emerged as one of the premier contemporary cinemas of the world, the emphasis is often on Iran's most renowned auteurs and their films. As such the media selection regularly scrutinized is imbued with the cult of personality of these filmmakers.

By stressing the contributions of this high culture of the intelligentsia, many scholars have underrepresented the importance of popular culture and the tastes of the masses. As Raymond Williams prudently contended, all culture is valuable and culture is ordinary because it is not limited to a certain group of people.[3] Williams understood culture as both traditional and creative, and rejected the distinction between high and low culture, stating:

What kind of life can it be, I wonder, to produce this extraordinary fussiness, this extraordinary decision to call certain things culture and then separate them, as with a park wall, from ordinary people and ordinary work ... Culture is ordinary: through every change let us hold fast to that.[4]

For Williams, the elite classes of society are not the sole arbiters in defining the cultural landscape. Instead, ordinary people, embodied by the working class, are equal agents in the production and consumption of culture. With this in mind, the following study focuses on media for its popularity rather than its critical acclaim.

Exploring popular Iranian cinema is significant for the content of the films as well as the symbolism of film itself. As Hamid Naficy argues in his seminal work, *A Social History of Iranian Cinema*, from the beginning, films and the introduction of and fascination with cameras by the Qajars, linked cinema to modernity, the encounter with Western powers, and Iranian national identity.[5] Like other foreign imports, the West did not simply impose cinema and modernity on Iran. But rather, as agents of culture and change, Iranians tailored and modified these new products and ideas to fit their palates. Cognizant of the power and influence that could be exerted by controlling such

[3] Raymond Williams, "Culture Is Ordinary," in Ben Highmore, ed., *The Everyday Life Reader* (London: Routledge, 1958), 91–100.
[4] Ibid., 94.
[5] Hamid Naficy, *A Social History of Iranian Cinema*, vol. 1, *The Artisanal Era, 1897–1941* (Durham, NC: Duke University Press, 2011).

a medium, both the Pahlavi monarchs and Islamic Republic used censorship and state-sponsored content to propagate their respective messages. However, as Naficy points out, no one group was ever able to "control" cinema. As a fundamental component of cultural expression, cinema was influenced by every level of society, and by internal and external forces. This exchange of ideas created a uniquely Iranian cinema, a fusion of local affinities, cultural traditions, transnational experiences, and the plurality of modernity.[6]

By using culture and identity as their weapon, Iranians constructed counter representations of their national aspirations. Naficy sums up this sentiment effectively:

Movies are important causes, effects, and instruments of modernity. Every movie is at once an individual expression and a collective one. As a result, movies are potent currency in ideological battles, affecting both modern individual subjectivities and collective national identities. The politics of Iranian modernity has always involved the politics of filmic perception, representation, and counter representation.[7]

In addition to films, popular television, literature, and even the Internet are part of a media apparatus that is used by individuals for expression, which is why the Islamic Republic continues to censor and exercise jurisdiction over all of these instruments of culture. However, the emphasis on cinema is because of its particularly compelling symbolism. In the 1970s as the revolutionary movement against the shah became increasingly powerful, cinemas became a prime target of anti-shah opposition. The content of the films was criticized for images of indecency and decadence, while the theaters were depicted as symbols of Western influence and seen as an encroachment on Iran's traditional Islamic values. Some oppositional forces actually used films as a means to critique the shah. Though censorship did not allow films to directly challenge the shah or his rule, filmmakers subtly got their message of rebellion across to viewers.[8]

Like the shah, the Islamic Republic understood how indispensable the role of media and cinema were in constructing a new and revolutionary Iranian identity. In fact, capturing the revolution, and later the war with Iraq, became a crucial use of films. In contrast to the cliché of

[6]  Ibid.    [7]  Ibid., 15–16.
[8]  Hamid Naficy, *A Social History of Iranian Cinema*, vol. 2, *The Industrializing Years, 1941–1978* (Durham, NC: Duke University Press, 2011).

the Iranian revolution as backwards or antimodern, the Islamic Republic embraced all the trappings of the modern nation-state, including the power to wield dominant narratives through cinema and television. According to Naficy, it took roughly four years for the transition to the Islamic Republic's "Islamicate cinema" and, under the Islamic Republic, Iran's film industry industrialized and modernized into a flourishing enterprise.[9]

The rest of this chapter looks at popular Iranian media after the revolution and the evolution of content and expression. Less an examination of the storytellers, it focuses on the stories being told and the people observing them. From stories centered on Iranian experiences to those that moved beyond borders, it becomes evident that Iranians continued to challenge censorship and enforced national narratives, and demonstrated a need for expression within the limited spaces they were given. While those in power tried to define Iranian identity on their own terms, Iranians illustrated the capacity of ordinary people to resist with the use of ordinary culture.

## 5.1 War Films: From Sacred Defense to Rejects

For its inherent defensive nature and fundamental need for cooperation and sacrifice, few events bring a nation together like war. Even a young nation-state will quickly rally behind its national identity as part of the counterattack in a war of aggression. But modern notions of war include more than battle tactics and weapons technology. In the twentieth century, image-making became an integral part of warfare and conflict.[10] As Paul Virilio presents in his study on war and cinema, the use of propaganda and film added another aspect to war strategy, as state authorities came to understand the utility of such devices.

In the case of Iran, the war with Iraq became the ideal representation of the new Iranian national identity and its culture of resistance. Though the anti-shah revolutionaries and the individuals that took power after the revolution understood the importance of pictures and symbols, it was the war that ultimately defined the Islamic Republic as

---

[9]  Hamid Naficy, *A Social History of Iranian Cinema*, vol. 3, *The Islamicate Period, 1978–1984* (Durham, NC: Duke University Press, 2011).

[10]  Paul Virilio, *War and Cinema: The Logistics of Perception* (London: Verso, 1989).

an image-making machine.[11] As Roxanne Varzi argues, the war helped consolidate the Islamic Republic by deflecting internal conflicts on to an "other," making Iraq an external target of engagement. In order to maintain the persona of revolution, independence, and resistance that the Islamic Republic advocated, filming the war became a central policy. While looking extensively at the documentary films of Mortezā Āvini, Varzi posits that though the footage of the war is real, the director was still engaged in the construction of a specific reality in order to convey a particular narrative of the events.

Along with the documentary footage of combat that saturated Iranian television sets during and after the war, the postrevolutionary rebirth of the Iranian film industry began with war cinema. Given the Islamic Republic's penchant for controlling images, it is no surprise that the first films the state supported and allowed were films depicting Iran's "Sacred Defense." Years after the war, as more space opened for expression, Iranian filmmakers memorialized the dark side of war and made films that highlighted the lingering loss, devastation, and futility felt by many Iranians.

The career trajectory of director Ebrahim Hatamikia exemplifies the transition and shifts in Iranian sentiments about the war. Hatamikia began his career as an ardent supporter of the revolution and his early films, such as *Mohājer*[12] (The Immigrant), focused on themes like bravery, martyrdom, and religious faith. In the film, young Iranian soldiers at the border are attempting to gather intelligence from the Iraqi side with the use of remote-controlled planes. Pictures of Khomeini adorn their control devices and their faith is paraded as they prostrate themselves before missions. The knowing path of martyrdom is taken without hesitation as one soldier pushes through to the Iraqi side, exposing himself, but also succeeding in his mission.

While Hatamikia's earlier work focused on an idealized vision, presenting the purity of faith and martyrdom, his later works underscored the consequences of war. In his film, *Bu-ye Pirhan-e Yusef*[13] (The Scent of Joseph's Shirt), Hatamikia explored the specters of war in

---

[11] Roxanne Varzi, *Warring Souls: Youth, Media, and Martyrdom in Post-Revolution Iran* (Durham, NC: Duke University Press 2006).

[12] Ebrahim Hatamikia, dir., *The Immigrant* (Tehran: Fānus Khiāl Channel, n.d. [1989]), DVD.

[13] Ebrahim Hatamikia, dir., *The Scent of Joseph's Shirt* (Tehran: N Records, 2010 [1995]), DVD.

the story of a missing soldier. Though his son's dog tag was found in the stomach of a shark, Ghāfur remains vigilant in the search for his son Yusef and believes he is still alive. The film recounts the biblical story of Joseph and his colored coat. Jealous that their father favors Joseph, his brothers plot a scheme to sell Joseph and tell their father he was torn apart by wolves. Like the false evidence of Joseph's bloodied colorful coat, Ghāfur is suspect of the dog tag and keeps hope alive of his son's safety. Ghāfur's torment shows one aspect of war that continues to haunt Iranian parents: missing soldiers and the anguish of not knowing the fate of their children.

Another film from the same period by Hatamikia, *Āzhāns-e Shishehi*[14] (The Glass Agency), scrutinized other negative features of the war and its human costs. In the film, Hāji, a war veteran, takes a travel agency hostage in order to help his sick friend. Hāji demands a seat on a plane to London for his companion, who is also a veteran of the war, so he can receive the medical care he needs. The story takes place years after the conflict ended and illustrates Iranian disaffection toward the war and its propaganda. At the same time, the film calls attention to the forgotten soldiers who sacrificed everything for their countrymen. Although the Islamic Republic transformed the public space during and after the war as a constant reminder of the "Sacred Defense," the film emphasized a distinct reality in which the government neglects veterans and fails to provide critically needed services. Additionally, it shows how Iranian civilians, jaded from the Islamic Republic's war narrative, often ignore the plight and hardships of Iran's war veterans. In both the later examples of Hatamikia's work, the role of the patriotic and faithful soldier is still venerated, but the critiques of the Islamic Republic and Iranian society is laid bare.

It should be no surprise that Hatamikia's films depicted martyrdom and national defense as heroic endeavors and later showed the darker side of war and national disillusionment. As opposed to a marked transition from youthful idealism to a sense of disenchantment with revolutionary and war ideology, Hatamikia's films illustrate the complexity of Iranians' relationship to the Islamic Republic's identity construction. In one of his more recent films, *Che*,[15] Hatamikia revisited

---

[14]   Ebrahim Hatamikia, dir., *The Glass Agency* (Tehran: Jahān Tasvir, 2001 [1998]), DVD.
[15]   Ebrahim Hatamikia, dir., *Che* (Tehran: Honar Aval, 2015 [2014]), DVD.

the idea of radical heroism, personified by the legendary revolutionary and martyr, Mostafa Chamran. The film follows Chamran as he tries to quell the Kurdish separatist rebellion after the revolution and bring peace to the city of Pāveh. In the film, when asked why he left his life as a physicist in the United States, Chamran replied simply, "This is my homeland." Chamran is depicted as pious and humble; he prays, speaks eloquently, and works steadily to maintain peace and prevent the loss of life.

For Chamran, Pāveh is part of Iran, despite the Kurdish background of its residents. This stresses the nationalist character of Chamran in Hatamikia's portrayal. He struggles to hold the nation-state together, which is imperative to the continued success of the revolution. The film underlines Iranian nationalism and Chamran's valiant nature. Using the first letter of his name as the title for the film, Hatamikia unequivocally connects Chamran to another famed revolutionary, Che Guevara. Like Che, who was involved in transnational rebel movements across Latin America, Chamran participated in resistance movements in Lebanon and Palestine. Hence, while Hatamikia is critical of the Islamic Republic and made a career out of condemnatory war films, he simultaneously upholds the values central to the revolution and Iranian resistance culture, which is infused with Shiite symbolism and nationalist pride.

Beyond the filmmakers, Iranian audiences are also significant mediators of identity construction and cultural production through their consuming habits. Despite the serious nature of war and the Islamic Republic's attempts to focus on a somber treatment of the subject, Iranian films began to handle the topic with less tragic overtones. While the easing of restrictions on artists in the 1990s made some progress possible, these changes were also facilitated by the reception of Iranian audiences. Kamāl Tabrizi's 1996 film, *Leyli Bā Man Ast*[16] (Leily Is with Me), was a turning point in the depiction of the war in films. The comedic style of the film was a refreshing change from despondent war themes that were pervasive in Iranian society. The brilliant comedic performance of Parviz Parastui as Sādeq, a man seeking a bank loan to fix his home, left a memorable impression on Iranian audiences and made the film widely popular and well known, even today.

---

[16] Kamāl Tabrizi, dir., *Leily Is with Me* (Tehran: Tasvir Donyā-ye Honar, 2008 [1996]), DVD.

In the film, Sādeq's simple request for a loan is complicated by the fact that banks primarily give loans to people with connections or war veterans. While attempting to secure a loan, Sādeq befriends a colleague from his work in television, Mr. Kamāli, who is known for filming the war from the front lines. The comedy and action of the film follow Sādeq's ruse, as an enthusiastic compatriot, escorting Mr. Kamāli to film the war at the front. All the while as Sādeq is trying to flaunt his fervor for the war effort in the hopes of getting his loan, in reality he is carefully avoiding going to the front lines and dreads being harmed. While these are the antics that make the film comical, at a deeper level Sādeq's disingenuous commitment raises questions about the war and the mixed sentiments of Iranian citizens. Though the war was actually defensive and, in many ways, brought the nation together under the new Islamic Republic, after eight long years that ended in cease-fire, many Iranians came to resent what they saw as the Islamic Republic's profligacy and failure. Sādeq's exploit, to use the war to his advantage, resonated with Iranians who felt similarly cheated by the promises of the Islamic Republic and the unfulfilled victory of the "Sacred Defense."

In spite of his duplicity, Sādeq experiences a genuine shift in attitude when, against his will, he finally reaches the front lines. As he witnesses first-hand the bravery and sacrifice of young Iranians, who are driven by their religious faith as well as the love for their country, Sādeq is absorbed by the magnitude of the moment. In the end, he is swept up by the zeal and courage of the men he meets and decides that he would be honored to film at the frontlines anytime. Sādeq's dramatic reversal can be understood as a gesture to acknowledge the real fallen heroes of the war, who gave their lives for their nation. Like the films of Hatamikia, *Leyli Bā Man Ast* exposes the multifaceted character of Iran's contemporary national narrative. For all its efforts, the Islamic Republic failed to instill a one-dimensional view of Iranian identity or the nature of the war with Iraq, which it deployed as a mainstay of its narrative. Instead, filmmakers and audiences rejected *and* adopted different parts of the competing narratives they were presented. In the case of *Leyli Bā Man Ast*, the film's ability to be lighthearted and sincere captured the complex reality that Iranians felt in the aftermath of war. For the first time, the war was treated in a humorous manner and Iranians were allowed to laugh at an otherwise tragic event in their recent collective history.

The film's positive reception paved the way for more films of this nature.

As Michel Certeau posits, another form of production is in fact consumption.[17] As such, how ordinary people consume or use products is consequential to cultural production and the appropriation of public space. Certeau gives agency to common people and their everyday choices and practices. In this sense, Iranian audiences were not simply passive observers, but rather, their choices of what films to consume and how to use them influenced the production of films. The importance of audience consumption is exemplified in the dissimilar reception of two films.

Following the tumultuous events of the contested 2009 election and the subsequent Green Movement, Iranians experienced one of the most politically charged eras since the 1979 revolution. With heightened censorship, especially in relation to the fateful election, it was difficult to make a movie that depicted the events of 2009. However, the 2012 film *Qalādeh-ha-ye Talā*[18] (The Golden Collars) tackled the topic of the election results and its aftermath head-on. The film portrays the events after the election as a conspiracy by outsiders and spies, using the trope of surreptitious British meddling and Iranian double agents. The plot suggests that the protests and violence that erupted after the election were the result of foreign collusions to undermine the legitimacy of the Iranian system and topple the Islamic Republic.

With nationalist undertones, the last scene of the film shows protests in front of the United Kingdom's embassy with the audio track of Salar Aghili's "Vatanam" (My Homeland). Far from the reality of the events on the ground, the film was perceived as propaganda and largely rejected by Iranians, many of which called for a boycott. As one Iranian artist[19] recalled:

The film was not taken seriously by filmmakers or regular people. Mostly the film became infamous for its attempt to tarnish the protestors and many called for boycotting it. In fact, it took some time for Amin Hayāyi's career to

---

[17]  Michel de Certeau, *The Practice of Everyday Life* (Berkeley: University of California Press, 1988).

[18]  Abolghasem Talebi, dir., *The Golden Collars* (Tehran: Donyā-ye Honar, 2013 [2012]), DVD.

[19]  The interview was conducted in Tehran in September 2015 with a prominent member of the Iranian film industry who chose to speak anonymously.

recover. He's a very famous actor, but people saw him as a sellout of sorts when he played in this movie.

Here, the implications of the film and its reception among Iranian audiences are more relevant than the story. As the cover of the DVD claims, it was the "most political film in the history of Iranian cinema." Consequently, the case of this film reveals two crucial points: first it confirms the Islamic Republic's recognition of the weight of cinema and image-making; and second, it proves that despite the control over production exerted by state authorities, the power over consumption remains in the hands of the public.

In contrast to the boycott and dismissal of *The Golden Collars*, Masoud Dehnamaki's 2007 film *Ekhrāji-ha*[20] (The Deportees), though critically lambasted, was publicly admired. Like *Leily Is with Me*, the film is a comedy-drama about the "Sacred Defense." Made nearly twenty years after the end of the war, *Ekhrāji-ha* set new box office records in Iran for ticket sales and was widely popular. Though the film's director is known for his conservatism and critics received the film poorly, *Ekhrāji-ha* was so successful that characters and catch-phrases from the film became part of the Iranian youth vernacular at the time and the film went on to have two sequels.

The film follows the story of Majid "Suzuki," who, after being released from prison, is eager to go back to his old neighborhood and marry a young woman. However, Majid's hopes are dashed because he is seen as an inadequate mate. In order to have an honorable reputa-tion, making him a more acceptable suitor, Majid decides to join the war effort. The plot's comedic repartee comes from the shenanigans of Majid and his friends, as this unsuited band of misfits attempts to join the military effort. Majid and his pals are initially rejected for training, because they do not fit the noble and pious image of war heroes and martyrs.

From the beginning, it is clear that war is not Majid's main concern. His decision to join is simply to impress his love interest, which he comes to find has another male suitor, Mortezā, who is also training at the military base. In a telling exchange, Mortezā asks Majid, "Is this not your country as well?" As the story moves forward, Mortezā decides to train this group of eccentrics himself, in order to make

---

[20] Masoud Dehnamaki, dir., *The Deportees* (Tehran: Tasvir Donyā-ye Honar, 2008 [2007]), DVD.

"real" soldiers out of them. Though interlaced with consistent comic relief, the film shows the transformation of the characters as they experience the realities of war together. Like Sādeq in *Leily Is with Me*, witnessing the war and the valor of their fellow countrymen first-hand changes the perception of Majid and his friends. As the group of rejects takes the opportunity to display their bravery, Mortezā and other military officials are forced to recognize their own prejudices. In the progression from rejects to heroes, both sides see how they have misjudged the other, as they come together to fight for the homeland.

Mixed with religious and nationalist symbolism, the film plays on recurring motifs of Iranian nationalism. In the end, Majid's metamorphosis comes full circle as he willingly takes the path of martyrdom. To restore his reputation, Majid commits the most honorable act as a martyr for his country, his faith, and his brothers in arms. The success of *Ekhrāji-ha* illustrates again the meaningfulness of these themes in Iran's national narrative. That so many people chose to watch the film, unlike *The Golden Collars*, demonstrates the public's agency in negotiating their image.

Though the war was used by the Islamic Republic to consolidate its power and promulgate a distinct image of the Iranian state, it is still an integral part of every contemporary Iranian's personal narrative. A 2015 film, by Paymān Haqāni, encapsulates the impact of the war on Iranians and how it shaped their lives. In the avant-garde film, *316*,[21] Haqāni presents the story of one woman's life in a series of chapters. Using only one actor to narrate the story, the film shows mostly images of people's shoes, interweaved with edited footage as the woman narrates her life story over these snapshots. The chapters mark typical events in one's life such as birth, childhood, marriage, and old age; however, two periods stand out in the tale. In a life that consists of ten chapters, two are dedicated to external events: chapter four is the revolution and chapter five is the war.

While narrating her perspective of the revolution, actual footage from 1979 is edited to show scenes of protest and celebration, along with chants of "Death to the Shah," "Allah O Akbar," and images of Khomeini. The chapter on the war is somber, as the narrator recounts the hardships people faced, as well as the devastation and loss. For the storyteller, the experience of war at such a young age had an enduring

[21] Payman Haghani, dir., *316* (n.p., 2015), DVD.

effect: "The sounds have never left me alone, they are always with me." Thus, contemporary Iranians, in a sense, cannot consider their individual life without noting the repercussions of these two key events. Just as the Islamic Republic uses these events to define the contours of Iran's national narrative, Iranians use them to define their identity.

## 5.2  Challenging Narratives: Alternative Histories and Satirical Disguises

Over the last two centuries, Iran's weakened position vis-à-vis Western powers created a desire to bolster its image. Loss of land and foreign concessions over the management of Iran's resources were the physical evidence to support an Orientalist view that inflicted the Iranian psyche with a sense of inferiority. In their attempts to build a modern nation-state, both the Pahlavi and Islamic Republic states tried to reconstruct a national story that reimagined Iran's place in the world on a more equal footing. Each government utilized the parts of Iran's past that satisfied their respective ideas and framed tangible narratives. History was used as a tool to control the national story in order to establish a homogenous internal sense of fraternity and an outward appearance of supremacy. However, control over Iran's historical narrative was not only contested by opposing rulers and foreign powers, but rather, it was called into question by Iranian people.

At home and abroad, Iranians strive to exert authority in telling the story of their nation, culture, and history. An anecdote from Nasrin Rahimieh highlights these efforts, as she recounts her involvement as director of the Persian Studies Center at the University of California, Irvine. During her tenure, Rahimieh faced the passion of diaspora Iranians as they tried to influence their public image in an academic setting.[22] Often rejecting features they deemed undesirable, Iranians in the diaspora stressed the notion of a true or authentic identity, which they wished to see reflected in the educational and cultural material of the university. Rahimieh emphasizes a penchant for idealizing the past, especially after the turbulent transformations of the revolution. While the study of the Iranian diaspora is beyond the scope of this project, Rahimieh's experience demonstrates the capacity of ordinary people to

---

[22]  Nasrin Rahimieh, *Iranian Culture: Repression and Identity* (New York: Routledge, 2016).

shape social and institutional structures. Here the focus will remain on the agency of those residing in Iran and how their views, anxieties, and hopes are reflected in their popular culture.

Iran's historical chronicle is crucial to the Iranian psyche and their sense of identity. As such, themes like altering the past or how the past influences the present are exhibited in popular Iranian literature and media. Rahimieh explicates the link between time travel and Iranian identity by paralleling the metaphorical time travel of the shah to the fictional time travel of the character Mashallah, from Iraj Pezeshkzad's novel *Mashallah Khan at the Court of Harun al-Rashid*.[23] In the novel, Mashallah, a bank guard, travels to eighth-century Baghdad to change the fate of the Persian vizier to the Abbasid caliph, and changes his own ordinary fate through his adventures and mishaps. Just as Mashallah plays with fiction and reality, the shah's view of history and events surrounding his rule were infused with a mix of fiction and truth. As Rahimieh puts it:

In the realm of fiction, where the real can be suspended, Mashallah is a type, not unlike Cervantes' seventeenth-century creation, Don Quixote, who becomes obsessed with tales of chivalry and attempts to replicate them in reality. In the context of Iran in the mid decades of the twentieth century, a literary type with grandiose and implausible ambitions resonates with what was taking place on the Iranian social, political, and cultural scenes. For example, the young Shah whose ascension to the throne was the handiwork of the Allied forces and the distrust of the Shah's father and who was restored to power again in 1953 with American and British support came to believe his own imagined grandeur, ancestry, and might.[24]

Like the works of artists during the Pahlavi reign, the works of post-revolutionary artists in Iran continued to elucidate the anxieties and aspirations of Iranians.

Also similar to the Pahlavi era were the efforts of the Islamic Republic to control the account of Iran's history and secure its position of power within the current geopolitical structure of the world. Due to censorship and restrictions, contemporary artists used satire and period pieces to critique the Islamic Republic and rethink their national story. With the success of *Leily Is with Me*, the director/actor duo of Kamāl Tabrizi and Parviz Parastui brought another brilliant comedic

[23] Ibid.    [24] Ibid., 24.

film to Iranian audiences in 2004's *Marmulak*[25] (The Lizard). The story follows the character Reza, played by Parastui, as he is arrested for burglary and sent to prison. In prison, in spite of the fact that Reza is seemingly faithless and critical of his culture's religious leanings, the warden believes he can rehabilitate Reza with a "spiritual diet." Later, when Reza finds himself in the prison hospital, he befriends a man in the neighboring bed, who, unbeknown to Reza, is a cleric. In contrast to the warden's forced ideas of religiosity, the cleric presents a softer image of piety that diverges from the clichéd impression of clerics that Reza often condemns. For instance, in the course of his interactions with Reza, the cleric chooses to read from Saint-Exupéry's *The Little Prince* for inspiration. When Reza learns that his new companion is a cleric, he conveys his surprise, which the cleric receives with a humble smile.

The substance of the plot unfolds after Reza escapes from prison wearing the cleric's robes and impersonates him to elude authorities. The comedy revolves around Reza's attempts to imitate the very figure he has regularly criticized, as he tries to leave the country undetected. As a cleric, Reza experiences both negative and positive treatment from the people he encounters along the way. His newfound station opens doors for him that are closed to others and he is often treated with more respect and favoritism. This position of entitlement for the clerical body reflects a central issue for Iranians in their grievances against the Islamic Republic. In keeping up the charade, Reza is forced to listen to people's thoughts and concerns on religion and, in doing so, the audience is also exposed to these different views. At times, Reza is piqued by the artificial piety of some, such as a man who enquires about the legality of temporary marriage to satisfy his own needs. On the other hand, he is pleasantly surprised by the devotion of many of the locals he comes to know while he is acting as a new small-town cleric and trying to secure a passport in order to flee. As he gains the respect of the locals and the mosque attendees expand, Reza is noticeably moved and feels a deeper personal change.

At its core, the film is about unpacking the idea of faith and separating what is disingenuous from what is sincere. The film has insightful

---

[25] Kamāl Tabrizi, dir., *The Lizard* (n.p., 2004), DVD. Note that the film was pulled from theaters by Iranian officials for inappropriate content, but was widely watched at home and commonly known.

political implications and at the same time it is careful not to paint all clerics or religiously minded people with the same brush. Though the film certainly shows negative sides of religion and politics, it is not an outright rejection of Islam. Such nuance throughout the film helps expose the complex feelings of Iranians toward the Islamic Republic and its Islamic narrative of Iran's intricate culture and history. By focusing on a religious figure in a country that is governed by clerics, the film takes aim at the highest authorities of the state. However, its satirical style and comedic plot allow space for more subtle critiques of the Islamic Republic and ideas of religiosity.

Like he did with his character in *Leily Is with Me*, Parastui skillfully captures Reza's transformation from outspoken skeptic to thoughtful advocate. The last sentence of the film is Reza's narration over the image of a mosque full of worshippers, as he paraphrases an adage from the cleric he took the robes from in prison: "There is no person in the world that does not have a path to find God." Again, we see how Iranians distinguish political discourse from their traditional roots. Despite the religious overtones, the film was popular for its ability to show the degrees of faith and provide a relevant social commentary with critiques of the Islamic Republic's clerical leadership, which was made more possible through satire.

The most well-known and popular satirist in Iran is the writer, director, and actor Mehran Modiri. Working in television and films, Modiri is an icon of Iran's contemporary popular culture landscape, especially in the field of comedy. Though Modiri was active as an actor and director in the 1990s, he reached stardom in the first decade of the 2000s with his work in television. His shows are not only popular for their comedic relief, but also for their social commentary. The satirical style often disguises social and political scrutiny that is difficult to express under the Islamic Republic's restricted media structure. As a result of his popularity and content, Modiri became an active and important voice in Iran's public discourse.

Two of Modiri's most popular television shows focus on time and space outside contemporary Iran and, by doing so, create a space that is less susceptible to the legal limitations placed on Iranian artists. His most popular show to date is the 2005 smash hit *Shab-ha-ye Barareh* (Barareh Nights). The tale of *Shab-ha-ye Barareh* takes place in a fictional rural village named Barareh during the time of the Pahlavi dynasty. Consequently, the events and story are placed outside of the

concrete reality of Iran's present, both physically and temporally.[26]
The show opens with the arrest of its central character, a journalist
named Kiānush Esteqlāl-Zādeh, for writing an article about government corruption. The idea of state corruption is evinced further with
Kiānush's attempts to bribe his way out of trouble. After a humorous
mishap in court, Kiānush's bribe mistakenly sets another man free,
while Kiānush is found guilty and banished from Tehran. By opening
the story with a dialogue about censorship and corruption, the show
tackled issues applicable to contemporary Iranians under the Islamic
Republic. However, by setting the story in the historical context of the
Pahlavi monarchy, the show could appear to maintain the very narrative that the Islamic Republic had long promoted.

The story is set up in the first episode after Kiānush is banished and
finds himself trapped in a small village he has never heard of called
Barareh. The plot and comedy follow Kiānush's encounter with an
unfamiliar place and people. Despite the fact that the village is still
a part of Iran, the interaction of Kiānush with locals seems like a clash
of cultures where both sides are baffled by the other's naiveté. For
instance, the locals are shocked to hear that Kiānush is unfamiliar
with their prestigious corner of the world and they emphasize several
cases of Barareh's exceptionalism, such as having the best chickpeas in
the world or their famed sweet water.[27] One villager explains the
historical value of Barareh with a story of Alexander the Great's
expedition to this noteworthy village, which is commemorated with
a hole in the ground known as "Alexander's Pit."[28]

In many ways the show highlighted the class differences and elitist
attitude of metropolitan Iranians versus Iran's more traditional and
rural elements. By exploring these different viewpoints, the show also
illustrated the struggle of Iranians in their encounter with the West and
their endeavor to build a modern nation-state. The emphasis on historic tales demonstrates the importance of history and image-making.
Like Iranians who constructed grand historical narratives to challenge
Orientalist views of their inadequacy, the locals in Barareh seemed

[26] "Barareh Nights (Episode 1)," YouTube video, last accessed March 21, 2021, www.youtube.com/watch?v=UNh0cb5mlWc.
[27] "Barareh Nights (Episode 2)," YouTube video, last accessed March 21, 2021, www.youtube.com/watch?v=_c8Qfj3Yhmo.
[28] "Barareh Nights (Episode 3)," YouTube video, last accessed March 21, 2021 www.youtube.com/watch?v=6jvVbPJl2Cg.

compelled to communicate the village's long and distinguished history for Kiānush. Much as the shah recounted a hyperbolic Iranian narrative of an unbroken 2,500-year history, Barareh locals described their 3,200-year history. When Kiānush asks about the village's past, one local narrates the origins of Barareh from a magical bean, recalling the legend of *Jack and the Beanstalk*. The use of an English fairy tale in local lore is telling, as it speaks to the anxieties of Iranians in constructing a national history that could impress Western powers. Seen in this light, Barareh is like a window into the Iranian national psyche that has been tormented by its own sense of inferiority in relation to foreign powers.

In another satire by Modiri, *Qahveh Talkh* (Bitter Coffee), Iranian concerns about the state of their country and the importance of history are again evident. Centered on the story of a history professor, Nimā Zande-Karimi, *Qahveh Talkh* travels from the present to the past in order to disguise its social commentary in comedy and historical settings. The story begins with Nimā calling a radio station to correct a misleading historical fact that he overheard them announce.[29] As he does with his students and the people around him, Nimā tries to get the producers at the radio station to care about history. Though he is persistent and strong in his conviction, Nimā struggles to get anyone to value history as a subject or the significance of its influence. Frustrated with people's apathy and his own financial hardship, Nimā eventually decides to quit and go back to his hometown. Before going home, he receives a mysterious phone call telling him to go to the Niāvarān Palace. While at the palace waiting, Nimā drinks a bitter cup of coffee that transports him back in time to eighteenth-century Iran, before the rise of the Qajar dynasty.

Like *Barareh Nights*, the comedy revolves around Nimā's mishaps and shenanigans in a space outside present-day Iran. The main plot unfolds as Nimā attempts to alter Iran's history by preventing the rise of the Qajar monarchy. The idea that the Qajar kings were responsible for Iran's fall from grace was a staple of the Pahlavi narrative, which portrayed Reza Shah as Iran's champion that saved the country from the incompetency of the Qajars. While the Pahlavi chronicle showed the anxiety of Iranians in the twentieth century as they wrestled to

---

[29] "Ghahve Talkh – Bitter Coffee," YouTube video, last accessed September 6, 2018, www.youtube.com/watch?v=wIOvq2Cayag.

explain the reason for their subordinate position to the West, the story of *Qahveh Talkh* indicated a continued struggle to understand and change their situation. Despite Nimā's experience with people apathetic to history, the show illustrates how Iranians actually see history, and the telling of their national history, as a crucial point of contention.

Though it is set in the far-off past, *Qahveh Talkh* reflected relevant issues in contemporary Iran. As one Iranian commentator states in their review of the show:

Although *Qahveh Talkh* started out as a historical comedy, after a few episodes it became a mirror which reflected the problems and issues of modern Iran. I, as a person who was born and who has lived most of my life in Iran, became very much glad to watch this show. When I watch *Qahveh Talkh* I really don't feel that I am watching some historical comedy. Instead I feel it is showing, i.e. in a funny way, how we live in this country. It is actually trying to show today's problems and issues of Iran so that maybe we become more aware of them and maybe change ourselves.[30]

Even though Nimā has the knowledge of the future and the ear of the king, he struggles to implement any of the reforms he is trying to push through to improve Iran's history, so it can find its rightful place among the most advanced and powerful nations in the world. Though he has traveled back in time, he cannot change its course. The futility of Nimā's efforts can be read many ways. In one sense it echoes the reality that we cannot change past events and, therefore, Iranians should focus on the present and future of their nation. It can also be seen as a critique of the efforts of the state to construct a past that they find suitable as another fruitless endeavor.

While the content of the show can be interpreted in different ways, one thing is evident: history and history telling are essential to the Iranian national consciousness. How people regard and express their historical narrative continues to be a point of contention among Iranians as they challenge the accounts of those in power. Contrary to Nimā's experience, history is quite important, and Iranians assert their view in how it is told. Satire and historical settings allow them to push the boundaries of the Islamic Republic's restrictions and convey

---

[30] "Illustrating Modern Iran under the Veil of History," IMDb review, last accessed September 6, 2018, www.imdb.com/review/rw2377339/?ref_=rw_urv.

not only social and political critiques, but also actively partake in image production.

## 5.3 Need for Expression

As the previous examples illustrated, Iranian artists and audiences cleverly find ways to get around the Islamic Republic's restrictions in order to tell their stories. Not only do these stories challenge the Islamic Republic's cultural hegemony and control over Iran's national narrative, they also demonstrate the need for expression that is critical to the Iranian national psyche. As state authorities attempted to regulate media, Iranians continued to push back and defy their limitations. The longing to be heard, especially in a context of repression, is often proclaimed by the youngest members of society. Thus, counterculture in Iran is a form of political resistance. As Hebdige argues, youth subcultures confront hegemony by moving away from established behaviors and carving out a niche for themselves to adopt fresh symbols and styles.[31] Such subcultures emerged in the Iranian social milieu over the decades after the revolution, which is evident in the outer appearance of many young people, as well as their tastes in entertainment such as music and media.

The intersection of film and music is exemplified by Bahman Ghobadi's 2009 film *No One Knows About Persian Cats*.[32] The film follows the story of two young underground musicians in Tehran as they try their hand at forming a band and making music. Since the music they can produce in Iran is restricted by Islamic Republic regulations, the pair attempts to leave the country in order to make their music more freely abroad. Along the way, as they meet other underground musicians in Iran, the audience is exposed to the variety of musical tastes and subcultures, such as rock and rap, which exist just below the surface of the Islamic Republic. The film reveals the complexity of expression in an environment with strict boundaries through the story of the musicians as well as their emotive songs. A cameo by well-known rapper, Hichkas, provides a track that discusses the corruption of money and the struggle of lower classes in Iran.[33] The film

---

[31] Dick Hebdige, *Subculture: The Meaning of Style* (London: Methuen, 1979).
[32] Bahman Ghobadi, dir., *No One Knows About Persian Cats* (n.p., 2009). DVD.
[33] "Hichkas – Ekhtelaaf in No One Knows About Persian Cats," YouTube video, last accessed September 6, 2018, www.youtube.com/watch?v=U7L9y-Wmz1o.

goes deeper than a critique of musical restrictions by using the songs and lyrics as a medium to draw attention to other social issues. Iranian youths created a necessary space for expression in the absence of an open public forum. Ghobadi's film navigates a thin line between fiction and documentary, incorporating real musicians and actors to play out a staged story that is also a stark reality for young Iranian artists.

The idea that one must leave Iran to be uninhibited is seen in another film with a very different subject matter. The 2011 film *Ayeneh-ha-ye Ruberu*[34] (Facing Mirrors), directed by Negār Āzarbayjāni, tells the story of Edi, a transgender male who is trying to leave Iran in order to escape a pending marriage that his father is forcing upon him. Though Edi identifies as male, his female birth is all that his father understands, making the possibility of his transition at home unbearable. While the Islamic Republic legally recognizes transgender identities, their draconian policies on gender and sexuality – which discriminate against women and criminalize homosexuality – promote a conservative cultural mentality. The film explores the idea of gender and traditional gender roles through the story of Edi and Rana, a female taxi driver who is working to support her son while her husband, Sādeq, is in prison. The characters stories converge when Rana picks up Edi, who needs a driver to help him get his affairs in order and leave Iran promptly. Edi promises to pay off Sādeq's debt so he can be freed in exchange for Rana's assistance.

As the story moves forward, it raises questions about women's place in society and the notion of gender itself. As a taxi driver, Rana is working in a traditionally male occupation. Additionally, the fact that she is the sole earner working to pay off her husband's debt reverses the conventional role of men as the head of the household. Despite her situation, Rana maintains a traditional way of thinking, which is questioned further by Edi, a man born in a woman's body. The dialogue between Edi and Rana throughout the film confronts the established mindsets of Iranians and provides a powerful social critique of the Islamic Republic's treatment of women, sexuality, and gender.

With a cast and crew made up primarily of women, it is not surprising that traditional notions of gender are at the center of the film's discussion. Iranian women after the revolution took up positions

[34] Negār Āzarbayjāni, dir., *Facing Mirrors* (Tehran: Rasāne-ha-ye Tasviri, 2014 [2011]), DVD.

behind the camera in order to actively challenge their subordinate station in the Islamic Republic's legal system and voice their opposition to the status quo. Like the musicians in Ghobadi's film, these women, and men like Edi, often look beyond their own borders in hopes of finding a more open space for expression. However, despite their strong criticisms and repudiation of Islamic Republic policies, the idea of homeland is never far from their hearts and minds. As Edi confesses to Ranā: "My wish is to stay, be able to stay in my own country, to tell someone I love them, even behind bars ... It's not until you are forced to leave that you realize the value of your own country."[35] As this example shows, Iranians engage in social debates that undermine the dogmas and narratives of the Islamic Republic without conceding their national identity or love for their motherland. It is important to recognize that Iranians make use of even the narrowest spaces they are given to articulate not just their dissatisfaction and anxieties, but rather their hopes and desires as narrators of their own stories.

While the exodus motif focused on the need to escape restrictions by leaving, Iranian artists and audiences also showed the need for more openness within Iran. A lighter take on the demand for access and expression is seen in the comedic film *Dāyereh-e Zangi*[36] (Tambourine), in which illicit media such as foreign films and satellites are part of everyday life in Iran. The film takes place in an apartment building in Tehran and depicts some of the routine occurrences of middle-class life. The plot unfolds as Mohammad, a repairman, arrives at the apartment building to fix the satellite dishes of various tenants. Each tenant of course insists that Mohammad fix their dish first and as the film moves forward, the audience is exposed to the day-to-day life of these assorted families who share the same building. Although satellite dishes are not allowed under Islamic Republic prohibitions and the sale of foreign films is not permitted, the film demonstrates how both practices are commonplace in Iran and how the image of satellite dishes on rooftops is ubiquitous.

With the restrictions imposed by the Islamic Republic, the trivial act of watching a film or surfing the Internet become both defiant and liberating. Access to materials and information, especially media, are

[35] Ibid.
[36] Parisa Bakhtavar, dir., *Tambourine* (Tehran: New Century, 2008), DVD.

essential for an open society. As the film reveals, notwithstanding the reality of suppression, Iranians secure their access to these mediums through their resourcefulness and ensure a steady supply to fulfill their demands. Moreover, the film shows that these "unlawful" practices do not appear to be criminal at all; instead, the characters display a nonchalant attitude toward what have become ordinary customs.

Additionally, through the stories and dialogue of the families, the film exposes other facets of contemporary Iranian society that lie beneath the Islamic Republic's methodical surface. A conversation between one of the buildings tenants, Abbas, and his father-in-law, illustrates the generational gap in political thinking. While discussing an expensive phone bill due to international calls, Abbas tells the father not to make calls to politically motivated satellite programs abroad that actively desire regime change in Iran. His wife then steps in to assure the father that his phone calls, and cursing of the government, will not change the political landscape. Though the older father figure expresses his political indignation, the uninterested attitude of Abbas and his wife provide a marked contrast. Abbas is more concerned with the phone bill than a political debate. With this exchange, the film reveals how many contemporary Iranians are critical of the state's policies, but are often more concerned with the management of the their daily lives than seeking radical solutions.

The Islamic Republic's restrictions may be codified, but Iranian people show continued resilience and ingenuity in the face of such constraints. Iranian filmmaker Jafar Panahi personifies the spirit of Iranian fortitude in his ironically titled film *This Is Not a Film*.[37] Following the disturbances of the 2009 election and ensuing Green Movement, Panahi was one of the many artists who displayed his support for the protestors. The Islamic Republic's crackdown on protests included significant political and cultural figures, such as Panahi, who was first detained in July 2009. Though released promptly, Panahi was later arrested again in March 2010 and this time charged with crimes against the state. Panahi eventually received a six-year prison sentence, to be served under house arrest, and a twenty-year ban on making films, traveling, or giving interviews. The fact that the restrictions placed on Panahi's filmmaking were more severe than his prison sentence speaks volumes to the Islamic Republic's mentality toward

---

[37] "Jafar Panahi – 2011 This Is Not a Film," YouTube video, last accessed September 6, 2018, www.youtube.com/watch?v=UHfQ35ltakY.

film. Cognizant of the power of filmmakers as agents of cultural and social change, the Islamic Republic exploited the legal system as a way to curtail the influence of Panahi as an artist.

However, as the Islamic Republic learned over the decades following the revolution, the agency of people cannot be easily stifled. While under house arrest and barred from making films, Panahi found a way to channel his creativity and prove once again the power of expression. With the help of a friend who worked the camera, Panahi, imprisoned at home, recorded his daily routines and his legal battle. In the film, Panahi reads a screenplay for a project he was working on and discusses his previous films. He cleverly notes that while the judgment bans him from making films and giving interviews, it does not specify anything about acting or reading screenplays. He also draws attention to the process of filmmaking in Iran, which is mired in censorship and red tape, and discusses his legal issues on camera. Regardless of his cunning loophole, Panahi's documentary was not authorized. It was eventually smuggled out on a USB and shown on screens and in festivals outside Iran.

The case of Panahi's film is analogous to an Iranian populace that resists the limitations placed on it by the Islamic Republic with strength, grace, and humor. Though the state has not officially lifted Panahi's ban as of this writing, they slowly eased his restrictions and allowed him space to move more freely. When faced with the defiance and agency of the people, Iranian authorities showed a capacity both to modify and accommodate some demands, and to forcefully silence them. Even with this ever-present pressure, Panahi reasserted his position in 2015 by stating:

I'm a filmmaker. I can't do anything else but make films. Cinema is my expression and the meaning of my life ... Nothing can prevent me from making films as when being pushed to the ultimate corners I connect with my inner-self and in such private spaces, despite all limitations, the necessity to create becomes even more an urge.[38]

The fact that Panahi continued his work as a filmmaker without hesitation recalls the casual attitude of Iranian apartment dwellers with illegal satellites. Through unapologetic expression, Iranians

---

[38] Ali Jaafar, "Iranian Filmmaker Jafar Panahi Releases Statement Despite Ongoing Ban," *Deadline* (January 26, 2015), last accessed September 6, 2018, http://deadline.com/2015/01/jafar-panahi-iran-berlin-ban-1201359221/.

continue to challenge the Islamic Republic and its shaky control over image production.

## 5.4 Beyond "Iranian" Stories: Asghar Farhadi

Hamid Naficy argues that Iranian cinema was transnational from the beginning, as it grew from exchanges with other national cinemas and the global travel of Iranians.[39] Though Iranian auteurs and audiences alike were heavily influenced by foreign cinema and culture, what we typically see on screen are Iranian stories. They are Iranian because the plots, physical spaces, images, and sensibilities of the characters are all specific to the Iranian setting. The prominence of Iranian stories can be understood as a need to assert a national identity and push the boundaries of their limitations in order to contest the Islamic Republic's hegemonic practices. However, as the Islamic Republic was forced to accommodate some public demands, and with the passage of time, space opened up for a wider variety of stories to be told. While the cases given examined stories that primarily focus on topics specific to Iran, recent popular works have shifted attention to broader themes that encompass the extensive scope of human experiences.

No other Iranian director or artist demonstrates this transition like Asghar Farhadi. Now internationally recognized for his award-winning films, Farhadi epitomizes the notion of Iran's transnational cinema. His work is not only transnational for its global reach and collaboration with international artists, but because the stories he tells are universally meaningful and resonate across borders. What separates Farhadi from other critically acclaimed Iranian filmmakers is the reach of his films within Iran. Unlike the high art of the intelligentsia that often represents Iranian cinema in the world, Farhadi's films appeal to a broader audience for its relatable depictions of everyday middle-class life. Farhadi's brilliance as a writer/director is in capturing and conveying human stories in a way that is emotive and palatable to larger audiences.

Common themes within his films explore social and class issues, gender roles, marriage, and the human proclivity to lie. In his 2009 film *Darbāre-ye Elly*[40] (About Elly), Farhadi presents the story of

[39] Hamid Naficy, *A Social History of Iranian Cinema*, vol. 4, *The Globalizing Era, 1984–2010* (Durham, NC: Duke University Press, 2011).
[40] Asghar Farhadi, dir., *About Elly* (Tehran: Tasvir Donyā-ye Honar, 2010 [2009]), DVD.

a group of young middle-class Iranian families as they take a vacation to the Caspian Sea. One of the friends, Sepideh, brings along a new acquaintance, Elly, to introduce her to the group's recently divorced friend, Ahmad. The friends appear to be having a good time as they dance, sing, and enjoy common frivolities. However, the drama unfolds when Elly disappears by the water, where she is supposed to be watching the children as they play. In a confused effort to piece together what has happened to Elly, tensions mount and the friends begin to argue. As the group attempts to unravel the mystery surrounding their new companion, they point fingers and hold each other accountable for her potential drowning in the sea.

The dialogue rather than the action drives the film forward as the characters slowly reveal small lies and deceptions they have been hiding. Ahmad admits he asked Sepideh to bring Elly along in the hope of making a connection. When someone claiming to be a family member tries to contact Elly, the friends are forced to invite him to the villa and tell him what has come to pass. At this point, Sepideh is compelled to reveal that the man soon arriving is Elly's fiancé, a fact that she has hidden from her friends, including Ahmad. Anxieties and emotions rise when the fiancé arrives to identify a body that was found in the water and demands answers about why Elly was there in the first place. The film raises moral questions about the nature of duplicity, as the friends contemplate whether they should be honest with Elly's distraught fiancé or lie to protect his feelings. The notion of who is the victim and who is to blame is blurred in Farhadi's film because the characters cannot be easily divided into protagonists and antagonists. Instead, the audience is presented with nuanced subjects that do not fit common archetypes. While the Iranian context is still present in the film's texture, the story could be set anywhere with a comparable effect.

*About Elly* was a success in Iran and abroad, reaching international box offices and garnering several awards. As one young urban Iranian noted, the scene in which the friends are at the villa enjoying a game of pantomime is a measure of the film's status: "This became a popular activity after the movie came out. People at parties, young and old, would start a game of pantomime."[41] But it was Farhadi's next effort that skyrocketed him to fame both domestically and internationally.

---

[41] Interview conducted in Iran in September 2015. The subject was middle class, female, and in her late twenties.

His 2011 film *A Separation* was widely watched in Iran and went on to win the most prestigious awards in the world,[42] including the 2012 Oscar for best foreign film, the first for an Iranian film.

In *A Separation*, Farhadi explores some class differences with urban middle-class as well as urban working-class Iranians. The film presents a cast of diverse characters, each of which have the capacity to gain the audience's sympathy and animosity. The plot revolves around the separation of Nāder and Simin and the future of their adolescent daughter, Termeh. While Simin wishes to leave Iran and immigrate to Canada, with the hope of a better life for her daughter, Nāder feels obligated to stay in Iran, especially to care for his father who is suffering from Alzheimer's. Since Simin is staying with her parents during the separation, Nāder is forced to hire a caretaker for his father while he is at work. The introduction of Razieh, the caretaker, offers a view and critique of class distinctions in Iran. The economic and cultural divide of the middle and working class is a thread throughout the film's story.

The action of the film moves forward after a scuffle between Nāder and Razieh, when Nāder comes home to find his father alone, frail, and tied to his bed. Though Razieh has tried her best to care for Nāder's father, she finds herself overwhelmed with the work. Nāder and Razieh argue intensely and Nāder appears to push Razieh out the front door with some force. Shortly after their dispute, when it is revealed that Razieh has suffered a miscarriage, Nāder worries that his shove may have been the catalyst for her condition. From here the courts become involved as Razieh, and her out-of-work, ill-tempered husband, accuse Nāder of causing her miscarriage.

Like *About Elly*, Farhadi examines the complexity of thoughts and emotions that drive people to lie and deceive. Termeh feels pressure to lie to the magistrate about her father's knowledge of Razieh's pregnancy, while Nāder lies about knowing that Razieh was pregnant. At the same time, Razieh hides the fact that she was knocked down by a car the same day as her incident with Nāder and does not know for certain what caused her miscarriage. None of the characters can be categorized in simple terms; they all mislead but feel compelled by their circumstances to do so. The events surrounding Razieh and her miscarriage exacerbate the tensions between Simin and Nāder, who are also in

---

[42] Asghar Farhadi, dir., *A Separation* (Culver City, CA: Sony Pictures Classics, 2012 [2011]), DVD.

court to decide the fate of their marriage and their daughter. As Farhadi weaves his story together without taking explicit sides in any case, he puts the audience in a difficult position in picking sides as well.

In the end, the magistrate allows Termeh to decide for herself which parent she will live with, but the audience is not privy to the path Termeh chooses. The ambiguity of the story's ending is not just an artistic choice on the part of Farhadi, but rather an honest revelation into the director's psyche. As Farhadi himself explains, Termeh's choice in the end is not between mother and father, but about choosing between two different paths for a future.[43] For Farhadi, this is the question that haunts Iranian society: what future will this generation of Iranians choose? In the film the question remains unanswered because the larger question is still unanswered for Farhadi as an Iranian.

Farhadi discussed how growing up in Iran, especially during the Iran–Iraq War, influenced his taste in films. With screens in Iran, big and small, inundated with scenes of war, Farhadi was drawn to more peaceful stories: "I had a reaction to these films, I wanted to see films that were calmer, with no vestiges of war. This is why films that had more life in them were attractive to me."[44] While Farhadi's talents are in telling broader human stories, his Iranian culture remains a central part of his films. For instance, Iranian religiosity is clearly portrayed in Razieh's character, when she is told to swear on the Quran that Nāder's push was the cause of her miscarriage. In this poignant scene, Razieh tells her furious husband that she cannot in good conscience oblige by this request. Despite their desperate need for the money Simin and Nāder are offering to settle the matter, Razieh is unable to relent on her beliefs. Razieh's piety is an honest representation of one segment of Iran's mixed population, while Nāder and Simin provide a picture of a different sector within the same society.

As these examples illustrate, Farhadi skillfully creates space for multifaceted depictions of the Iranian populace. Consequently, he provides authentic portrayals of his countrymen that run counter to the one-dimensional images prevalent in Western societies. While Farhadi is interested in telling human stories about life, he is also

[43] Auberi Edler, dir., *Masterpieces of European Cinema: A Separation* (Paris: Folamour Productions, 2014), Amazon video streaming.
[44] Ibid.

concerned with telling stories that show Iranians as humans. As he recollected winning the Oscar in 2012, Farhadi noted:

What made Iranian people happy wasn't just that a film had won an Oscar, because Iranian cinema has won many awards. This happened at a time when the world's image of Iran was bad … When I went there for a cultural event to speak to the world, or at least part of the world, about Iran's culture, it made people very happy.[45]

When accepting the Golden Globe for best foreign picture in 2012 for *A Separation*, Farhadi voiced his adoration for his compatriots:

When I was coming up on the stage, I was thinking, "what should I say here?" Should I say something about my mother, my father, my kind wife, my daughters, my dear friends? My crew, great and lovely crew? But now, I just prefer to say something about my people. I think they are a truly just loving people.[46]

For Farhadi, like other Iranians, his nation-state is a core part of his identity and portraying images that challenge the narrative of both foreign powers and the Islamic Republic are crucial to his work.

Yet, it is Farhadi's ability to create characters and stories that transcend the confines of a nation's borders that resonates with so many international viewers. Even as spectators outside the Iranian cultural milieu, people can connect to the subjects in his films because the issues he raises are universal. Simultaneously, his Iranianness is still part of the stories he tells, working its way into the details of his films. His 2013 film *Le Passé*[47] (The Past), which takes place in France with almost exclusively French characters, is the best illustration of his transnational scope.

The film is neither "Iranian" nor "French," but rather it is a film about people and the complications that arise in relationships of family and love. In characteristic form, the film explores how little deceptions, even well intentioned, can have grave consequences. Farhadi does not choose between Iranian distinctiveness and transnational metropolitanism, instead his films reflect the heterogeneity of contemporary Iranian society and how people across the world are connected. As an

---

[45] Ibid.

[46] "'A Separation' Film from Iran Won the Best Foreign Language Film in Golden Globe Awards 2012," YouTube video, last accessed September 7, 2018, www .youtube.com/watch?v=hPWCBDVVzf0.

[47] Asghar Farhadi, dir., *The Past* (Culver City, CA: Sony Picture Classics, 2014 [2013]), Amazon video streaming.

Iranian storyteller, Farhadi represents an Iranian identity that embraces pluralism and challenges the bifurcated narratives of the past. Though Iranian identity remains a significant issue, Farhadi's multidimensional characters represent the complexity of identity and the manifold ways in which human stories are shared.

## 5.5 Conclusion

Since the artists are Iranian and produce projects with an Iranian audience in mind, the shows and films presented in this study offer a window into the country. What most of these stories have in common is the context of Iran, with its particular history, politics, and culture. Unlike Hollywood films, which often take you outside the borders of the United States or into an alternate reality, in Iranian cinema the space for storytelling is typically closer to home. For Iranian artists, their muse is often their nation, not in spite of the legal restrictions the Islamic Republic imposes, but because of those very constraints.

Art, culture, politics, nation, and identity converge at a crossroads where various groups clash over control and defining Iran's future. The nexus of these forces is exemplified in a tweet from Iran's former Foreign Minister, Javad Zarif, after Farhadi's 2017 Oscar win for *The Salesman*: "Proud of cast & crew of 'The Salesman' for Oscar & stance against #MuslimBan. Iranians have represented culture & civilization for millennia."[48] Like Farhadi, who did not attend the 2017 Oscar's ceremony in protest after President Trump's infamous "Muslim Ban," Zarif used the award as an occasion to draw attention to a larger international political concern. With one brief sentence, Zarif shrewdly inserted national pride for Iran's contributions to world civilization, as well as a critique of foreign powers. The intersection of nationalism, politics, and popular culture is illustrated by Zarif's tweet, which used the nationalist enthusiasm of Iranians, after a major victory for one of its films, to promote a political agenda.

The link between popular culture, political confrontation, and national identity is also evident in how Iranian actors use their position as cultural symbols to shed light on their shared struggles. For instance, the fiery speech of young actress Bārān Kosari at a Rouhani rally during

[48] Javad Zarif, Twitter post (February 26, 2017, 10:45 PM EST), last accessed September 7, 2018, https://twitter.com/JZarif/status/836059730397315073.

the 2017 Iranian presidential election drew roaring applause from a massive crowd.[49] Standing among the crowd of Rouhani supporters, Kosari took a microphone and delivered a passionate statement on her choice to vote and participate in the electoral process, despite calls from Iranian dissidents to boycott the elections. As a voice for her generation, Kosari expressed the sentiments of other young Iranians who looked at the election as another opportunity to engender progress in Iran. Not mincing her words, Kosari invoked the reform movement that began with President Khatami, as an appeal to continue the battle for change. The video of her speech was shared on social media because of its content and the speaker's fame.

Iranian artists illustrate the connection between popular culture and the nation in less overt political contexts as well. In his acceptance speech for best actor at the 2016 Cannes Film Awards, Shahāb Hosseini made the standard rounds in thanking his director and fellow actors in *The Salesman*. However, Hosseini used the ceremony as an opportunity to thank his fellow countrymen and dedicated the award to them, stating, "I give this award with the whole of my existence and love from the depth of my heart, to the people of my land."[50] Though Hosseini's nationalism is obvious from his dedication and the appeal to his land, he began his speech by thanking God and acknowledging his father's happy soul in heaven. Nation, religiosity, art, and humanity; like the characters he has portrayed so well, Hosseini embodies this plurality of Iranianness.

In addition to the stories they help create, Iranian artists use numerous platforms to confront the dominance of the state. Fighting censorship and communicating ideas that may not be in line with the Islamic Republic's restrictions or narrative are part of the fabric of contemporary Iranian culture. In this sense, ordinary Iranians also utilize everyday expression as a means to challenge authorities and, as a consequence, appropriate the state's culture of resistance for their own purposes. While the Islamic Republic's broad message of resistance culture may be meaningful to Iranian proclivities, it is a double-edged sword that Iranians employ in their state of perpetual defiance.

---

[49] Facebook video, last accessed September 7, 2018, www.facebook.com/ehsanz/videos/10155797295762080/.

[50] "Prix d'interprétation masculine : Shahab Hosseini – Cannes 2016," YouTube video, last accessed September 7, 2018, www.youtube.com/watch?v=gHETrHWgQMM.

# 6  Conclusion

After the establishment of the Islamic Republic and the consolidation of power among a small group of the revolution's architects, Iranians continued their campaign for freedom and control over the nation's identity and future. Having gone through the trials and tribulations of the revolution and its aftermath, many Iranian patriots chose to engage with the system and sought reforms to fulfill the believed promises of the revolution and the hopes for a better future for their nation. An examination of internal movements for cultural and political reform illustrates the evolution of Iranians' national engagement.

However, before looking at the people's resistance, it is prudent to note the continued impact of the national narratives promoted over the last century. Royalist rhetoric cannot be dismissed as vestiges of the past. Instead, more than forty years after the revolution that toppled the shah, some Iranians romanticize the idea of monarchy and the image of Persian dominion represented by the heirs of the Pahlavi throne. The fact that Iranians use symbols from earlier eras to challenge the Islamic Republic is understandable, especially given the use of oppositional narratives by Iranian revolutionaries. As Mansoor Moaddel argues with his Episodic Discourse Model, the contexts in which ideas emerge influence the development of those positions.[1] Accordingly, Iranians produced ideas within a specific social and political space using the histories, images, and discourses accessible to them. Since ideologies are often competing, the nature of production is oppositional, as Moaddel elaborates:

Ideological production is a function of the kinds of discourses that are dominant in the social environment. Ideological producers develop their ideas vis-à-vis the conceptual framework, symbolic order, and ritualistic practices, that is, the discursive fields of competing ideologies. In addressing

---

[1]  Mansoor Moaddel, *Islamic Modernism, Nationalism, and Fundamentalism: Episode and Discourse* (Chicago: University of Chicago Press, 2005).

social problems, they reevaluate, revisit, or reject the claims, the arguments, and often the conceptual foundations of competing ideologies. At the same time, ideological producers beget responses, rebuttals, and counterarguments from their adversaries.[2]

As such, Iranians confronting the Islamic Republic in pursuit of meaningful reform, including its national narrative and policies, utilized the tools at their disposal to express their grievances. Descendants of the Pahlavi dynasty appropriated these protests in order to advance a wholly different agenda of regime change.

## 6.1 The Paradox of Imperial Democracy and the Foreign Prince

From the moment the shah was placed back into power by foreign agents in 1953, he discounted the clamoring political voices calling for independence. His nationalist project, which built off of the work of his father, also ignored the demands of Iranian people in their quest for national sovereignty. Despite the façade of independence and revolution that the shah carefully designed, Iranian discontent toward the system of monarchy became palpable as they struggled for democracy and liberation. The people's protests culminated in the revolution that tore down the monarchy and its pretense. Still, in the aftermath of the revolution, the dying shah with his last appeals to the world made a case for *imperial* democracy. In his *Answer to History*, the shah maintained that:

Democratization at all levels of Iranian life can flourish only under the aegis of a constitutional monarchy. Iran had always been and remains an *empire*, that is, an assemblage of people whose ethnic character, language, manners, and even religious beliefs are different. (Muslims constitute an imposing majority.) Hence, the necessity of a sovereign who would bring unity from above in order to realize a true *imperial democracy*.[3]

Again, the shah exposed his naiveté as he completely disregarded the demands of a large portion of Iranians who understood democracy and monarchy as mutually exclusive institutions.

The lessons of the twentieth century taught many Iranians that true democracy could not be achieved with an unelected official at the top.

---

[2] Ibid., 15.
[3] Mohammad Reza Pahlavi, *Answer to History* (New York: Stein and Day, 1980), 129 (emphasis added).

Unfortunately, for Iranians who fought for democratic principles and the end of monarchy, the revolution fulfilled only half of that promise. One unelected official replaced the other at the top, while Iranians continued to aspire for a future with freedom through the vicissitudes of their national saga. Though the shah failed to unite Iranians around his nationalist enterprise and the paradox of imperial democracy, Pahlavi discourse remained a part of the Iranian national story.

After the shah's death in July 1980, the heir to his would-be throne, his eldest son Reza Pahlavi, took the lead in sustaining his family's legacy. On his twentieth birthday, October 31, 1980, Reza Pahlavi held a press conference in Cairo declaring himself the legal king of Iran, Reza II.[4] His announcement came three months after his father's death and over a month after Iraq's invasion of Iran, which began the eight-year Iran–Iraq War (1980–88). Pahlavi's language echoed that of his father, as he spoke of Iranian independence, history, and civilization. However, also akin to his father, Reza Pahlavi did not share in the experience of ordinary Iranians. Of course, as a prince, his life was distinct from that of his fellow countrymen in numerous ways. But his time spent abroad, especially training in the US Air Force in 1978,[5] fit the Pahlavi penchant for foreign approval. As tensions rose in Iran over the shah's relations with foreign powers, particularly the United States, such incidents highlighted the Pahlavi disconnect with the Iranian public.

Despite the popular revolution that ousted the shah in 1979, Reza II appealed to Iranians from exile by affirming the same discourse that had failed his father. Throughout his reign, the shah reinforced the narrative of the Pahlavi dynasty as the source of light in Iran's darkest times. He maintained this idea until the very end stating, "I think of all those compatriots who, under the reign of my father and myself, pulled Iran out of darkness and servitude and transformed it into the great nation it was in 1978."[6] It is no coincidence that, after the revolution and his father's death, Reza Pahlavi saw himself as a liberator since Iran had fallen into darkness again, without the guiding light of the Pahlavi

---

[4] "SOGANDE REZA PAHLAVI – 1980 (1359)," YouTube video, last accessed September 17, 2018, www.youtube.com/watch?v=udvlRgE_m0w&t=203s.

[5] "About Reza Pahlavi," rezapahlavi.org, http://en.rezapahlavi.org/aboutrezapah lavi/.

[6] Mohammad Reza Pahlavi, *Answer to History* (New York: Stein and Day, 1980), 190.

monarchs. Speaking at his self-coronation from Cairo, Reza II stated, "My fellow countrymen and brothers, I begin this responsibility, which is given to me after the burning emptiness of my great father's passing, during one of the darkest eras of Iran's history."[7] However, the prince's appeals to his compatriots and self-declared ascendancy to a throne that no longer existed placed him outside the everyday concerns of Iranians, who were grappling with the aftermath of their revolution and an Iraqi invasion on their soil. For many Iranians, who had valiantly fought to overthrow their foreign king, a foreign prince was not a suitable alternative.

As Iranians struggled for their lives during the war and for freedom within the new republic, Reza Pahlavi continued the rhetoric of the past from his new home in the United States. Disconnected literally and figuratively from the Iranian masses, the prince took comfort in the support of former monarchists and others in the Iranian diaspora, which he surmised reflected the Iranian nation back home. As such, the self-proclaimed king also became the self-appointed representative of the Iranian nation-state. While speaking about his communications with political factions in Iran in 1989, and the efforts to create a national front in opposition to the Islamic Republic, Pahlavi claimed, "The response that I have obtained *from a majority of my countrymen*, ranging from virtually every faction of the political spectrum ... has been overwhelmingly positive."[8] Although Pahlavi has not lived in Iran for over forty years, he continues to use such strong language in terms of the Iranian political scene and his role as a representative.

In fact, over these decades living in the United States, Pahlavi persistently met with political figures in the United States, acting as a mediator for the Iranian people. Despite not holding an official position or any kind of referendum by the Iranian people that grants him such authority, Pahlavi continued to make similar claims. For instance, in 2017 while in a meeting with US lawmakers in Washington, DC, Pahlavi stated:

It is a little bit awkward that in all these years the dialogue with Iran has been limited to the current regime and its representatives, and that the *majority of*

---

[7] "SOGANDE REZA PAHLAVI – 1980 (1359)," YouTube video, last accessed September 17, 2018, www.youtube.com/watch?v=udvlRgE_m0w&t=203s.
[8] "Reza Pahlavi Interview in 1989," YouTube video, last accessed September 17, 2018, www.youtube.com/watch?v=qkrqliMO2sI (emphasis added).

*the Iranian people* who are against this regime and the secular democratic opposition that can speak for them is yet to be directly engaged in any kind of dialogue ... One of my primary functions has been over the years to be a voice on behalf of my compatriots.[9]

Though Pahlavi maintained that Iranian civil society should decide its own fate, as he continued his speech, he went on to lobby US legislators to assist Iranians, thereby inviting the intervention of outsiders. Appeals to foreign powers are reminiscent of his father's policies, which were vehemently protested by Iranians.

The 2017 interview reveals another facet of Reza Pahlavi's long-held view that the Islamic Republic does not legitimately represent any segment of the Iranian populace. While the Islamic Republic has governed Iran for over forty years, Pahlavi often spoke of its imminent demise. On speaking tours throughout the United States over the decades after the revolution, Pahlavi argued that the Iranian people would soon depose the Islamic Republic, culminating in Iranian democracy, with Pahlavi himself as the conduit. In 1989, speaking in front of an audience at Georgetown University, Pahlavi asserted, "Now let me say a few words about how I see the future. I have no doubt that the Iranian people are taking the first steps to dispose of the Islamic Republic. Many Iranians now believe that the Khomeini regime has reached the end of its life."[10] Thirty years later Pahlavi continues to make the same predictions based on the belief that the Islamic Republic will soon be gone, and that his role as leader will finally be fulfilled after decades of efforts to that end. At Georgetown he continued his speech:

I see my own role in this process as that of a strategic leader and a political catalyst. I represent the oldest institution in my country, an institution with deep and solid roots in our culture. This institution must stand above politics, if it is to perform its historical mission properly ... Our goal is to restore to the Iranian people their sovereign right to choose freely and deliberately their preferred system of government ... If they choose constitutional monarchy, I shall be honored to perform my duties as their king and servant.[11]

---

[9] "Iranistas' Update on Prince Reza Pahlavi's day on Capitol Hill," YouTube video, last accessed September 17, 2018, www.youtube.com/watch?v=XGqgMDifGJY (emphasis added).

[10] "Democracy in Iran after Khomeni," video, C-Span, last accessed September 17, 2018, www.c-span.org/video/?6200-1/democracy-iran-khomeni.

[11] Ibid.

For Pahlavi then, monarchy, though constitutional, was still seen as a legitimate alternative to the Islamic Republic. In another interview given in 1990, Pahlavi doubled down on his idea of constitutional monarchy by claiming that the crown would be the preferred choice among Iranian voters, stating:

I believe that if the people of Iran today could choose between a democratic republic or an authoritarian monarchy, they would choose a democratic republic. However, if the people of Iran today had the option between a democratic republic and a democratic monarchy, they would vote for monarchy.[12]

In contrast to the Iranian revolutionaries who successfully dismantled the rule of kings, Pahlavi discussed monarchy and democracy as complimentary institutions, consequently propagating the late shah's image of imperial democracy.

Like his father, who was unaffected by the cacophony of dissent among his people, the younger Pahlavi often demonstrated the gap between his vision and that of the Iranian populace. In April and July of 2015, as people in Iran celebrated in the streets after the historic Iran nuclear agreement,[13] Pahlavi's active Twitter account restrained from showing any enthusiasm for the deal. In the May 2017 Iranian presidential election, as Iranians engaged in the political system by voting in massive numbers,[14] Pahlavi promoted civil disobedience[15] and called for an uprising against the government.[16] These disparities belie the self-made image of Reza Pahlavi as the spokesperson for the Iranian nation.

Moreover, Pahlavi consistently fostered the historical production of his titular dynasty. In April 2018, after the remains of a body suspected to be Reza Shah was found in Iran, Pahlavi quickly wrote a letter to

[12] "Meeting Reza Pahlavi – 1990," YouTube video, last accessed September 17, 2018, www.youtube.com/watch?v=vewPWJCnt_w.
[13] BBC News, "Iranians Celebrate Nuclear Agreement," YouTube video, last accessed September 17, 2018, www.youtube.com/watch?v=eY9lwZCfW_Q.
[14] Al Jazeera English, "Iran: More Than 40 Million Vote in Presidential Elections," YouTube video, last accessed September 17, 2018, www.youtube.com/watch?v=PucK15rtIFs.
[15] FOX News, "Eric Shawn Exclusive: Freedom for Iran," YouTube video, last accessed September 17, 2018, www.youtube.com/watch?v=9pzhx_wsD8E.
[16] Reza Pahlavi, Twitter post, May 20, 2017, 11:46 PM EST, last accessed September 17, 2018, https://twitter.com/PahlaviReza/status/866138206689013761.

UNESCO asking for their assistance in preserving and reburying the body. In his letter, Reza Pahlavi recounted precisely the national narrative that his father had cultivated during his reign, declaring:

> *Known as the father of modern Iran*, Reza Shah is regarded by Iranians as one of the most impactful and visionary monarchs in our history ... The discovery of Reza Shah's body is not merely a family matter; rather, it carries great historical and cultural significance for all Iranians. For that reason, *I write you today on behalf of the Iranian people* to urge UNESCO to direct attention and resources toward preservation and proper re-burial of Reza Shah's body ... On behalf of my compatriots, I ask you to take prompt action to help the Iranian people ensure preservation of Reza Shah's body as a matter of critical importance to our national heritage.[17]

Again, the assertion of his role as a representative of the Iranian polity is noteworthy given that there is little evidence of his mass popularity among those living in Iran.

Rather than heeding the voices of Iranian protesters that ousted his father, Pahlavi remained steadfast in his commitment to the monarchic tale of Iranian glory and the establishment of the modern Iranian state by Reza Shah. Though this royalist discourse may only represent a minority of Iranian voices, it is important to recognize the lasting impact of Pahlavi rhetoric. One dissident image (see Figure 6.1) illustrates how the Pahlavi national narrative, embedded with the ideas of independence and revolution, continues to influence the Iranian social and political climate and, as a result, Iranian identity formation.

The irony of an image calling for a revolution back to monarchy should not be overlooked. Yet, the idea of revolution linked to the crown was a central part of Mohammad Reza Pahlavi's nationalist construction. However, the Pahlavi failure to solidify a resonant identity created the space for identity formation from below, among the oppositional and revolutionary forces. The Islamic Republic then seized this sentiment for its own agenda of political power. While some aspects of the revolution succeeded, such as independence and the overthrow of monarchy, Iranians' long-awaited liberation and democracy remained wanting. From revolution to evolution, how Iranians tackled these issues is telling.

---

[17] Reza Pahlavi, Twitter post, May 30, 2018, 2:32 PM EST, last accessed September 17, 2018, https://twitter.com/PahlaviReza/status/99102250911285 6577 (emphasis added).

#RegimeChange in #Iran
#IranProtests
#RezaPahlavi #WeWillReclaimIran

♡ 1          ⟲ 5          ♡ 9

**Figure 6.1** Reza Pahlavi: "Revolution." This image was posted on Twitter in January 2018 in support of protests in Iran and in opposition to the government of the Islamic Republic. The image shows three generations of Pahlavi men, including Reza Shah, the Shah Mohammad Reza Pahlavi, and Reza Pahlavi. The word "Revolution" appears in Persian with the monarchic flag.

## 6.2  The People's Resistance

Iranian civil society developed over more than a century, as ordinary people discovered common interests and the will to act collectively in order to stake a claim in their future. Significant moments in the twentieth century highlight these efforts, such as the Constitutional Revolution (1905–11), the period of burgeoning political growth from 1941 to 1953 in absence of a strong monarch, and the 1979 revolution. In all these cases, activity from below, among the emergent "Iranian" populace, achieved important changes to the society and the political make-up of the budding nation-state. By 1979 the indomitable voices of this civil society formed a national narrative and identity in opposition to the ruling class that culminated in a people's revolution.

However, the revolution did not deliver on all its assurances, leaving the Iranian people with the need to continue their efforts to see the full promises of the revolution come to fruition. In doing so, many Iranians resisted the absolutism of the Islamic Republic by focusing on engagement with the political system. The first of such tests came in the early years of the Islamic Republic with the invasion by Iraq. Saddam

Hussein's major miscalculation was that he believed he could benefit from Iranian discontent and bring down the Islamic Republic with domestic assistance. But it was the strength of Iranian national identity that facilitated the revolution and was a force the Islamic Republic capitalized on to rally Iranians behind their new government. Despite concerns with the Islamic Republic, foreign aggression evoked the central premise of the revolution's message and brought back emotive images of struggle and eternal resistance. Rather than bringing the Islamic Republic to a quick end, the Iran–Iraq War solidified its power.

Saddam Hussein's misstep can be understood if we look at the progression of Iranian national identity and the emergence of the Iranian nation-state in 1979. At its core, the revolution was a conquest over foreign powers and the assertion of Iranian control. As one middle-class woman from Tehran vented:

Yes, we have problems, social, economic, political, you name it. But they are ours to fix. If change comes, or when change comes I should say, we will be the ones to do it. Iranians don't trust outside powers, they've never acted in our interest; only we can act in our own interest. Look, if my father acts poorly, I don't like it, but if you say something about my father, I will defend him with my life. It's my father. This is my country, I can see a lot of bad things, but I don't think anyone on the outside can fix it.[18]

For Iranians, kin, nation, and pride are all closely tied together; they are also quite aware of their history, which makes them wary of external interventions.

After the revolution Iranians continued to air their grievances with the state of affairs. While civil disobedience was one tactic deployed to voice their concerns, disapproval was often manifested through civic engagement as well. When the children of the revolution came of age and could finally vote they did so in droves. In the 1997 presidential election, 80 percent of the voting population went to the ballots.[19] The message of change from reformist candidate Mohammad Khatami inspired people across the political and social spectrum, resulting in his landslide victory. According to Ervand Abrahamian, the majority of

---

[18] I conducted this interview in Tehran in September 2015. The subject was in her early thirties.

[19] Ervand Abrahamian, *A History of Modern Iran* (Cambridge: Cambridge University Press, 2008).

Khatami's support came from the new middle class and young college students. Though many of these young students and professionals had serious objections to the Islamic Republic and the state of the country and its political affairs, they chose to actively participate in the system in the hope of reforming it from within.

It is also noteworthy that Khatami, who was re-elected in 2001, is part of the clerical class. By choosing someone from the clergy for the executive office, young Iranians indicated that the president's religiosity was not an issue, but rather, it was the policies of the individual that were critical. Moreover, the election of Khatami illustrated how young, secular-leaning Iranians could differentiate between an Islamic state and an Islamic candidate. Though a cleric, Khatami represented a movement toward reform and away from Iran's hardliners, underscoring the importance of an independent governing body that was elected by the people. In many ways, Khatami simply echoed the possibilities of the revolution; both identified as being Islamic, but appealed for a people's republic.

Khatami's tenure brought increased openness and an easing of social restrictions in Iran, while elevating Iran's place in the international community. However, Iranians grew disappointed with his inability to maneuver around the structural boundaries of his position. Within the Iranian system the elected government is beholden to the unelected Guardianship of the Islamic Jurist, known as *Velāyat-e Faqih*. The Supreme Leader – who was Ayatollah Khomeini after the revolution and Ayatollah Khamenei since Khomeini's death in 1989 – represents the highest authority in this structure. As the hardliners stifled Khatami's attempts at greater reforms, Iranians became frustrated by the political system and participated less in the 2005 presidential elections. As a consequence of low participation, the conservative-leaning candidate, Mahmoud Ahmadinejad, was elected as president.

In contrast to Khatami's position as a cleric, Ahmadinejad's lay status revealed again the complexity of Iranian identity and politics. Although Ahmadinejad was not a cleric, he took up the mantle and cause of the revolution as his central message. Going back to the fundamentals of the revolution and speaking for the dispossessed classes, Ahmadinejad fell into the conservative camp of Iranian politics. His victory in 2005 was often attributed to schisms among the reformers and Iranians apathetic to political involvement. Yet, despite this presumed indifference, fieldwork in Iran in the mid-2000s exposed a more complicated picture of the political and cultural spheres.

Traveling in Iran in the mid 2000s, mostly in Tehran among middle class urbanites,[20] I would often hear talk of the futility of the political system. Though the majority of subjects I spoke with were not Ahmadinejad supporters and had strongly secular leanings, they also felt betrayed by the promises of the reformers, much as they felt betrayed by the promises of the revolution. What was remarkable was the volume of political and social commentary in a so-called apathetic environment. Rather than indifference, it was agency that drove many not to vote in the 2005 election. The choice to vote and the choice *not* to vote should both be considered politically motivated actions in this context. On that account, not voting became another act of resistance, a message to the reformers to unify and produce more tangible results.

Iranians quickly felt the changes under Ahmadinejad, as urban middle-class youth sensed the increased social restrictions. Many of the subjects I spoke with expressed a desire for secularism and better economic opportunities, and they were often critical of the Islamic Republic's Islamic posturing. In direct conversation some communicated a reluctance toward religion and religiosity. However, in observing everyday behaviors it became evident that Islamic culture was so engrained in the society that these same urban youth partook in activities related to Islam. For instance, the works of Rumi, a thirteenth-century Persian Islamic scholar, poet, and mystic, were popular in written form and music. Also, during the holy month of Muharram, many young people participated in the large processions and activities (see Figure 6.2).

Muharram is significant for Shiites because of Ashura, the tenth day in Muharram in which the legendary martyrdom of Imam Hossein took place. On one occasion during Muharram I joined a small group of Tehran youths as they drove through the city listening to the songs of Koveytipur, a singer known for his songs of lamentation during the

---

[20] The majority of the subjects I spoke with were also the postrevolutionary generation, mostly born soon after the revolution. However, subjects varied in age as well, including some middle aged and older people. These subjects were met through various methods, including friends and family networks and using snowball sampling, as well as through months of living in Iran in various everyday interactions.

**Figure 6.2** Muharram in Tehran, 2006. The top photo shows the portrait carried at the beginning of a long procession through the streets, with men playing drums and striking their backs with chains in the bottom photos.

Iran–Iraq War and for Muharram. Lightly beating their chests and moving to the rhythmic melody they sang along:

> *The curtain was lifted and I saw all that is and is not*
> *Indeed, the things that cannot be seen are spectacular*
> *The heart's harp plays an alluring song*
> *There is a wailing love that sets fires*[21]

---

[21] The song has over 697,000 plays on Radio Javan and several videos with hundreds of thousands of views on YouTube. "Kuwaitipour – Change Del," Radio Javan, last accessed September 18, 2018, www.radiojavan.com/mp3s/mp3/Kuwaitipour-Change-Del?start=49051&index=1.

While they listened to this music almost ironically, their frivolity gave in just enough to take in the depth of emotion that the music induced. War, martyrdom, religiosity, and spirituality are imprinted in contemporary Iranian culture, even for those who oppose the Islamic Republic's discourse.

This helps explain the paradox of Khatami versus Ahmadinejad, or the reformer cleric versus the lay conservative. Like in Jewish and Christian contexts, for Muslims it is undoubtedly possible to identify with the religion and be secular. It is also conceivable to identify and partake in religious culture, without being particularly pious. The lines between "tradition" and "modernity" become blurred because they are not fixed categories of meaning. Individuals can identify and participate in aspects of both at the same time, or at different times. Rather than a clean dichotomy, there is integration and plurality. Iranians continue to contest simple or one-dimensional renditions of their long and intricate narrative. Additionally, they continue to challenge the control of those in power through political participation.

After Ahmadinejad's first term, Iranians took to the polls again to demonstrate their discontent with his policies. In the 2009 election, Khatami was eligible to run for president again, but instead of running himself, Khatami stepped aside and backed Mir Hossein Mousavi. In what came to be known as the Green Movement, Mousavi aligned himself with Khatami and other reform-minded Iranians. The momentum that built up around Mousavi's campaign was reflected in Iranians donning the color green in the streets and in popular culture as well. In fact, a pop song by Amir Tatalu, "Irān-e Sabz," released before the election, directly endorsed Mousavi. The song stressed the significance of taking part in the system and, as a consequence, helping to shape Iran's future. Tatalu started by stating plainly, "If you don't want to vote it means you've given up, you don't want to be counted. So, we will all vote together, for freedom, for reform, for a green belief."[22] The song's lyrics maintained this reasoning and reiterated the themes of martyrdom and nation so familiar in the Iranian nationalist repertoire. Imploring people to vote, Tatalu sang:

*For the progress of Iran, all together without weariness*
*We, the remnants of the blood of the martyrs, are all brave*

---

[22] "Amir Tataloo Iran e Sabz," YouTube video, last accessed September 27, 2018, www.youtube.com/watch?v=wIultGdBjgk.

*Let the world know we are always behind Iran*
*The destroyer of poverty and corruption, Mir Hossein-e Mousavi*
*We, all the youth of Iran, are in line [to vote] to support you*

As discussed earlier, the 2009 election had another massive voter turnout, which for Iranians almost guaranteed a reformist victory. When the results showed Ahmadinejad as the winner, Iranians immediately took to the streets feeling cheated and demanding their votes be counted. Protests and calls for tallying the votes exemplified the Iranian demand for accountability from the Islamic Republic.

Though the protests were violently extinguished by authorities and Ahmadinejad served a second term as president, Iranians came back to the polls in large numbers in 2013 to reaffirm their civic commitment and demand change.[23] Again, it was a cleric who represented such calls for change, which further substantiates the idea that religiosity was not an impediment to transformation. Similarly to how Mousavi used the color green to symbolize his campaign in 2009, Hassan Rouhani was characterized by the color purple. Rouhani was seen as a successor to Mousavi and Khatami, all of whom embodied a movement within the Iranian polity to reform the Islamic Republic, engage the international community, and implement the aims of the Iranian people. One graphic that a subject in Iran shared with me illustrates the explicit connection between the Green Movement and the election of Rouhani (see Figure 6.3). After facing the forceful suppression of the Green Movement, rather than capitulating, Iranians resolutely went back to the site of attack. In 2013 they used the ballot box to stake their claim and this time around there was little space for fabricating the election results.[24]

With a stagnant economy and strained international relations, Rouhani's government set its sights on negotiating a deal with world powers that would curb Iran's nuclear program and ease sanctions in order to bring economic relief to Iranians. The historic "Iran Deal" was reached in July 2015 and Iranians took to the streets and social media to

[23] Al Jazeera English, "Polls Close in Iran's Presidential Election," YouTube video, last accessed September 18, 2018, www.youtube.com/watch?v=E1ArI93qVeI.
[24] Al Jazeera, "Hassan Rouhani Wins Iran Presidential Election," YouTube video, last accessed September 18, 2018, www.youtube.com/watch?v=2DUkkKT717I.

**Figure 6.3** Graphic connecting the Green Movement and the election of Rouhani. The Persian reads a bit more poetic: "Sabz va banafsh nadāreh, Jonbesh edāmeh dāreh."

show their excitement.[25] For Iranians, the deal vindicated their hopes that the system, though deeply flawed, could work in their favor. The apparent détente with the United States was seen as a turning point for the Islamic Republic.

Riding the wave of this optimism, more reformers emerged as candidates in the legislative elections of 2016. While legislative elections typically do not attract as many voters as presidential elections, young and hopeful Iranians pushed voting campaigns and reformers made significant gains in parliamentary seats. Iranians used social media to urge people to vote with a straightforward campaign that stated "I will vote" (see Figure 6.4). The comments attached to these images reveal the connection between political participation, Iranian identity, and how Iranians see their role in guiding the nation's future, as one commentator stated:

The toughest critics of voting in Iran cannot deny that such viral campaigns are about hope and democratic aspirations of the Iranian people. The naysayers and those who hypocritically claim to be for a "true democracy" cannot deny that

[25] BBC News, "Iranians Celebrate Nuclear Agreement," YouTube video, last accessed September 18, 2018, www.youtube.com/watch?v=eY9lwZCfW_Q&t=2s.

**Figure 6.4** Instagram voting campaign, February 2016. The large text reads, "I will vote," while the smaller text states, "For all the people in both lists of reformers."

even a beloved "democratically elected" prime minister like Mossadegh was vetted and appointed by a monarch of essentially a one-party system. They cannot deny that there is a difference between moderation and extremism. *They cannot blame anyone but themselves when backwards hardliners come to define their identities as Iranians* – with the idiotic "death to" chants and illegal embassy occupations. And they sure as hell can't ask "where is my vote" if the votes are stolen! Because even a stolen vote is more valuable and admirable than a no-vote.[26]

Another commentator on the same image added, "I will vote ... I will define my identity as an Iranian and I will build the future of Iran."[27] Such remarks support the claim that civic engagement, such as voting, is an integral part of contemporary Iranian identity construction, and

[26]   The URL of the original post is not available; the quote I provided was taken from a screenshot of the comment from the original post (emphasis added).
[27]   This quote is from the same post; therefore, the URL is not available. However, the comment was also taken from a screenshot.

that ordinary people are cognizant of the government's role as representative of the people. Additionally, Ahmadinejad's presidential terms showed Iranians the importance of participation and the distinct impacts between different administrations.

Mass participation was again evident in Iran's 2017 presidential election. With the victory of reformers in the parliamentary election the previous year, the incumbent president ran a campaign focused on their platform of Iranian unity and nationalism, the importance of civil liberties, and the historic achievement of the nuclear deal. Speaking at the European Parliament Committee on Foreign Affairs in February 2016, Iran's then foreign minister, Javad Zarif, spoke of president Rouhani's commitment to the rights of citizens:

No country can claim that is has a perfect record, even a good record, in human rights, and I don't claim that Iran has that. We criticize many of the abuses that take place. We believe that a lot of improvement is needed in Iran. We are the first to admit that. The president [Rouhani] has declared as a campaign promise that he wants to bring about a charter of citizens' rights. And he will be issuing that charter and will take legislative measures, will present legislation to the parliament in order to protect better the rights of Iranian citizens.[28]

In tackling the idea of citizenry and a charter of their rights, Rouhani attempted to address a central plea among Iranians who had long yearned for greater freedom.

The realization of the nuclear deal brought a renewed sense of hope and the 2017 election became a rallying point for Iranian nationalism. The nationalist atmosphere was palpable at Rouhani's rallies as people sang along with Hojat Ashrafzādeh's stirring song "Iran Again,"[29] which promoted Iranian unity and rejuvenation. With more than 40 million people partaking, another large voter turnout elected Rouhani for a second term.[30] As images poured in showing celebrations after Rouhani's victory, the colors green and purple were visible across the crowds.[31] The

---

[28] "Dr. Zarif Speech & Q&A at the European Parliament Committee on Foreign Affairs. 16 Feb. 2016," YouTube video, last accessed September 18, 2018, www.youtube.com/watch?v=zFE8RmPrxq4.
[29] "Iranian Women, 2017 Election in Iran," YouTube video, last accessed September 18, 2018, www.youtube.com/watch?v=hOVzsS8GPrs.
[30] CNN, "Iran Holds Pivotal Presidential Elections," YouTube video, last accessed September 18, 2018, www.youtube.com/watch?v=3oCagmVivIc.
[31] AP Archive, "Iranian's Celebrate Moderate Election Win," YouTube video, last accessed September 18, 2018, www.youtube.com/watch?v=5SE3nDpnHX0.

connection between these colors and the people they represent is substantial. They are emblematic of a reform movement that began with the children of the revolution, a group that time and again chose to challenge the Islamic Republic through proactive participation. While the generation that ushered in the revolution succeeded in demolishing the system, the postrevolutionary generation continues to build from the rubble.

## 6.3 Conclusion

The 1979 revolution was a watershed moment in Iranian history, marked by its independence from foreign powers as represented by the shah and the monarchy. As a new beginning, 1979 also marked a key moment in the emergence of Iran as a nation-state, as it coincided with the materialization of national identity formation from below. One of the principal undertakings among oppositional groups was a search for an Iranian identity that reflected the shared ideas and values of the public and diverged from an idea of Iranianness that felt forced upon them by interlopers. As such, identity itself became a point of resistance for Iranians and counternarratives were an important tool in contesting the authority of the shah.

   With the continuity of authoritarianism after the revolution, similar confrontations took place against the resistance narrative of the Islamic Republic, which was usurped from the revolutionary forces. However, in contrast to the shah, the revolution and its identity construction was a local process that involved a large cross-section of Iranian society. When people rose up over the decades to oppose the Islamic Republic, they often advocated for reform within the system. In the decades since the revolution, the Islamic Republic and the Iranian people continued navigating the contours of national identity and its political implications. While the Islamic Republic maintains the discourse of perpetual resistance,[32] it is forced to grapple with the strength of Iranian citizens

---

[32] The Islamic Republic and its officials continue to use the rhetoric of defense and resistance against world powers by highlighting the plight of those outside the Iranian context. On February 21, 2017, when Iran hosted a conference in support of the Palestinian intifada, Ayatollah Khamenei took a moment before his speech on Palestine to recognize the anniversary of what he called the "martyrdom of Malcolm X." This moment underscores the core of Islamic Republic discourse. In one action Khamenei drew attention to the struggle of Palestinians and the plight of Black Americans and Muslim Americans, while alluding to the philosophy of martyrdom. "We Are with Every Group That Is

and their influence in cultural and political shifts. Changes in the Islamic Republic, or what it "allows" as part of its narrative such as the gradual acquiescence of pre-Islamic Iranian cultural motifs, should be understood in the context of the Iranian people's ability to negotiate their own terms and appropriate public spaces for expression. As we have seen, this is evident in popular culture, where Iranians have progressed in how they portray themselves, what stories they tell, and how they tell them.

Such development manifests in various ways and is also visible in public spaces where changing landscapes have more than just aesthetic consequences. After the revolution, city facades were transformed in order to reflect the new identity of the state. Street names, billboards, architecture, and artwork were all curated to promote the Islamic Republic's position. However, like the cautious acknowledgment of Iran's non-Islamic heritage, the Islamic Republic conceded physical changes to the cityscape as well. In the early 2000s, the Municipality of Tehran's Beautification Bureau began projects to rejuvenate the life of the city. One of its lead artists, Mehdi Qadyānlu, painted over 100 murals depicting a variety of themes and concepts from everyday life.[33] Qadyānlu's work breaks from the styles and images of war murals popular in the early decades of the revolution. Other revamping projects, such as the Nature Bridge (see Figure 6.5), were sanctioned by the Islamic Republic and publicized on state run news programs.[34] The implications of these projects go beyond surface renovations; instead they are indicative of the concerted efforts of Iranian citizens to assert their agency. In this sense, transforming public space becomes analogous to transforming public discourse, which has long been exploited by those in power.

Steadfast on the Path of Resistance: Ayatollah Khamenei," Khamenei.ir (February 21, 2017), last accessed March 21, 2022, https://english.khamenei.ir/news/4644/We-are-with-every-group-that-is-steadfast-on-the-path-of-Resistance.
[33] CNN, "Iranian Painter Beautifies Tehran Streets," YouTube video, last accessed March 21, 2022, www.youtube.com/watch?v=G9cN92pVw2I; World Economic Forum, "Public Art: Spaces of Hope – Mehdi Ghadyanloo," YouTube video, last accessed March 21, 2022, www.youtube.com/watch?v=r5drwAsaymE.
[34] Press TV ran several segments focused on beautifying projects. See Press TV, "Tehran's Nature Bridge," Facebook video, last accessed March 21, 2022, https://sw-ke.facebook.com/IranPressTV/videos/nature-bridge/337699250350935.

**Figure 6.5** Photos taken during my fieldwork in September 2015. The bridge connects two parks that are divided by a large freeway. The bridge has multiple levels for walking, some cafes and shops, and provides a view of the city. Thus, its design is intended to connect places as well as people.

Despite the efforts of the Islamic Republic to maintain control over Iran's national identity and narrative, Iranians continue to gravitate toward a version of their own making. Contrary to the notion that nationalism and nation-states are waning, the Iranian case illuminates the continued impact of nation-state formation and historical production. The revolution remains as a moment of rupture, where time for Iranians became framed as "before the revolution" and "after the revolution." It also remains a turning point for the nation-state, as the people proclaimed their independence from foreign powers. As they continue the struggle for freedom, the question of national identity is still relevant. Moving away from an identity centered on Shiite Islam – though religiosity is certainly a fundamental part of the society – Iran becomes self-identifying. More than Islam or monarchy, or Cyrus or Hossein, the idea of Iran is tied to the people, a community that despite political and social differences will quickly rally behind the idea of *vatan*.

This sentiment is unmistakable and can be seen in various settings from politics to sports. In two unrelated interviews from 2018, Iran's first postrevolutionary president, Abolhassan Bani-Sadr, and Iran's national soccer team coach, Carlos Queiroz, both stressed the resilience of Iranians and their love of the nation. In discussing the Iranian team's obstacles leading to the 2018 World Cup, Queiroz stated:

I've never, in all my career, seen players deliver so much after receiving so little as I have with these Iran boys ... We struggle to travel, to have training camps, to bring opponents, to buy equipment. Even buying shirts is a challenge, but these challenges helped me fall in love with Iran. These difficulties become a source of inspiration to the people, it makes them more united, to fight for their country.[35]

In discussing the US withdrawal from the Iran Nuclear Deal in 2018, Bani-Sadr offered some insightful analysis:

However, if the United States were to attempt or support military intervention to change the regime in Iran, it would face a disaster many times worse than that experienced in Iraq and Afghanistan. *Everyone, irrespective of whether they are reformers or hardliners or apolitical, will rise up against a foreign invader.*[36]

The legacy of the revolution resounds with these words, as Iranians refuse to submit to foreigners and, in the face of aggression, earnestly protect their homeland.

Such defiance was exemplified during Muharram commemorations in 2018. Again, denoting Iran's culture of resistance when confronted

---

[35] Andy Mitten, "How Carlos Queiroz Took Iran to the World Cup," *GQ Magazine* (June 13, 2018), last accessed September 18, 2018, www.gq-magazine.co.uk/article/how-carlos-queiroz-took-iran-to-the-world-cup.

[36] Nathan Gardels, "Former Iranian President: Trump Just Strengthened Iran's Hardliners," *The Washington Post* (May 10, 2018), last accessed September 18, 2018,www.washingtonpost.com/amphtml/news/theworldpost/wp/2018/05/10 /iran-nuclear-deal (emphasis added).

with mounting pressure from foreign powers, one Madāhi performer zealously roared,

> *The world has become ready for a World War*
> *The devilish screams of imperialist Jews [Israel]*
> *Come from the throat of a Saudi king*
> *Takfiris, Wahhabis, and Daesh have become collaborators*
> *Under the plan of the great Satan [U.S.]*
> *When we feel the spirit of God in the heart of this land*
> *The enemy can have no peaceful night*
> *Soon Hossein's voice will be heard everywhere …*
> *This is the legacy of Khomeini …*
> *Do not threaten us with war, we are alive*
> *We will answer you with the sword*
> *The word "surrender" has been erased from our belief*[37]

Though the religious nature of Ashura observances is axiomatic, Madāhi performers deliberately connected the narrative of Karbala to the political climate facing Iran vis-à-vis other nation-states.

More recent events in Iran illustrate the same dynamics. After the United States, under the Trump administration, abrogated the Iran nuclear deal and imposed harmful sanctions, Iranians struggled in a devastated economy. Suffering at the hands of their own government's mismanagement and repression, and the cruel political maneuvering of the United States, Iranians expressed their frustrations toward both antagonists. The events of January 2020 exemplify the complexity of Iranian national consciousness and the depth of its political landscape.

After news broke of the US assassination of Iran's top general, Qasem Soleimani, the world held its breath in fear of an impending war. In many ways, Soleimani personified the carefully tailored narrative of the Islamic Republic. A young soldier in the Iran–Iraq War, Soleimani rose through the ranks and spent his entire life defending his country. Despite being a top official of the Iranian Revolutionary Guard Corps (IRGC) – which many Iranians strongly criticize as corrupt and repressive and whose raison d'être is to protect the revolution and the supreme leader – Soleimani, as the commander of the Quds

---

[37] "Madāhi-ye Tufāni Va Siyāsi-ye Hossein Tāheri," *Ākharin Khabar* (September 16, 2018), last accessed September 27, 2018, http://akharinkhabar .ir/interestings/4595026.

Force – which focuses primarily on military operations outside of Iran – was seen as a national guardian. In this role Soleimani consistently maintained great admiration, and was arguably the most popular official in Iran.[38] His veneration was evident in the images of Iranians pouring into the streets to mourn and express their anger at the assassination.[39]

This outpouring was significant to show, yet again, the miscalculations of foreign powers unfamiliar with Iranian history and national culture. At a time when Iranian discontent had reached a boiling point,[40] this act of foreign aggression facilitated a show of support for one of the state's most respected figures. Like Imam Hossein, Soleimani became a martyr for his people, who he had spent a lifetime protecting. Also similar to Hossein, and the philosophy of martyrdom the Islamic Republic had honed in the Iran–Iraq War, Soleimani was victorious in death. To die at the hands of the United States in a cowardly attack while in a car – after the United States had betrayed its promises in the nuclear deal – was the ultimate tale of martyrdom that evoked the story of Karbala and reasserted the image of the United States as Yazid. But the reaction of Iranians went beyond religious tropes because Soleimani was viewed as a national hero. As a figure of national security and defense, the attack on Soleimani was seen by Iranians as akin to an attack on the nation itself.[41]

[38] According to polling in Iran by the University of Maryland, Soleimani consistently remained the most popular figure, but the survey does not offer the Supreme Leader Khamenei as an option. University of Maryland School of Public Policy, "Iranian Public Opinion under 'Maximum Pressure,'" last accessed May 20, 2020, https://cissm.umd.edu/research-impact/publications/iranian-public-opinion-under-maximum-pressure.

[39] Assal Rad, Twitter post, 6 January 2020, 12:38 AM, last accessed May 20, 2020 https://twitter.com/AssalRad/status/1214058732906172417?s=20.

[40] Just two months earlier, in November 2019, protests broke out across the country sparked by a sharp spike in gas prices. Though brutally suppressed by the state, the protests were indicative of growing frustration over economic despair due to Islamic Republic mismanagement and corruption, and US sanctions.

[41] Beyond interviewing people in Iran after the assassination, footage from Iran shows highly nationalistic music and songs accompanying images of Iranians in the streets. Lyrics to these songs include familiar themes of *vatan* and sacrifice: "My life I sacrifice for Iran" and "My homeland I have to call for you, I must stay beside you. You are poetry and passion my homeland." Assal Rad, Twitter post, January 6, 2020, 3:19 AM, last accessed May 20, 2020, https://twitter.com/AssalRad/status/1214099181276545026?s=20.

Only a week after Soleimani's assassination, Iranians rose in protest again, but this time the target was their own government. In retaliation for Soleimani, Iran carried out a missile attack on an American base in Iraq on January 8, 2020. Though the attack avoided American causalities and averted a full-blown war, egregious negligence by Iranian officials allowed commercial flights to continue, leading to the shooting down of a Ukrainian airliner, killing all 176 civilians on board. The government's ineptitude, coupled with an initial attempt to cover-up its mistake, outraged Iranians, who took to the streets demanding accountability for the officials responsible for the tragedy and expressing their broader grievances with the state.

These recent episodes demonstrate what has been a central argument in this study; that despite caricatures to the contrary, Iranians cannot be easily reduced to simple dichotomies. Even the pronouncements of the Iranian government carry more complexity than the hostile rhetoric often associated with the Islamic Republic. On March 20, 2020, in a Nowruz (Iranian New Year) message, President Rouhani wrote a letter for Americans, calling on them to urge their government to ease sanctions during the Coronavirus pandemic. Appealing to their humanity in a time of global crisis, Rouhani's message carefully conveyed the desire of the Iranian populace to be part of the international community. However, the message also emphasized Iranian national pride and its resistance to foreign aggression: "We are a glorious and proud people with millennia of civilization. We react to the language of force with the language of resistance and to the language of dignity with the language of respect."[42]

The idea that Iranians would defend a nation with a government they are deeply dissatisfied with may appear counterintuitive, however, as this study has contended, Iranian nationalism has many layers to unravel. Beneath the state lies the nation itself, the cherished *vatan*. The Iranian nation and its people continue to be a mystery to many in the world, as one WikiLeaks cable from crown prince bin Zayed of Abu Dhabi shows: "Any culture that is patient and focused enough to spend years working on a single carpet is capable of waiting years and even

---

[42] "President in a Message Addressing the American People," Website of President of Iran (March 20, 2020), last accessed May 28, 2020, http://president.ir/en/114343.

decades to achieve even greater goals." His greatest worry, he said, "is not how much we know about Iran, but how much we don't."[43]

To understand Iran, we must relinquish the outdated binary of tradition versus modernity, or the crude outlook that an Iranian is either for or against the state, which lacks informed nuance. A more comprehensive understanding requires a deeper look at the nation-building project in Iran over the last 100 years. It is important to acknowledge the lasting impact of creating nations and nationalisms. Though imagined or constructed, the fraternity of nationalism binds people together in very real ways.

Looking at the word "patriot," Hobsbawm claimed its original implication was of people who showed devotion to their country by wanting to renew it through reform or revolution.[44] Thus, the Iranian patriots of the twentieth century struggled against an imposed nationalism to find their own voices in a revolutionary movement, which deposed the antiquated institution of monarchy and the monarch linked to foreign powers, and established the modern nation of Iran. Despite the hopes of the revolution, Iranians continued to face obstacles and showed devotion to their country with their unrelenting demand to see its promises of freedom and democracy fulfilled.

---

[43] David E. Sanger, James Glanz and Jo Becker, "Around the World, Distress Over Iran," *The New York Times* (November 28, 2010), last accessed September 18, 2018, www.nytimes.com/2010/11/29/world/middleeast/29iran.html.

[44] Eric J. Hobsbawm, *Nations and Nationalism Since 1780: Programme, Myth, Reality* (Cambridge: Cambridge University Press, 1992), 87.

# 7 | *Epilogue*

One of the central ideas posited in this study is the need to look beyond the political discourse of both the United States and Iran if one is to understand a complex nation of over 80 million people. By examining Iranian national identity formation from both the top-down and the bottom-up, we start to piece together the varying threads that, weaved together, make up the rich tapestry of Iranian identity. While this study explored the construction of national identity in Iran at the hands of the Pahlavi monarchy and the Islamic Republic – both of which curated the idea of "Iranianness" to their own tastes as they silenced competing histories – and how these narratives were negotiated by Iranian people, the ultimate objective of this project is to add to our understanding of contemporary Iran.

As we have witnessed the shifts of US policy on Iran from President Obama to President Trump and President Biden, an understanding of the Iranian side of the debate in Washington is crucial to implementing cogent policies. Current discussions on Iran policy range from the merits of the JCPOA – also called the Iran Nuclear Deal – and Iran's behavior in the Middle East, to hawks calling for regime change and the looming possibility of war. Often neglected in these deliberations is the country in question and the views of its 80+ million people. Ironically, it is this very same dismissal by Western powers and capitulations at their hands that has colored the history of Iran and the opinions of many of its citizens. A consideration of this history and how Iranians forged an identity of resistance to protect themselves – not only from the abuses of their authoritarian rulers, but also the trespasses of foreign forces – is imperative to executing a strategy that is advantageous for the United States, Iran, and the global community.

History teaches us how we have come to where we are today. In that respect, this book has tried to explain how the Iranian psyche has developed into this contemporary moment. Such insights can facilitate a clearer picture of the challenges the United States faces – or may yet face – in a conflict with Iran, or serve to facilitate a more peaceful path in how the United States approaches diplomacy with Iran. This deeper knowledge then, can assist in how we interpret the often-dynamic actions of Iran. As such, the intention of this project is to fill a gap between academia and the policy world of Washington, while offering a look into contemporary Iran for a broad American audience.

The epilogue serves that purpose by looking at more recent events that have evoked nationalist sentiments and responses among Iranians. These events include the landmark Iran Nuclear Deal of 2015, Iran's 2017 presidential election, the US withdrawal from the nuclear deal in 2018, and others. I have used Twitter accounts as my archive – the social media platform provides an opportunity to focus on female voices. Though Iranian women have always been part of the story, played an active role in the revolution, and continue to be agents of resistance and change in Iran, the Internet created a new space for public expression that Iranian women were quick to capitalize on. The accounts surveyed here are all Iranian women inside Iran, with active accounts, and a range of followers and political views. From activists such as Bahareh Hedayat to journalists like Saba Azarpeik,[1] these women provide a deeper look at how Iranians view and interpret the events unfolding around them in different ways.

## 7.1 New Ways to Communicate: The Internet Revolution

While the promise of the Internet as a tool to set the world free may have been overly ambitious, the new technology was indeed revolutionary for connecting people across the world like never before and providing the masses with unprecedented access to information. In an authoritarian state like Iran, where the state acts precisely to limit such access and puts restrictions on people's freedoms in public spaces, the Internet offered a digital public space that gave many Iranians, especially women, a needed outlet to express themselves.

---

[1] Both Hedayat and Azarpeik have been targeted by Iranian security forces, facing arrests and imprisonment, Hedayat for her work as a student activist and Azarpeik for her work as a journalist exposing government corruption. Not all the subjects chosen have suffered in the same manner, but they have been chosen for their use of social media platforms to express their wide-ranging views on events significant to Iranian society and politics.

One of the first uses of this new space that Iranians gravitated toward was blogging. A blog is essentially a personal website where individuals could write, share, interact with others, and construct their online identities. In the early 2000s, an Iranian-Canadian immigrant by the name of Hossein Derakhshan[2] – who had written about the Internet in a column for a reformist newspaper as a journalist in Iran – began his own Persian-language blog, which quickly grew to popularity. Seeing the potential of blogs for the political scene in Iran, Derakhshan wrote instructions in Persian on how to create a blog.

As Derakhshan himself explains, blogging became very popular at a rapid pace in Iran to meet the high demand for a platform for free expression. By 2005, there were hundreds of thousands of Persian-language blogs in what came to be known as "Weblogistan" or the Iranian blogosphere.[3] This explosion of Iranian blogging was important for providing an inside look and wealth of information on Iranian society and politics. However, it is noteworthy that blogging and the internet did not simply create activism where none existed, but rather, these were new tools to *continue* the activism, resistance, and identity formation and expression that Iranians, including Iranian women, had long shown in others spaces. Iranian women were agents of change in the 1979 revolution, essential to aiding Iran's war efforts in the 1980s against Iraq, and creators and consumers of culture long before the advent of the Internet or blogging.

As scholars like Sima Shakhsari and Niki Akhavan have aptly observed, Weblogistan reflected the same activism, debates, contesting ideas of Iranianness, and inequities that were happening offline. In their study of Weblogistan, Shakhsari argues:

It is important to remember that the exchange of ideas (what has been referred to as "practicing democracy") in Weblogistan was actually enabled by a history of struggle that preceded the "internet revolution" in Iran. Indeed, the much tweeted and subsequently televised 2009 election was not the first time that the student movement, the women's movement, and other social movements in Iran had demanded social freedoms.[4]

---

[2] The information I provide about Hossein Derakhshan comes directly from an interview I conducted with him on May 7, 2021. Derakhshan was integral to the proliferation and popularity of Iranian blogging.

[3] Sima Shakhsari, *Politics of Rightful Killing: Civil Society, Gender, and Sexuality in Weblogistan* (Durham: Duke University Press, 2020).

[4] Ibid., 75.

The work of Shakhsari and Akhavan are also crucial for challenging the mainstream Western narratives of Iranian blogging that tended to exclude the voices of Iranian women that did not validate their narrative of a secular, woman-led political opposition in Iran prepared for regime change.

In reality, the same plurality and nuance that can be seen in other mediums within popular culture are reproduced in the digital space as well. As my own study has illustrated, Iranian identity and society is far more complex than what can fit into neat dichotomies or easy categories. Not only is there diversity across the spectrum of Iranian society, individuals exhibit fluidity in their own views. Like any other peoples, Iranians are not static or monolithic, their ideas on contemporary Iranian society cannot be reduced to being "pro" or "anti-regime."

As Akhavan explains,[5] not only do dominant narratives of Iranian-women bloggers tend to ignore women with religious inclinations, but they also overlook the fact that critical stances of the state are found in both opponents and supporters of the government, and that even some who are critical of the state participate in activities like elections. These findings fly in the face of simple dichotomies. Moreover, most mainstream narratives of Iranian-female bloggers focus on politically oriented blogs, while a significant portion of Persian-language blogs are apolitical. A 2016 study of Persian blogs found that software and technology, religious and Persian poetry, sports, and arts were also popular blog topics.[6]

While content on Iranian politics and society is also quite popular and abundant, it is important to look at the breadth of these discussions to get a fuller understanding of the complicated and ever-changing picture of Iranian society. It should be noted that it is not only Iranian people and society at large that display such complexity. As Narges Bajoghli's groundbreaking study of Iran's Islamic Revolutionary Guard Corps (IRGC) reveals, even a center of state power that is often portrayed in mainstream Western media and politics as monolithic has its own ideological and generational divisions.[7] Apart from the fact that the "pro"

[5] Niki Akhavan, "Exclusionary Cartographies: Gender Liberation and the Iranian Blogosphere," in Roksana Bahramitash and Eric Hooglund, eds., *Gender in Contemporary Iran: Pushing the Boundaries* (Abingdon: Routledge, 2011), 78.
[6] Abolfazl Al-e Ahmad, "irBlogs: A Standard Collection for Studying Persian Bloggers," *Computers in Human Behavior* 57 (2016), 195–207.
[7] Narges Bajoghli, *Iran Reframed: Anxieties of Power in the Islamic Republic* (Redwood City: Stanford University Press, 2020).

and "anti-regime" binary is unfounded and misleading, Bajoghli's work complicates the very notion of what it means to be "pro-regime."

Even the individual Iranian is not fixed in their views, which can fluctuate and change over time and context. The case of Hossein Derakhshan is a fascinating example of the spectrum of Iranian views in one individual. Though he was raised in a religious household, young Derakhshan exhibited condemnatory views of religion, was a staunch critic of the Iranian government, rejected the reform movement in Iran, and immigrated to Canada in 2001. However, his time as an Iranian immigrant living abroad gave him a fresh perspective. Especially in the wake of 9/11 and the invasion of Iraq, Derakhshan's position quickly changed to recognize the hypocrisies and inequalities that existed in Western nations.

After extensive study, Derakhshan's refined understanding of geopolitics and Iran's modern history led him to draw different conclusions about the 1979 revolution, the continued impact of colonialism and foreign force, and the state of Iranian political discourse. After returning to Iran in 2008, Derakhshan was arrested and served six years in Evin prison. Eventually Derakhshan left Iran again to continue his studies abroad. Despite these experiences, Derakhshan can neither be described as "pro-regime" or "anti-regime"; such a crude view of Iranians contradicts the very real complexities of Iranian society.

To further our understanding, I turn now to an examination of social media reactions to a set of specific events in recent years. These incidents often elicited national sentiments in Iran, and observations about Iranian society and politics within domestic and international contexts. Like blogs, social media is another tool that creates a sense of community – whether "real" or "imagined" – in which people who will never meet in person can meet online to be part of the same discussion. As researchers Laura Gurak and Smiljana Antonijevic explain, the nature of Internet communications like blogs and social media "as simultaneously private and public enables the formation of both individual and group identities."[8] Thus, observing how these Iranian women reacted to such events online can provide another view of their relationship and understanding of their individual and collective Iranian identity.[9]

[8]  Laura J. Gurak and Smiljana Antonijevic, "The Psychology of Blogging: You, Me, and Everyone in Between," *American Behavioral Scientist* 52, no. 1 (2008), 60–68.
[9]  As noted earlier, the list of women is far from comprehensive. These women were selected for having active and engaging twitter accounts, consistent commentary

## 7.2 History Made: The 2015 Iran Nuclear Deal

After nearly four decades of enmity and hostile rhetoric on both sides, the United States and Iran – along with members of the international community – engaged in negotiations and reached a mutually advantageous agreement on July 14, 2015. While on paper the Iran Nuclear Deal – officially called the Joint Comprehensive Plan of Action or JCPOA – was a model for global nonproliferation efforts and promised economic relief from sanctions for Iran, the historical weight of this moment ran much deeper for many Iranians. Images of thousands of Iranians pouring into the streets to celebrate the deal[10] were broadcast in the United States and by international news agencies. The celebrations were accompanied by a hero's welcome for Iran's foreign minister, Javad Zarif, who was a central figure in the success of the JCPOA.

The joy and relief many Iranians felt at the time went beyond sanctions relief. After decades of isolation on the global stage, détente with the United States was seen as a diplomatic and historic breakthrough, one that was tied to the efforts of Iranian people and their decades-long struggle to resist the imposed narratives of their rulers, which in the case of the Islamic Republic had carried an anti-US bent. One Twitter user, Amene Shirafkan, described the scenes of merriment stating, "There are people in the middle of Vanak Square celebrating and chanting 'Ya Hossein, Mir Hossein.'"[11] With this chant, which refers to reformist presidential candidate Mir Hossein Mousavi, we see again the links between Rouhani's election, the Green Movement, and a desire of millions of Iranians to reform their country into a more open society that is connected to the international community. Another Twitter user, Shokoofeh Habibzadeh, echoed the hopeful sentiments this historic moment had inspired with a picture of a sea of white balloons rising to the sky and caption "This

---

on important events affecting Iranian politics and society, and a range of backgrounds. This section is meant to add to the whole of the study, provide more female voices, and another source base for examining contemporary Iranian society and identity.

10  Saeed Kamali Dehghan, "Thousands Take to Iran Streets to Celebrate the Historic Nuclear Deal," *The Guardian* (July 14, 2015), last accessed June 8, 2021, www.theguardian.com/world/2015/jul/14/joy-in-tehran-at-end-to-isolation-but-hardliner-reaction-to-nuclear-deal-feared.

11  Amene Shirafkan, Twitter post (July 14, 2015, 1:00 PM EST), last accessed June 8, 2021, https://twitter.com/shirafkan82/status/621001247731154944?s=20.

picture is being shared on virtual platforms with the hope of peace and reconciliation."[12]

For some commentators, the deal's appeal to peaceful resolution and Iran's newfound ability to partake more in the world economy was seen as a positive opening for the Iranian nation. As this study has shown in other contexts, nostalgia for the past and the idea that Iran's current state of affairs is a far cry from its historic greatness is a common motif in the Iranian conceptualization of their identity. As Iranian blogger and journalist Zahra Keshvari put it:

The last paragraph of the Guardian editorial sounds as if we wrote it: After almost four decades, this agreement, which has come a long way, has given rise to the hope that *one of the world's greatest civilizations* will have countless benefits – not just for Iranians, but also for its neighbors, who are being destroyed by conflict and tension. Get out of isolation. This opportunity must be appreciated.[13]

Still others looked at the more practical outcomes of the deal that would benefit the Iranian people at large. Journalists Zeinab Esmaeili[14] and Emily Amraee[15] both commented on the opportunity the deal presented for Iran to purchase new commercial aircrafts and help flight safety after years of sanctions had prevented Iran from improving its commercial airplanes.

Despite the overwhelming support for the deal and an atmosphere of renewed hope,[16] there were still apprehensive voices that scrutinized

---

[12]   Shokoofeh Habibzadeh, Twitter post (July 15, 2015, 5:20 PM EST), last accessed June 8, 2021, https://twitter.com/shokoohabibzade/status/62142923 6532969472?s=20.

[13]   Zahra Keshvari, Twitter post (July 15, 2015, 3:10 AM EST), last accessed June 8, 2021, https://twitter.com/zahrakeshvari/status/621215140374020096?s=20 (emphasis added).

[14]   Zeinab Esmaeili, Twitter post (July 14, 2015, 4:42 AM EST), last accessed June 8, 2021, https://twitter.com/z_siver/status/620876058078937088?s=20.

[15]   Emily Amraee, Twitter post (July 15, 2015, 12:57 PM EST), last accessed June 8, 2021, https://twitter.com/EmilyAmraee/status/621362856869687296?s=20.

[16]   During my field research in summer 2015, after the nuclear deal had been reached, there was a palpable energy of positivity and hope. This feeling was articulated by many of the Iranian interlocutors I engaged with in the course of my research. These findings are corroborated by the reporting on Iranians celebrating the deal and polling done by the University of Maryland on Iranian opinions on the deal. University of Maryland School of Public Policy, *Iranian Public Opinion on the Nuclear Agreement: A Public Opinion Study* (September 2015), last accessed June 8, 2021, https://cissm.umd.edu/sites/default/files/201

Iran's position and the accountability of other parties to the deal to ensure that Iran was not capitulating to foreign powers. Like nostalgia for past glory, resisting foreign powers and maintaining Iran's independence are common threads in the Iranian national psyche. While writer and lawyer Sharareh Dehshiri quipped[17] about the contradicting narratives of Iran's hardliners – who claimed the JCPOA as a victory in Arabic-language outlets and simultaneously criticized it in Persian-language papers – others raised serious questions surrounding the deal.

Well before the election of Donald Trump in the United States and his decision to abrogate the Iran Nuclear Deal in 2018, seasoned journalist Fereshteh Sadeghi presciently asked in July 2015, "If Iran fails to implement the deal sanctions will be snapped back. How if the US, EU fail to keep their word?"[18] Not only was Sadeghi questioning the imbalance in accountability, but she also hit on a key theme of the Islamic Republic's discourse that has long argued the United States and the West could not be trusted. In another tweet, Sadeghi acknowledged the popular support for the deal among Iranians with the caveat that the deal be respectable and "within Iran's red lines."[19]

Although the deal had mass support among Iranians, the examples here show that the reasons varied for different people, as well as the levels of enthusiasm. But whether in favor or skeptical, the reactions to the deal were often understood within the context of the Iranian nation and how its people could benefit from an agreement they themselves helped bring to pass through their agency at the ballot. The motivation to take action on behalf of their nation and future was tested again by the 2016 election of Donald Trump – a staunch critic of the deal – as the forty-fifth US president.

## 7.3 The Era of Trump: Iran's 2017 Presidential Election

In May 2017, Iranians went to the polls again to elect their president. In answer to the election of Trump in the United States, Iranians turned

9-07/CISSM-PA%20Iranian%20Public%20Opinion%20on%20the%20Nuclear%20Agreement%2020090915%20FINAL-LR.pdf.

[17] Sharare Mishavam, Twitter post (July 15, 2015, 10:14 AM EST), last accessed June 8, 2021, https://twitter.com/SharareMishavam/status/621322046161747969?s=20.

[18] Fereshteh Sadeghi, Twitter post (July 14, 2015 7:09 PM EST), last accessed June 8, 2021, https://twitter.com/fresh_sadegh/status/620913059243130880?s=20.

[19] Fereshteh Sadeghi, Twitter post (July 11, 2015 12:06 PM EST), last accessed June 8, 2021, https://twitter.com/fresh_sadegh/status/619900513493106688?s=20.

out in mass to re-elect President Rouhani and reaffirm their commitment to diplomacy, the JCPOA, and détente with America. But beyond the immediate goal of maintaining the nuclear deal, the way many Iranians framed their participation in the election revealed broader objectives of reform and change, as well as feelings about serving the nation.

Several of the women examined here connected the re-election of Rouhani again to the Green Movement. Emily Amraee recounted a story from the collective devastation over the 2009 election and the renewed hope felt in 2017:

Eight years ago on a Saturday morning, [on the day after the 2009 election] on a day like this, I passed Haft-e Tir Square and came face to face with a random pedestrian, we both shed tears and hugged each other. I wish I could find her and embrace her tomorrow [Saturday morning after the 2017 election].[20]

The simple act of Mir Hossein Mousavi and his wife, Zahra Rahnavard, voting was considered important to highlight and reported by journalist Zeinab Safari.[21] However, journalist and activist Saba Azarpeik went a step further by sharing a screenshot (see Figure 7.1) of the Instagram account of Mousavi's daughter Zahra, which showed a political cartoon of caged birds casting their votes, while a free bird outside the cage raised their head and closed their eyes announcing they would not vote. A powerful image meant to juxtapose Mousavi and his wife voting from under house arrest with Iranians who planned to boycott the election, it was accompanied with Azapeik's own text that stated, "Share this wide, until it reaches our boycott friends."[22]

Thus, a figure such as Azarpeik, who had made a career investigating state corruption and found herself targeted by Iranian security forces, could be critical of the state while also participating in Iran's elections in order to bring about change. This desire for reform predates the Green Movement in Iran, as one Twitter user, Farzaneh Ebrahimzadeh, illustrated in her post recounting Iran's first reformist president,

[20]  Emily Amraee, Twitter post (May 19, 2017 5:02 PM EST), last accessed June 9, 2021, https://twitter.com/EmilyAmraee/status/865674090870439936?s=20.
[21]  Safari Zeinab, Twitter post (May 19, 2017 3:29 PM EST), last accessed June 9, 2021, https://twitter.com/SafariZeinab/status/865650555686748160?s=20.
[22]  Saba Azarpeik, Twitter post (May 18, 2017 5:08 PM EST), last accessed June 9, 2021, https://twitter.com/sabaazarpeik/status/865313070427414528?s=20.

**Figure 7.1** 2017 election cartoon. Screenshot shared by Saba Azarpeik of Zahra Mousavi's post.

Mohammad Khatami: "Twenty years ago, on May 23rd 1997, I passed under the same sign [polling place] and with fear and hope, I voted for Khatami and I never regretted it. #IranElections2017."[23] The idea of reforming the state has been a decades-long effort on the part of Iranian people, and one of the avenues to do so has been to participate in elections.

For others, partaking in elections was about being involved in civic engagement and addressing domestic issues such as gender equality. As one blogger by the name of Marzieh noted, "There is a lot of determination and passion among the community groups active in the election, hopefully after the election we won't stop and we will continue the work of civil society."[24] The passion in the election that Marzieh points

[23] Farzaneh Ebrahimzadeh, Twitter post (May 19, 2017 4:44 AM EST), last accessed June 9, 2021, https://twitter.com/febrahimzade/status/865488925271 367681?s=20.

[24] Marzieh, Twitter post (May 20, 2017 5:31 AM EST), last accessed June 9, 2021, https://twitter.com/marzie_r/status/865862453342556160?s=20.

to was seen in the boisterous festivities that ensued after Rouhani was re-elected. Echoing the scenes from the 2015 Iran Nuclear Deal announcement, Iranians took to the streets again in hopeful celebrations that were so striking, even a more skeptical voice like Fereshteh Sadeghi noted their significance: "Someone studying Social Science should write a dissertation on why *the nation* is dancing and singing in the streets."[25]

In fact, the idea of the nation and Iranians participating for the country and its people was a common thread. Amene Shirafkan shared a picture of her and two friends holding up their inked finger as a sign they had just voted, with a caption that simply read, "For Iran."[26] A blogger and translator, by the name of Shahrzad reiterated the same sentiment with a picture of the Iranian flag and accompanying text that said, "Don't get tired of standing in line, we must stand up for the right to vote, for Iran."[27] In another tweet, Shahrzad shared a picture of an older Iranian man walking up to a polling station with his cane and wrote, "An older gentleman came by himself, for Iran."[28] Emily Amraee went as far as equating caring about Iran with the act of voting by stating, "Iran was important to 39,500,000 people,"[29] in reference to those who voted.

After Rouhani's victory had become clear, many of these women congratulated the nation and its people more so than Rouhani and his administration. Film critic Faranak Arta tweeted, "Nation and people of Iran, kudos to you,"[30] while journalist Marjan Laghaee stated firmly, "The credit does not belong to Rouhani, the credit belongs to the [Iranian] people."[31] Saba Azarpeik summed up much of the shared

25  Fereshteh Sadeghi, Twitter post (May 21, 2017 5:11 PM EST), last accessed June 9, 2021, https://twitter.com/fresh_sadegh/status/866400974256164864? s=20 (emphasis added).

26  Amene Shirafkan, Twitter post (May 19, 2017, 2:16 PM EST), last accessed June 9, 2021, https://twitter.com/shirafkan82/status/865632351270748161? s=20.

27  Shahrzad, Twitter post (May 19, 2017, 12:02 PM EST), last accessed June 9, 2021, https://twitter.com/Shahr2ad/status/865598434711130113?s=20.

28  Shahrzad, Twitter post (May 19, 2017, 5:05 AM EST), last accessed June 9, 2021, https://twitter.com/Shahr2ad/status/865504878046584832?s=20.

29  Emily Amraee, Twitter post (May 19, 2017, 3:53 PM EST), last accessed June 9, 2021, https://twitter.com/EmilyAmraee/status/865656694621319168?s=20.

30  Faranak Arta, Twitter post (May 19, 2017, 10:14 PM EST), last accessed June 9, 2021, https://twitter.com/FaranakArta/status/865752653233631234?s=20.

31  Marjan Laghaee, Twitter post (May 20, 2017, 6:59 AM EST), last accessed June 9, 2021, https://twitter.com/MarjanLaghaee/status/865884744684318721? s=20.

feelings of success and hope in a tweet that said, "The results will be announced, but we share our happiness with all the people of Iran ... happiness belongs to everyone tomorrow [when the results would be officially announced]."[32] As such, the victory did not belong to those who voted, but to the whole of the nation.

That many Iranians understood these events as a collective struggle for the betterment of their homeland and society at large should come as no surprise. The election of a US president who had set his sights on Iran as an enemy both in his rhetoric and actions – for example, the Muslim ban, which predominantly affected Iranians – was the perfect backdrop to galvanize Iranians to defend the nation. In this case, they did so by voting for a candidate who represented everything Trump disavowed, the very diplomatic breakthrough that promised to open up the world to Iran and the Iranian people.

## 7.4 #PersianGulfForever

Less than five months after Rouhani's re-election, President Trump took his first steps to dismantle the JCPOA and in the process insulted Iranian national pride by calling the Persian Gulf the "Arabian Gulf" and setting off an Iranian backlash. On October 13, 2017, President Trump delivered remarks from the White House to say he would not be certifying the nuclear deal, painted Iran as a threatening menace, evoked the 1979 hostage crisis, and set the United States on a course of heightened tensions and hostilities with Iran, despite the historic détente achieved by his predecessor. While many Iranians were appalled by his general aggressive language and his decision not to certify the deal – which did not withdraw the United States from the deal, but gave Congress greater power over it – one part of his statement stood out, "[Iran] harasses American ships and threatens freedom of navigation in the *Arabian Gulf*."[33]

Reviving the nationalist responses that we saw earlier when the Persian Gulf was referred to as the *Arabian* Gulf, in the context of Trump's speech, the deal, and rhetoric against Iran, this choice of

---

[32] Saba Azarpeik, Twitter post (May 20, 2017, 7:20 AM EST), last accessed June 9, 2021, https://twitter.com/sabaazarpeik/status/865708831124443136?s=20.

[33] The White House, "President Trump Delivers Remarks on the Iran Strategy," YouTube video, last accessed June 10, 2021, www.youtube.com/watch?v=1X Q-TrAh-XQ (emphasis added).

words was seen as an intentional slight by many Iranians. Their reaction to this particular incident follows several patterns in the Iranian national psyche, which recall the fears of land loss, pride over the homeland, historical significance, and resistance to foreign force. Indeed, the reactions to Trump's speech illustrated these same themes and elicited displays of national pride.

In order to highlight the authenticity of the name "Persian Gulf," in a tweet Farzaneh Ebrahimzadeh utilized a 1,000-year-old historical text by Ebrahim Estakhri.[34] The accompanying historical map was proof enough of the name "Persian Gulf," which Ebrahimzadeh used as a hashtag. For many Iranians, history is itself a source of pride as Iran's vast saga and various empires reflect a kind of internalized value attached to Iranian national identity. Ebrahimzadeh also demonstrated themes of homeland and external confrontation in another tweet, in which she stated, "Traitors of the homeland that receive funds straight from Arab unions and Israeli allies, stay silent in the face of Trump's significant insult #PersianGulf."[35]

Other commentators echoed Ebrahimzadeh's reaction, such as Faranak Arta, who tweeted that Saudi Arabia had "bought" the United States,[36] Shahrzad, who lambasted Trump's lack of basic knowledge and geography,[37] and Saba Azarpeik, who challenged Trump's discourse on Iran directly by tweeting, "Trump: We stand with the Iranian people. No, my dear, you are standing by sanctions profiteers and war hawks #NeverTrustUSA."[38] Like Ebrahimzadeh, who deployed Iran's bygone record, Fereshteh Sadeghi posted an image of a picturesque and historic Iranian building with the caption, "Great

---

[34] Farzaneh Ebrahimzadeh, Twitter post (October 13, 2017, 3:26 PM EST), last accessed June 10, 2021, https://twitter.com/febrahimzade/status/91892086880 5431296?s=20.

[35] Farzaneh Ebrahimzadeh, Twitter post (October 13, 2017, 1:08 PM EST), last accessed June 10, 2021, https://twitter.com/febrahimzade/status/91888605171 5919874?s=20.

[36] Faranak Arta, Twitter post (October 13, 2017, 5:47 PM EST), last accessed June 10, 2021, https://twitter.com/FaranakArta/status/918956492807688193?s=20.

[37] Shahrzad, Twitter post (October 13, 2017, 1:28 PM EST), last accessed June 10, 2021, https://twitter.com/Shahr2ad/status/918891312996331526?s=20.

[38] Saba Azarpeik, Twitter post (October 13, 2017, 1:29 PM EST), last accessed June 10, 2021, https://twitter.com/sabaazarpeik/status/918891429975408640?s=20.

work of art and design created by forefathers of this 'terrorist' nation. #Iran #Trump #History."[39]

In defense of the nation, Sadeghi's comment went beyond the backlash over the Persian Gulf and addressed Trump's broader anti-Iran rhetoric, which had long been a staple of US foreign policy culture. Decertifying the deal and Trump's Persian Gulf insult were only the precursors of what was to come. As Marzieh acutely observed at the time, "The frustrating part of the story is that Trump is only in his first year. I wish we could leap forward and he would melt with the first snow."[40] The US position vis-à-vis Iran changed dramatically over the course of Trump's presidency, going from a fragile rapprochement to the brink of war. While his decision to officially withdraw from the deal in 2018 set those events in motion, Iranian reactions to Trump's withdrawal were more complex than a simple rebuke of Trump.

## 7.5 Trump Quits the Iran Deal

On May 8, 2018, President Trump officially announced the US withdrawal from the landmark Iran Nuclear Deal. Trump started his statement[41] by suggesting his efforts were intended to prevent Iran from acquiring a nuclear weapon. The irony, of course, was not lost on commentators and Iranians themselves who understood the deal for accomplishing that exact objective. While Trump's hyperbolic remarks painted Iran as a global menace and a threat to the United States, his belligerent language and talk of maximum economic sanctions appeared to make the United States the bullying party.

However, following a direct threat to the Iranian state, Trump appealed to the Iranian people as a friend: "If the regime continues its nuclear aspirations, it will have bigger problems than it has ever had before. Finally, I want to deliver a message to the long-suffering people

---

[39]  Fereshteh Sadeghi, Twitter post (October 14, 2017, 8:47 PM EST), last accessed June 10, 2021, https://twitter.com/fresh_sadegh/status/919182962511568896? s=20.
[40]  Marzieh, Twitter post (October 13, 2017, 3:51 PM EST), last accessed June 10, 2021, https://twitter.com/marzie_r/status/918927080926085125?s=20.
[41]  CBC News, "Trump Pulls Out of Iran Nuclear Deal Full Speech," YouTube video, last accessed June 12, 2021, www.youtube.com/watch?v=Rap1oAvQpy8.

of Iran. The people of America stand with you." That Trump withdrew
from a deal that had widespread popular support among Iranians,
insulted their national integrity with foreign force, and threatened
them with economic devastation while claiming to support them, was
not lost on Iranian people. Shokoofeh Habibzadeh captured the sentiment of many Iranians when she tweeted, "To Trump and his allies:
The Iranian people do not need the pity of the world-devouring
powers."[42]

Iranian Twitter users circulated a hashtag that read "#untrUStable"
to censure the United States and indicate that the Trump administration's decision to rescind America's participation in the nuclear deal
was a betrayal of their word. Journalist Mahsa Jazini lamented the
continuous injustice inflicted upon the nation of Iran: "History owes no
nation more 'ifs' than Iran. If there was a Republican besides Trump. If
the Democrats had won instead of the Republicans. If it was Clinton
instead of Trump. If, if, if . . . #untrUStable."[43] It is noteworthy that the
idea that the United States could not be trusted has been a primary
argument of Iranian hardliners, especially those who were against any
deal with the United States. Yet, Iranians who were angry at Trump for
quitting the deal shared their outrage against all the parties that were
opposed to the deal, including Iranian hardliners, other foreign powers,
and even the Iranian diaspora opposition.

Addressing Iranian hardliners who had opposed the deal, but criticized Trump for leaving the JCPOA, Farzaneh Ebrahimzadeh lumped
these different groups together and tweeted, "If the Iran deal was bad,
why are you angry that the U.S. quit, when you were happy. Like
Netanyahu, MEK, Rajavi, you destroyed the deal. Like Saudi Arabia
and UAE, you celebrate the sanctions against your people."[44] While
Shahrzad mocked[45] another key oppositional diaspora figure, Reza
Pahlavi, for using Trump's withdrawal as an opportunity to advocate

---

[42] Shokoofeh Habibzadeh, Twitter post (May 8, 2018, 2:37 PM EST), last
accessed June 12, 2021, https://twitter.com/shokoohabibzade/status/9939228
09377296388?s=20.

[43] Jazini Mahsa, Twitter post (May 8, 2018, 2:40 PM EST), last accessed June 12,
2021, https://twitter.com/JaziniMahsa/status/993923508521586688?s=20.

[44] Farzaneh Ebrahimzadeh, Twitter post (May 9, 2018, 5:17 AM EST), last
accessed June 12, 2021, https://twitter.com/febrahimzade/status/99412932437
7825286?s=20.

[45] Shahrzad, Twitter post (May 9, 2018, 3:43 AM EST), last accessed June 12,
2021, https://twitter.com/Shahr2ad/status/994120635856060416?s=20.

regime change, Zahra Keshvari reiterated the place of Iranian hard-liners along with foreign powers by tweeting, "Now should we con-gratulate Iranian hardliners, Israel, Saudi Arabia, and America all together? #untr_US_table."[46]

Though President Trump and the United States were significant targets of backlash among Iranians, their resentment ran deeper to include anyone who had undermined the deal and as a result betrayed the will of the Iranian people, their livelihoods, and their right to independence and peace. Saba Azarpeik encapsulated the various strands of Iranian senti-ment in her tweet:

We support Zarif and Rouhani's peace and diplomacy. We were not advo-cates of war, and we were not and are not allies of hardliners that opposed the JCPOA. *We are the people of Iran's streets and bazaars*, and we have the right to a peaceful life, without tension and war, and the right to independ-ence without surrendering to force.[47]

Thus, support for the deal and what it promised to Iranian people became akin to support for those very people and the well-being of the nation. In just a couple sentences, Azarpeik distanced herself from Iranian hardliners, defended the Iranian people, and resisted foreign powers who – in her view – seek Iran's surrender. In another tweet, Azarpeik shared a picture of the Iranian flag and illustrated the themes of resistance in Iranian national identity, with the need to defend the nation and its people from all aggres-sors, both foreign and domestic:

Tonight, it was proven, patriotism is not a face you can wear, it is rooted in a belief. Moments like tonight, when some cheer Trump and welcome sanctions, but for others, *their heart beats for the hardship of their coun-trymen and the suffering of their nation*. The time has come to take this flag from the hardliners, and give it to its real owners [Iranian people] #untrUStable.[48]

---

[46] Zahra Keshvari, Twitter post (May 8, 2018, 12:29 PM EST), last accessed June 12, 2021, https://twitter.com/zahrakeshvari/status/993890662385901568?s=20.

[47] Saba Azarpeik, Twitter post (May 8, 2018, 12:44 PM EST), last accessed June 12, 2021, https://twitter.com/sabaazarpeik/status/993894299266945025?s=20 (emphasis added).

[48] Saba Azarpeik, Twitter post (May 8, 2018, 5:09 PM EST), last accessed June 12, 2021, https://twitter.com/sabaazarpeik/status/993961169814720512?s=20 (emphasis added).

Finding themselves in a distressing situation, these Iranians still displayed an urge to protect the nation, and articulated their sense of betrayal in national, rather than personal terms. This is because, for many Iranians, the national is personal. People who participated in Iranian elections, despite its democratic limitations, did so for the nation. Those very same people can be critical of the Iranian state, denounce the critics of that state, and defend the state they condemn against foreign intimidation all at the same time. A thread that runs through all these outlooks is a sense of resistance, one rooted in Iranian history and culture, as we have seen. While the Islamic Republic wielded and exploited that culture of resistance for its own use, Iranians before and after the revolution resisted their own authoritarian states as well.

## 7.6 November 2019 Protests

As the Trump administration's "maximum pressure" policy on Iran began to take effect and the weight of sanctions hit Iran's economy, not only did it hurt millions of ordinary Iranians who now faced hyperinflation, devaluation of their currency and buying power, and a scarcity of goods, it also impacted government subsidies and fuel prices at home. On November 15, 2019, the Rouhani administration announced a sudden hike in gas prices – up to 300 percent – as well as a new rationing system.

Though the stated intention was to raise money for poorer Iranians suffering the most, the unexpected price change was met with angry protests across Iran. Sparked by the gas price hike, protests that began in southwest Iran – in its oil-rich province of Khuzestan – soon spread throughout the country and revealed intensely felt resentment that went well beyond the issue of gas prices. These protests were met with brute and deadly suppression by Iranian security forces, leaving hundreds dead and thousands injured and arrested. In an unprecedented move to keep the outside world in the dark, Iranian authorities shut down the Internet for several days, leaving Iranians in the dark as well, and unable to share what was happening on the ground.

Unlike many previous protests in Iran in which middle-class Iranians played a significant role, these protests were marked by the predominant participation of working-class and more destitute Iranians. They included the most vulnerable segment of society hurting from the country's economic woes, a phenomenon observed by Sharareh Dehshiri in a

tweet in which she lamented, "The middle class does not have the energy
to protest. The middle class is tired."[49] As some protestors called for
peaceful protest and not to vandalize, others destroyed property such as
banks and gas stations in acts of frustrated desperation, as they saw their
livelihoods diminished and their future in peril.

While Zahra Keshvari shared a video of an Iranian woman standing with protestors and asking them not to damage property, she
also noted the grim situation for so many Iranians: "Unemployment
is rampant in Khorramabad and Lorestan. When one or two factor-
ies in the province closed, many people sold everything they had to
buy a car to make a living as a driver. Now they are left with a car
and a frightening future."[50] The gravity of the situation was
reflected in another comment from Marzieh who stated, "The
truth is that the gas price hike is like another fire set under another
part of our youth."[51] In a moment of total despair, Iranians
expressed their outrage at multiple targets, wherein the very people
who had shown support for the Islamic Republic, or the Rouhani
administration, were now openly criticizing them for the current
state of affairs.

Fereshteh Sadeghi took aim not only at the Rouhani government,
which she was often skeptical of, but leveled criticism at the Islamic
Republic itself:

For now, public sentiment is simply anger, *considering the fact that as usual
the I.R. blamed its enemies* without considering the fact that the ground was
ready for protests to break down and Rouhani's government acted as an
instigator by raising gasoline prices.[52]

In other tweets, Sadeghi scolded Rouhani for the way the policy was
implemented and what she saw as a "lack of attention to public

[49] Sharare Mishavam, Twitter post (November 15, 2019, 3:10 PM EST), last accessed
June 13, 2021, https://twitter.com/ShararaMishavam/status/11954338848733470
77?s=20.
[50] Zahra Keshvari, Twitter post (November 16, 2019, 8:09 AM EST), last accessed
June 13, 2021, https://twitter.com/zahrakeshvari/status/11956902287087083
53?s=20.
[51] Marzieh, Twitter post (November 14, 2019, 6:18 PM EST), last accessed June
13, 2021, https://twitter.com/marzie_25/status/1195118889258115075?s=20.
[52] Fereshteh Sadeghi, Twitter post (November 24, 2019, 6:09 AM EST), last
accessed June 13, 2021, https://twitter.com/fresh_sadegh/status/11985593402
67003905?s=20 (emphasis added).

feeling."[53] But her critique of the Islamic Republic went after one of its core characteristics: deflecting blame and responsibility on to its enemies. In this sense, Sadeghi was calling on the whole of the governing system – from its elected officials to its unelected domineering figures – to take responsibility for the suffering of their people.

Like Sadeghi, Saba Azarpeik took aim at Iranian officials across the spectrum, blaming the Rouhani administration and Iranian hardliners who had undermined the JCPOA. Despite the fact that Azarpeik was a firm Rouhani supporter and encouraged others to partake in his election, she did not mince her words when calling him a coward and accusing him of being dishonest with the Iranian people.[54] Well-known activist Bahareh Hedayat articulated grievances that went beyond economic hardship and gas prices, to a crucial injustice felt by many Iranians. In particular, she pointed to a lack of consideration or accountability to the Iranian people:

Protest against a hike in gas price is because of a lack of legitimacy of a decision that was arbitrarily taken by the government, and not a purely economic debate of left or right. When you exclude the people from the process of decision-making, any decision you make is illegitimate … The people who must tolerate the pressure of higher gas prices – and even if prices didn't increase, they would have to suffer through inflation caused by printing notes – are caught in a lose-lose situation. No one asked them: are you okay with facing difficulties caused everyday by government decisions?[55]

It makes sense that most of the condemnation at that moment was against the Iranian state and government, especially given the brutality and repression that the state imposed against protestors and the whole of Iranian society with the Internet blackout. Yet, others also alluded to groups and people outside Iran who may have hoped for building such pressure inside Iran as a result of Trump's Iran policy. Sharareh

[53] Fereshteh Sadeghi, Twitter post (November 24, 2019, 6:09 AM EST), last accessed June 13, 2021, https://twitter.com/fresh_sadegh/status/11985593365 80239360?s=20.

[54] Saba Azarpeik, Twitter post (November 16, 2019, 1:01 AM EST), last accessed June 13, 2021, https://twitter.com/sabaazarpeik/status/119558266992241868 8?s=20.

[55] Bahareh Hedayat, Twitter post (November 15, 2019, 8:48 PM EST), last accessed June 13, 2021, https://twitter.com/HedayatBahare/status/119533773 4308737025?s=20; and Bahareh Hedayat, Twitter post (November 15, 2019, 9:00 AM EST), last accessed June 13, 2021, https://twitter.com/HedayatBahare/ status/1195340920926932993?s=20.

Dehshiri tweeted, "The Farashgard members are celebrating on Saudi Arabia International."[56] The reference she is making is actually to *Iran International*, which is a Persian-language satellite channel based in London and understood in the Iranian community to be funded by individuals from Saudi Arabia, Iran's regional rival. Farashgard refers to a dissident group outside Iran that collected around Reza Pahlavi in the hope of seeing the Islamic Republic toppled.

Dehshiri's comment recalls the contempt for external actors and strains meant to push Iran into submission and overlook the suffering of Iranian people. In fact, when asked about the need for military intervention in Iran, Reza Pahlavi had argued only five months earlier that pressure should be exerted on the Islamic Republic to force its collapse and if such pressure was not sufficient to do so, then other options would have to be considered: "If the proper pressure does not exist at this time to force this regime to collapse, then, of course, it would become unavoidable to consider other options."[57] Twitter user Shahrzad posted a comment that summed up the frustration of some Iranians toward these outside forces as well as their own government:

We have a patriotic community that is attacked by monarchists, they fight with regime changers, argue with the opposition, agree with critics of the government, and they suffer attacks from MEK when they talk about reforms in Iran. After all this, suddenly, the government destroys them with one decision [to increase gas price].[58]

In the end, the violent state crackdown against protestors left at least 304 people dead, according to Amnesty International.[59] Pressure from

---

[56] Sharareh Dehshiri, Twitter post (November 16, 2019, 6:14 AM), last accessed June 13, 2021, https://twitter.com/SharareMishavam/status/11956613972098 62145?s=20.

[57] Jonathan Gratch, "Exiled Iranian Crown Prince to i24NEWS: 'The Time Has Come for Final Complete Change of Regime,'" *I24NEWS* (June 27, 2019), last accessed June 13, 2021, www.i24news.tv/en/news/middle-east/1561629316-e xiled-iranian-crown-prince-to-i24news-the-time-has-come-for-final-complete-c hange-of-regime.

[58] Shahrzad, Twitter post (November 16, 2019, 10:17 PM EST), last accessed June 13, 2021, https://twitter.com/Shahr2ad/status/1195722613273837568?s=20.

[59] "Iran: Details Released of 304 Deaths during Protests Six Months after Security Forces' Killing Spree," *Amnesty International* (May 20, 2020), last accessed June 13, 2021, www.amnesty.org/en/latest/news/2020/05/iran-details-released- of-304-deaths-during-protests-six-months-after-security-forces-killing-spree/.

the outside continued to be matched by internal pressures, all of which impacted millions of Iranian people stuck in the crossfire. As these examples illustrate, Iranians do not fit neatly into fixed ideologies. Instead, they navigate changing sociopolitical dynamics with matching fluidity. The November 2019 protests plainly showed a serious level of discontent that questioned the legitimacy of both the elected government and the state. However, the target of anger and how Iranians expressed their grievances were varied. To some observers it may have appeared that Iranian society was uniformly against the state and its officials as a whole, but events less than two months later presented an entirely different face of the nation.

## 7.7 January 2020: A Nation Mourns

On January 3, 2020, President Donald Trump ordered the assassination of Qasem Soleimani. Serving as the commander of Iran's Quds Force – a division of the IRGC that is primarily in charge of operations outside Iran – Soleimani was seen by many Iranians as the key person responsible for keeping the borders of their nation safe. The Shiite motifs of martyrdom that the assassination evoked have already been discussed, as well as Soleimani's legacy, which was enshrined as a martyr to his people akin to that of Imam Hossein. As the world feared an impending war, many were also stunned by the sheer volume of Iranians who had taken to the streets to express their grief and rage. While some political commentators stressed the idea that Soleimani was hated by many Iranians as a symbol of the state, it was impossible to deny the popularity of a figure who had elicited such an outpouring of emotions with his death.

The reaction of Iranians followed the familiar patterns presented throughout this study. From devoted sentiments about protecting the homeland, to antagonism toward foreign powers that had carried out this crime and toward Iranian diaspora dissidents who had cheered them on, Iranians couched their grief in terms of nation, defense, and resistance. For instance, Saba Azarpeik posted an image of ISIS leader, Abu Bakr al-Baghdadi, and wrote:

At the time when the blood of people in different nations was being shed by ISIS in every corner of the world, was it not the name of the commander

[Soleimani] that instilled fear in the members of ISIS? Can we forget his role in restoring the peace lost by ISIS? History cannot be altered.[60]

Others drew comparisons between ISIS and prominent Iranian dissidents that celebrated the assassination of Soleimani outside Iran,[61] both for being happy at the news of his death. Marjan Laghaee called on others to ignore such "traitors,"[62] describing them as "bi-vatan," which literally means without homeland, but in this context suggests someone who has betrayed their homeland.

Similarly, Sharareh Dehshiri reacted to another diaspora Iranian who called Soleimani a terrorist and appealed to Iranian patriotism, saying, "Your country has not been Iran for a very long time. You are more rootless than these words."[63] As these reactions show, the assassination of Soleimani sparked a highly emotional debate that went beyond politics to the core of Iranian identity and belonging. Fereshteh Sadeghi reiterated these feelings with her tweet that simply stated, "Your terrorist is my *national hero*. I don't care what you think."[64] It is worth noting that individuals who displayed different views in other areas of Iranian social and political life found greater commonality in this instance.

Another common theme that rallied Iranians around the flag was the US role and the fear of war, which is inherently defensive in nature. From the Iranian perspective, the assassination of their commander was seen as nothing short of an act of war, as Zeinab Safari lamented: "It seems our destiny is linked with war. Our childhood was spent in war [Iran–Iraq War, 1980–88]. Our adolescence and youth were spent in fear and under the shadow of war. And now,

---

60 Saba Azarpeik, Twitter post (January 3, 2020, 4:49 AM EST), last accessed June 14, 2021, https://twitter.com/sabaazarpeik/status/1213034603100942336? s=20.
61 Sharareh Dehshiri, Twitter post (January 3, 2020, 2:10 AM EST), last accessed June 14, 2021, https://twitter.com/ShararehMishavam/status/12129946990127 80033?s=20.
62 Marjan Laghaee, Twitter post (January 3, 2020, 2:48 AM EST), last accessed June 14, 2021, https://twitter.com/MarjanLaghaee/status/1213004067368243 200?s=20.
63 Sharareh Dehshiri, Twitter post (January 3, 2020, 8:00 AM EST), last accessed June 14, 2021, https://twitter.com/ShararehMishavam/status/12130827248876 46208?s=20.
64 Fereshteh Sadeghi, Twitter post (January 13, 2020, 2:00 PM EST), last accessed June 14, 2021, https://twitter.com/fresh_sadegh/status/12167971756419891 21?s=20 (emphasis added).

we're at war again."[65] Faranak Arta tagged Trump and Pompeo in a tweet that showed an image of a side-by-side list of countries the United States had bombed, sabotaged, or attempted to overthrow versus Iran, whose list was blank.[66] The message here suggested that the United States had not only unjustly attacked Iran, but also that it is a global aggressor with a historical precedent of belligerence toward sovereign states.

Marzieh echoed the discourse of broader US imperialism in her tweet: "Instead of chanting 'no to war,' we should be chanting 'America, get the hell out of the Middle East.'"[67] While Shahrzad commended the bravery of US presidential candidate Bernie Sanders for speaking honestly on the issue of US foreign policy:

Sanders is a man of principles. Even now that he is running for president, he courageously states that the United States should not go to war with Iran, should leave the Middle East, and end the anti-Yemeni war and alliance with Saudi Arabia #Soleimani.[68]

Like the anti-imperialist images that were central to the identity of resistance Iranian revolutionaries infused into their counter narrative against the shah, when contemporary Iranians saw their country threatened by the United States, their condemnations took on US empire.

Within days of Soleimani's assassination, the target of Iranian outrage returned toward their own state. After shooting down a civilian airplane and killing all 176 people onboard in its attempted retaliation for Soleimani, Iranian officials tried to cover up their catastrophic error. Once news came that the downing of Ukrainian Airlines Flight PS752 was a result of their own egregious actions, Iranians took to the streets again in an act of collective mourning and rage. Iranian officials took responsibility in name alone and used the familiar rhetoric of the

---

[65] Safari Zeinab, Twitter post (January 8, 2020, 7:13 AM EST), last accessed June 14, 2021, https://twitter.com/SafariZeinab/status/1214701735475740673?s=20.
[66] Faranak Arta, Twitter post (January 3, 2020, 3:58 PM EST), last accessed June 14, 2021, https://twitter.com/FaranakArta/status/1213202959254900736?s=20.
[67] Marzieh, Twitter post (January 4, 2020, 12:06 PM EST), last accessed June 14, 2021, https://twitter.com/marzie_r/status/1213506934118240256?s=20.
[68] Shahrzad, Twitter post (January 4, 2020, 1:28 AM EST), last accessed June 14, 2021, https://twitter.com/Shahr2ad/status/1213346529521623040?s=20.

Islamic Republic. In their attempts to placate public anger, the Foundation of Martyrs and War Veteran Affairs declared the victims of the crash official martyrs, as reported by Fereshteh Sadeghi.[69] The futility of these empty gestures was evident in protest chants shouted by Iranians, which exposed profound discontent and resistance against years of injustice.

Activist Bahareh Hedayat joined protests and shared videos of Iranians crying out, "Faryād, faryād, az in ham-e bidād" (Shout, shout, from all this injustice).[70] In another video she shared, protestors are heard shouting, "Be man nagu fetneh gar, fetneh to-yi setam gar" (Don't call me a seditionist, you are sedition, the oppressor).[71] Hedayat added her own commentary in a tweet that stated, "You are rotten from head to toe. You are liars, deceivers, and killers. These are not insults, it is precisely what the situation is #BigLie."[72] The depth of frustration for many Iranians, even those who had urged participation in the system and hoped for change, was conveyed by Sharareh Dehshiri who tweeted, "We are angry for feeling foolish. As an ordinary citizen, who was still a little optimistic, I apologize to everyone."[73]

Flight PS752 was seen as a national tragedy, and so, not surprisingly, some of the commentary was imbued with national sentiment. While Twitter users like Marzieh shared their condolences[74] with the crash victims and their families, Shokoohfeh Habibzadeh expressed sadness for the whole of the nation and a series of heartbreaking events: "Is the shadow of death over Iran? One day assassination, one day a stampede at a mourning ceremony, one day a plane crash,

[69] Fereshteh Sadeghi, Twitter post (January 14, 2020, 1:00 PM EST), last accessed June 14, 2021, https://twitter.com/fresh_sadegh/status/121714447092125287 0?s=20.
[70] Bahareh Hedayat, Twitter post (January 11, 2020, 10:06 AM EST), last accessed June 14, 2021, https://twitter.com/HedayatBahare/status/121601363 7267136518?s=20.
[71] Bahareh Hedayat, Twitter post (January 11, 2020, 9:56 AM EST), last accessed June 14, 2021, https://twitter.com/HedayatBahare/status/1216011010487803 905?s=20.
[72] Bahareh Hedayat, Twitter post (January 11, 2020, 1:43 AM EST), last accessed June 14, 2021, https://twitter.com/HedayatBahare/status/1215887023518646 272?s=20.
[73] Sharareh Dehshiri, Twitter post (January 11, 2020, 1:18 AM EST), last accessed June 14, 2021, https://twitter.com/SharareMishavam/status/12158807574760 57088?s=20.
[74] Marzieh, Twitter post (January 8, 2020, 5:37 AM EST), last accessed June 14, 2021, https://twitter.com/marzie_r/status/1214858612159500288?s=20.

and now a bus accident kills more of our countrymen. Why? #Iran #PoorIran."[75] Similarly, Marjan Laghaee summed up the sorrow of a nation, stating, "Our dear Iran, our dear Iran, our dear Iran, our dear Iran. With all our differences, problems, wounds, we all hug [love] Iran."[76] In this sense, it was not just individual Iranians who were suffering, but Iran itself, and that shared tragedy brought the people together.

Despite the major upheavals of November 2019, in which many Iranians rose up to protest their discontent against the Islamic Republic and its officials, less than two months later Iranian people coalesced around the assassination of Soleimani as a moment of collective mourning and national resistance against foreign powers. However, their ire soon turned back toward their own state once the truth of Flight PS752 was revealed. Though each event brought out different sectors of the country, there were Iranians who actively participated in each outpouring of anger, sadness, shock, and mourning. The varied reactions of Iranians reveal both the diversity of beliefs and feelings among a population of over 80 million people, as well as the individual shifts in attitude that occur over time and circumstance. Any attempt to reduce Iranian society into simple binaries or neat categories belies its vast array of character, history, and culture.

## 7.8 Conclusion

It is tempting in a contemporary world of connectivity, fast flow of information and people, and global relations to believe that the age of nation-states is on the decline. But in reality, the nation-state is still in its early stages in terms of human history, and continues to be the dominant form of individual identity and international communications. For better or worse, a significant part of understanding the self, and "other," is still greatly tied to these "imagined communities." More than an intellectual exercise or thought experiment, how a nation-state defines itself, and its relation to the global community, carries real consequences.

---

[75] Shookoofeh Habibzadeh, Twitter post (January 9, 2020, 4:55 AM EST), last accessed June 14, 2021, https://twitter.com/shokoohabibzade/status/1215210 475190915072?s=20.

[76] Marjan Laghaee, Twitter post (January 8, 2020, 12:24 PM EST), last accessed June 14, 2021, https://twitter.com/MarjanLaghaee/status/1214961195549114 375?s=20.

While this study has outlined the evolution of that identity in the case of Iran, it holds greater implications in global affairs. Caricatured depictions of Iran and the broader Middle East are ubiquitous in US news and media. Iran continues to be at the heart of US foreign policy debates, except what is often missing in the discussion is a consideration for historical events or the Iranian point of view. Political decisions made in the absence of thoughtful analysis result in imprudent policy choices, which are detrimental to global security and cooperation. By understanding the cultural, political, and historical context of contemporary Iran, we can hope to undertake more practical and informed policy positions.

Even with the complex and often contrasting social and political spectrum that makes up Iranian identity, as evidenced, there are some discernible patterns and a limited set of motifs that Iranians choose from within their cultural and historical experience to define their Iranianness. At the center of that character is unwavering resistance, defense of their homeland and its people, and the adoration of *vatan*.

Perhaps the greatest individual figure in Iran over the last century to embody such qualities, and unify Iranians, is their famed vocalist Mohammad Shajarian. Born in Mashhad in 1940, Shajarian first learned Quranic recitation and later trained in the classical singing of Persian poetry. Though his classical style may have appeared outdated as modern musical genres and pop music gained popularity, Shajarian grew to enormous fame as one of the most treasured artists of Iran. His passing at a hospital in Tehran on October 8, 2020, at the age of 80, sparked an outpouring of grief in an already extraordinarily challenging year for Iranians. The torrent of emotions from Iranians all around the world was a testimony to his unmatched genius and his impact on Iranian society, politics, and culture.

Turning the prose of famed Persian poets such as Rumi, Ferdowsi, and Hafez into song, Shajarian's dulcet and powerful voice became a symbol of the nation. Not surprisingly, Iranians expressed their sorrow in a similar national language of collective mourning, such as Saba Azarpeik who posted a picture of Shajarian and tweeted, "We [Iranians] owe the tenderness of our souls to you."[77] Similarly, Zahra Keshvari posted a video of Shajarian and wrote, "Your pain became

---

[77] Saba Azarpeik, Twitter post (October 8, 2020, 8:57 AM EST), last accessed June 14, 2021, https://twitter.com/sabaazarpeik/status/1314188105558130690? s=20.

our [Iranians] soul."[78] Emily Amraee noted how he transcended the boundaries among Iranians of all stripes, "I knew people who didn't listen to music for religious reasons. But even they could not resist the force of Shajarian."[79] Illustrating his connection to the homeland, Farzaneh Ebrahimzadeh shared a picture of Shajarian's own portrait of the map of Iran.[80] Undeterred by the risks of the Covid-19 pandemic, Iranians gathered outside the hospital to sing the songs of their beloved vocalist in somber unison.

In 2018, his son Homayoun released a song by the name "Irān-e Man" (My Iran),[81] which was an homage to his country and also a tribute to his father. The song lyrics demonstrated an intense adoration for *vatan*:

> *Oh, the blood of **vatan** [homeland] runs through my veins*
> *Oh, may your is flag be our **kafan** [burial shroud]*
> *May Ahriman [evil spirit in Zoroastrianism] always be far from you*
> *My Iran, my Iran, my Iran, my Iran*

In a song about his homeland, the younger Shajarian tied his love and idea of Iran directly to his father, as the voice of a people who brought light to darkness. Echoing and replicating the lyrics that immortalized Mohammad Shajarian in his legendary "Morgh-e Sahar" (Bird of Dawn), the younger Shajarian calls on his father to sing once again:

> *Night-illuminating singer*
> *Cry out once more*
> *"Oh God, Oh Universe, Oh Nature*
> *Turn our dark night into Dawn"*

In mourning a nation's shared loss, Bahareh Hedayat invoked the same notion of "vatan" and aptly described Shajarian's undeniable place in

---

[78] Zahra Keshvari, Twitter post (October 8, 2020, 10:00 AM EST), last accessed June 14, 2021, https://twitter.com/zahrakeshvari/status/13142039904190709 78?s=20.

[79] Emily Amraee, Twitter post (October 8, 2020, 4:01 PM EST), last accessed June 14, 2021, https://twitter.com/EmilyAmraee/status/1314294923248762880? s=20.

[80] Farzaneh Ebrahimzadeh, Twitter post (October 8, 2020, 12:32 PM EST), last accessed June 14, 2021, https://twitter.com/febrahimzade/status/13142422349 97444610?s=20.

[81] "Homayoun Shajarian – Iran e Man," YouTube video, last accessed March 21, 2022, www.youtube.com/watch?v=IWwsnBPSbE4.

the Iranian psyche: "His voice was the meaning of *vatan* [homeland] #Shajarian."[82]

Both before and after the revolution of 1979, his songs often called for justice, engendered pride, and longed for better days ahead. In times of turmoil and despair, his songs were the soundtrack of Iranian resistance and a reminder to be hopeful for the coming of the dawn. Despite the many challenges that Iranians have faced, they continue to fight back as agents of change, use the tools at their disposal, and forge their own identity with all its variations.

Although the goal of this project is to contribute to the academic discourse on contemporary Iran, and to provide a broad overview for policymakers and the general public alike, ultimately, I wanted to tell a story. No story is ever whole or complete. But I wanted to tell a story that many Americans may have heard in passing, but know little about. The story of a people who have struggled for their independence and freedom, which has been dashed by foreign and domestic forces for well over a century. The story of a people as diverse as their rich history and culture would suggest.

---

[82] Bahareh Hedayat, Twitter post (October 8, 2020, 9:38 AM EST), last accessed June 14, 2021, https://twitter.com/HedayatBahare/status/1314198531826044 928?s=20.

# Select Bibliography

Abrahamian, Ervand. *The Coup: 1953, the CIA, and the Roots of Modern U.S.–Iranian Relations*. New York: The New Press, 2013.
  *Iran between Two Revolutions*. Princeton, NJ: Princeton University Press, 1982.
  *The Iranian Mojahedin*. New Haven, CT: Yale University Press, 1989.
  *Khomeinism: Essays on the Islamic Republic*. Berkeley: University of California Press, 1993.
  *A Modern History of Iran*. Cambridge: Cambridge University Press, 2008.
  *Tortured Confessions: Prisons and Public Recantations in Modern Iran*. Berkeley: University of California Press, 1999.
Adelkhah, Fariba. *Being Modern in Iran*. New York: Columbia University Press, 2000.
Aghaie, Kamran Scott. *The Martyrs of Karbala: Shi'i Symbols and Rituals in Modern Iran*. Seattle: University of Washington Press, 2004.
Ahmadpour-Turkamani, Ali, ed. *Simā-ye Āftāb*. Qom: Daftar-e Nashr-e M'āref, 2011.
Ajami, Fouad. *The Vanished Imam: Musa al Sadr and the Shia of Lebanon*. Ithaca, NY: Cornell University Press, 1986.
Akbari-Mozdabadi, Ali, ed. *Hazrat-e Yār*. Tehran: Yā Zahrā, 2015.
Akhavan, Niki. "Exclusionary Cartographies: Gender Liberation and the Iranian Blogosphere." In Roksana Bahramitash and Eric Hooglund, eds., *Gender in Contemporary Iran: Pushing the Boundaries*, 78–98. Abingdon: Routledge, 2011.
Al-e Aḥmad, Jalal. *Gharbzadegi [Weststruckness]*. Translated by John Green and Ahmad Alizadeh. Lexington, KY: Mazda Publishers, 1982.
Algar, Hamid. *Roots of the Islamic Revolution in Iran*. Oneonta, NY: Islamic Publications International, 2001.
Anderson, Benedict. *Imagined Communities: Reflections on the Origin and Spread of Nationalism*. New York: Verso, 2006.
Ansari, Ali. *Confronting Iran: The Failure of American Foreign Policy and the Next Great Conflict in the Middle East*. New York: Basic Books, 2006.
  *Modern Iran since 1921: The Pahlavis and After*. London: Pearson Education, 2003.

222

Arjomand, Said Amir. *The Shadow of the Hidden Imam: Religion, Political Order, and Societal Change in Shi'ite Iran from the Beginning to 1890.* Chicago: University of Chicago Press, 1984.

*The Turban for the Crown: The Islamic Revolution in Iran.* New York: Oxford University Press, 1988.

Bajoghli, Narges. *Iran Reframed: Anxieties of Power in the Islamic Republic.* Redwood City, CA: Stanford University Press, 2020.

Batutu, Hanna. *The Old Social Classes and the Revolutionary Movements of Iraq: A Study of Iraq's Old Landed and Commercial Classes and of Its Communists, B'athists, and Free Officers.* London: Saqi Books, 2000.

Bayat, Asef. *Life as Politics: How Ordinary People Change the Middle East.* Redwood City, CA: Stanford University Press, 2010.

*Making Islam Democratic: Social Movements and the Post-Islamist Turn.* Redwood City, CA: Stanford University Press, 2007.

*Street Politics: Poor People's Movements in Iran.* New York: Columbia University Press, 1997.

Behrooz, Maziar. *Rebels with a Cause: The Failure of the Left in Iran.* London: I. B. Tauris, 1999.

Blake, William. *The Marriage of Heaven and Hell.* Public Domain: iBooks, 2014.

Boroujerdi, Mehrzad. "Contesting Nationalist Constructions of Iranian Identity." *Critique: Critical Middle Eastern Studies.* 7, no. 12 (1998), 43–55.

Certeau, Michel de. *The Practice of Everyday Life.* Berkeley: University of California Press, 1988.

Chamran, Mostafa. *Binesh Va Niyāyesh.* Tehran: Bonyād-e Shahid Chamrān, 2004.

*Kordestān.* Tehran: Bonyād-e Shahid Chamrān, 2006.

Chehabi, Houchang E. *Iranian Politics and Religious Modernism.* Ithaca, NY: Cornell University Press, 1990.

Chelkowski, Peter, ed. *Ta'ziyah: Ritual and Drama in Iran.* New York: New York University Press, 1979.

Chelkowski, Peter, and Hamid Dabashi. *Staging a Revolution: The Art of Persuasion in the Islamic Republic of Iran.* New York: New York University Press, 1999.

Cole, Juan R. *Engaging the Muslim World.* New York: Palgrave MacMillan, 2009.

Cole, Juan R., and Nikki R. Keddie, eds. *Shi'ism and Social Protest.* New Haven, CT: Yale University Press, 1986.

Cordesman, Anthony H., and Abraham R. Wagner. *The Lessons of Modern War*, vol. 2, *The Iran–Iraq War.* Boulder, CO: Westview Press, 1990.

Dabashi, Hamid. *Iran: A People Interrupted*. New York: The New Press, 2007.

*Iran, the Green Movement and the USA*. London: Z Books, 2010.

*Iran without Borders: Towards a Critique of the Postcolonial Nation*. New York: Verso, 2016.

*Shi'ism: A Religion of Protest*. Cambridge, MA: Belknap Press of Harvard University Press, 2011.

*Theology of Discontent: The Ideological Foundation of the Islamic Revolution in Iran*. New Brunswick, NJ: Transaction Publishers, 2008.

Daneshvar, Simin. *Savushun*. Tehran: Kharazmi, 1976.

De Bellaigue, Christopher. *In the Rose Garden of the Martyrs: A Memoir of Iran*. London: HarperCollins, 2004.

Egan, Eric. *The Films of Makhmalbaf: Cinema, Politics and Culture in Iran*. Washington, DC: Mage Publishers, 2005.

Erikson, Erik H. *Identity: Youth and Crisis*. New York: W. W. Norton, 1968.

Fanon, Frantz, Richard Philcox, Jean-Paul Sartre, and Homi K. Bhabha. *The Wretched of the Earth*. New York: Grove Press, 2004.

Fischer, Michael M. J. *Iran: From Religious Dispute to Revolution*. Cambridge, MA: Harvard University Press, 1980.

Frith, Simon. *Popular Music: Critical Concepts in Media and Cultural Studies*. London: Routledge, 2004.

Ford Foundation. *The United Nations and the Iran–Iraq War: A Ford Foundation Conference Report*. New York: Ford Foundation, 1987.

Ghani, Cyrus. *Iran and the Rise of Reza Shah: From Qajar Collapse to Pahlavi Rule*. London: I. B. Tauris, 1998.

Ghazvinian, John. *America and Iran: A History, 1720 to the Present*. New York: Alfred A. Knopf, 2021.

*Goftogu-ye Chahār Jānebe*. Tehran: Enteshārāt-e Sadrā, 2014.

Golshenas, Saeed, ed. *Cherāgh-ha-ye Furuzān Dar Tāriki*. Tehran: Nashr-e Sobhān, 2005.

Gramsci, Antonio, Quintin Hoare, and Geoffrey Nowell-Smith. *Selections from the Prison Notebooks of Antonio Gramsci*. New York: International Publishers, 1971.

Hall, Stuart. *Representation: Cultural Representations and Signifying Practices*. London: Sage/Open University, 1997.

Hall, Stuart, and Paul Du Gay. *Questions of Cultural Identity*. London: Sage, 1996.

Halm, Heinz. *Shi'a Islam: From Religion to Revolution*. Princeton, NJ: Markus Wiener Publishers, 1997.

Handler, Richard, and Eric Gable. *The New History in an Old Museum: Creating the Past at Colonial Williamsburg*. Durham, NC: Duke University Press, 1997.

Hebdige, Dick. *Subculture: The Meaning of Style*. London: Methuen, 1979.

*Hekāyat-ha-ye Talkh Va Shirin*. Tehran: Mo'asese-ye Farhangi Honari-ye Qadr-e Velāyat, 2012.

Hiro, Dilip. *The Longest War: The Iran–Iraq Military Conflict*. London: Grafton Books, 1989.

Hobsbawm, Eric J. *Nations and Nationalism Since 1780: Programme, Myth, Reality*. Cambridge: Cambridge University Press, 1992.

Hosseini, Seyyede Azam. *Dā: Khāterāt-e Seyyede Zahra Hosseini*. Tehran: Sureh-e Mehr, 2015.

Iranian Students' Association in Northern California. *The Regime of the Shah Steps Up Political Repression in Iran as It Prepares for the Celebration of 2500 Year [sic] of Iranian Monarchy*. Berkeley: The Association, 1971.

Jackson, John L. *Real Black: Adventures in Racial Sincerity*. Chicago: University of Chicago Press, 2005.

Jahanbegloo, Ramin. *Iran – Between Tradition and Modernity*. Lanham, MD: Lexington Books, 2004.

Karsh, Efraim. *The Iran–Iraq War 1980–1988*. Oxford: Oxprey Publishing, 2002.

Kashani-Sabet, Firoozeh. "Cultures of Iranianess: The Evolving Polemic of Iranian Nationalism." In Nikki R. Keddie et al., ed., *Iran and the Surrounding World*, 162–81. Seattle: University of Washington Press, 2002.

Kasturi, Sumana. *Gender, Citizenship, and Identity in the Indian Blogosphere: Writing the Everyday*. Abingdon: Routledge, 2020.

Katouzian, Homa. *Musaddiq and the Struggle for Power in Iran*. London: I. B. Tauris, 1990.

Kazemi, Mohsen. *Yādāsht-ha-ye Safar-e Shahid Sayyād Shirāzi*. Tehran: Sureh-e Mehr, 2011.

Keddie, Nikki. *Modern Iran: Roots and Results of Revolution*. New Haven, CT: Yale University Press, 2003.

Keddie, Nikki, ed. *Religion and Politics in Iran: Shi'ism from Quietism to Revolution*. New Haven, CT: Yale University Press, 1983.

Khalidi, Rashid. *Palestinian Identity: The Construction of Modern National Consciousness*. New York: Columbia University Press, 1997.

Khomeini, Ruhollah, and Hamid Algar. *Islam and Revolution: Writings and Declarations of Imam Khomeini*. Berkeley, CA: Mizan Press, 1981.

Khomeini, Ruhollah. *Jām-e Zahr*. Tehran: Mo'asese-ye Farhangi-ye Khākriz-e Imān Va Andisheh, 2015.

Kia, Mehrdad. "Persian Nationalism and the Campaign for Language Purification." *Middle Eastern Studies* 34, no. 2 (1998), 9–36.

Kinzer, Stephen. *All the Shah's Men: American Coup and the Roots of Middle East Terror*. Hoboken: John Wiley & Sons, Inc., 2003.

Kurzman, Charles. *The Unthinkable Revolution in Iran*. Cambridge, MA: Harvard University Press, 2004.

Lam'ei, Shabanali, ed. *Eshārāt-e Sokhanān-e Gozide va Payām-ha-ye Kutāh-e Doktor Shariati*. Tehran: Ramand Publication, 2015.

Lenin, Vladimir Il'ich. *What Is to Be Done? Burning Questions of Our Movement*. New York: International Publishers, 1969.

Marashi, Afshin. *Nationalizing Iran: Culture, Power, and the State, 1870–1940*. Seattle: University of Washington Press, 2008.

McAlister, Melani. *Epic Encounters: Culture, Media, & U.S. Interests in the Middle East since 1945*. Berkeley: University of California Press, 2005.

McClintock, Anne, Aamir Mufti, and Ella Shohat. *Dangerous Liaisons: Gender, Nation, and Postcolonial Perspectives*. Minneapolis: University of Minnesota Press, 1997.

Merhavy, Menahem. *National Symbols in Modern Iran: Identity, Ethnicity, and Collective Memory*. Syracuse, NY: Syracuse University Press, 2019.

Moaddel, Mansoor. *Class, Politics, and Ideology in the Iranian Revolution*. New York: Columbia University Press, 1993.

*Islamic Modernism, Nationalism, and Fundamentalism: Episode and Discourse*. Chicago: University of Chicago Press, 2005.

Mohammadi, Ali, and Annabelle Sreberny-Mohammadi. *Small Media, Big Revolution: Communication, Culture, and the Iranian Revolution*. Minneapolis: University of Minnesota Press, 1994.

Motahhari, Mortezā. *Nām-e Tārikhi-ye Ostād Motahhari Be Imam Khomeini*. Tehran: Sadrā, 2010.

Motahhari, Mortezā, and Hamid Algar. *Fundamentals of Islamic Thought: God, Man, and the Universe*. Berkeley: Mizan Press. 1985.

Mottahedeh, Roy. *Mantle of the Prophet: Religion and Politics in Iran*. New York: Simon & Schuster, 1985.

Naficy, Hamid. "Islamizing Film Culture in Iran: A Post-Khatami Update." In Richard Tapper, ed., *The New Iranian Cinema: Politics, Representation and Identity*, 26–65. London: I.B. Tauris Publishers, 2002.

*A Social History of Iranian Cinema*, vol. 1, *The Artisanal Era, 1897–1941*. Durham, NC: Duke University Press, 2011.

*A Social History of Iranian Cinema*, vol. 2, *The Industrializing Years, 1941–1978*. Durham, NC: Duke University Press, 2011.

*A Social History of Iranian Cinema*, vol. 3, *The Islamicate Period, 1978–1984*. Durham, NC: Duke University Press, 2011.

Nakash, Yitzak. *Reaching for Power: The Shi'a in the Modern Arab World*. Princeton: Princeton University Press, 2006.

Nieguth, Tim. *The Politics of Popular Culture: Negotiating Power, Identity, and Place*. Montreal: McGill-Queen's Univ. Press, 2015.

Nooshin, Laudan. "Subversion and Countersubversion: Power, Control, and Meaning in the New Iranian Pop Music." In Annie J. Randall, ed., *Music, Power, and Politics*, 231–72. New York: Routledge, 2005.

"Underground, Overground: Rock Music and Youth Discourses in Iran." *Iranian Studies: Journal of the International Society for Iranian Studies* 38, no. 3 (2005), 463–94.

Norton, Richard August. *Hezbollah: A Short History*. Princeton: Princeton University Press, 2007.

Pahlavi, Mohammad Reza. *Answer to History: By Mohammad Reza Pahlavi The Shah of Iran*. New York: Stein and Day Publishers, 1980.

*Mission for My Country*. London: Hutchinson, 1960.

*The White Revolution of Iran*. Tehran: Imperial Pahlavi Library, 1967.

Parsa, Misagh. *Social Origins of the Iranian Revolution*. New Brunswick: Rutgers University Press, 1989.

Parsi, Trita. *Treacherous Alliance: The Secret Dealings of Israel, Iran, and the U.S.* New Haven, CT: Yale University Press, 2007.

Pateman, Carole. *The Sexual Contract*. Cambridge: Polity Press, 1988.

Pezeshkzad, Iraj. *My Uncle Napoleon*. n.p.: Modern Library, 2006.

Rahimieh, Nasrin. *Iranian Culture: Repression and Identity*. New York: Routledge, 2016.

Rahnema, Ali. *An Islamic Utopian: A Political biography of Ali Shari'ati*. New York: I.B. Tauris, 2000.

Ramazani, Rouhollah K. *Revolutionary Iran: Challenge and Response in the Middle East*. Baltimore: John Hopkins University Press, 1986.

Roy, Sara. *Failing Peace: Gaza and the Palestinian-Israeli Conflict*. London and Ann Arbor: Pluto Press, 2007.

Said, Edward W. *Culture and Imperialism*. New York: Vintage Books, 1994.

*Orientalism*. New York: Vintage Books, 1994.

Shaery-Eisenlohr, Roschanack. *Shi'ite Lebanon: Transnational Religion and the Making of National Identities*. New York: Columbia University Press, 2008.

Shakhsari, Sima. *Politics of Rightful Killing: Civil Society, Gender, and Sexuality in Weblogistan*. Durham: Duke University Press, 2020.

Shariati, Ali. *Marxism and Other Western Fallacies: An Islamic Critique*. Translated by R. Campbell. Berkeley: Mizan Press, 1980.

Shariati, Ali, and Hamid Algar. *On the Sociology of Islam: Lectures*. Berkeley: Mizan Press, 1979.

Siamdoust, Nahid. *Soundtrack of the Revolution: The Politics of Music in Iran*. Stanford, CA: Stanford University Press, 2017.

Trouillot, Michel-Rolph. *Silencing the Past: Power and the Production of History*. Boston, MA: Beacon Press, 1995.

Varzi, Roxanne. *Warring Souls: Youth, Media, and Martyrdom in Post-Revolution Iran*. Durham: Duke University Press, 2006.

Vaziri, Mostafa. *Iran as Imagined Nation: The Construction of National Identity*. New York: Paragon House, 1993.

Virilio, Paul. *War and Cinema: The Logistics of Perception*. London: Verso, 1989.

Warren, Roland L. "The Nazi Use of Music as an Instrument of Social Control." In R. Serge Denisoff et al., eds., *The Sounds of Social Change: Studies in Popular Culture*, 72–78. Chicago: Rand McNally, 1972.

Williams, Raymond. "Culture Is Ordinary." In Ben Highmore, ed., *The Everyday Life Reader*, 91–100. London: Routledge, 1958.

*Keywords: A Vocabulary of Culture and Society*. New York: Oxford University Press, 1985.

Yuval-Davis, Nira. *Gender & Nation*. London: Sage Publications, 1997.

Zahir, Sanam. "The Music of the Children of the Revolution: The State of Music and Emergence of the Underground Music in the Islamic Republic of Iran with Analysis of Its Lyrical Content." MA Thesis, University of Arizona, 2008.

Zia-Ebrahimi, Reza. "Self-Orientalization and Dislocation: The Uses and Abuses of the 'Aryan' Discourse in Iran." *Iranian Studies* 44, no. 4 (2011), 445–72.

# Index

Warren, Roland L., 14, 113
Westernization, 37, 43
White Revolution, 30–33, 36, 44, 59
  Khomeini and, 47–48
Williams, Raymond, 110, 140
women, 102, 107, 109, 195–197,
  198
  Iran–Iraq War and, 78
  Islamic Republic and, 117, 158–159
  nationalism and, 6, 72

rights of, 31
Rouhani's re-election and, 202, 204
World War II, 1, 47–48, 112

Yas, 119–120
Yazid, 11, 57–58, 84–86
  United States as, 191

Zarif, Javad, 167, 185, 199, 209
Zionism, 82, 84, 86